THE
PROFITEERS

THE
PROFITEERS

HOW BUSINESS PRIVATIZES PROFITS AND SOCIALIZES COSTS

CHRISTOPHER MARQUIS

PUBLICAFFAIRS
New York

PublicAffairs
Hachette Book Group
1290 Avenue of the Americas, New York, NY 10104
www.publicaffairsbooks.com
@Public_Affairs

Printed in the United States of America

First Edition: May 2024

Published by PublicAffairs, an imprint of Hachette Book Group, Inc. The PublicAffairs name and logo is a registered trademark of the Hachette Book Group.

The Hachette Speakers Bureau provides a wide range of authors for speaking events. To find out more, go to hachettespeakersbureau.com or email HachetteSpeakers@hbgusa.com.

PublicAffairs books may be purchased in bulk for business, educational, or promotional use. For more information, please contact your local bookseller or the Hachette Book Group Special Markets Department at special.markets@hbgusa.com.

The publisher is not responsible for websites (or their content) that are not owned by the publisher.

Print book interior design by Sheryl Kober

Library of Congress Cataloging-in-Publication Data

Names: Marquis, Christopher, Prof., author.
Title: The profiteers : how business privatizes profits and socializes costs / Christopher Marquis.
Description: New York : PublicAffairs, 2024. | Includes bibliographical references and index.
Identifiers: LCCN 2023044586 | ISBN 9781541703520 (hardcover) | ISBN 9781541703544 (ebook)
Subjects: LCSH: Social responsibility of business. | Corporate profits—Moral and ethical aspects. | Corporate profits—Social aspects.
Classification: LCC HD60 .M3656 22024 | DDC 658.4/08—dc23/eng/20240105
LC record available at https://lccn.loc.gov/2023044586

ISBNs: 9781541703520 (hardcover), 9781541703544 (ebook)

LSC-C

Printing 1, 2024

To Maggie and Chuck Setler,
whose example I have aimed to follow

CONTENTS

Contents

Introduction

"**M**y guest tonight is the most respected chief executive of the twentieth century," host Stuart Varney began. It was October 17, 2001, and I was lucky enough to be in the room for this live taping of the PBS television show *CEO Exchange*. The venue was the University of Michigan's Power Center for the Performing Arts, and the CEO he was about to interview was Jack Welch, who had just retired from General Electric (GE). I wasn't a particular fan, but I didn't want to miss a chance to see a legend in the flesh. My seat was just a few rows from the front.

Casually shifting from side to side, his left hand firmly planted in his pants pocket, Varney revisited some of the highlights of Welch's twenty-year reign. He'd led the firm through six hundred acquisitions, increasing its market value forty-plus times, from $13 billion to more than $550 billion.[1] Welch's success, Varney said, underlining his words with right-handed karate chops, was due to his "breaking just about every rule there is to break."

When Welch joined him on the stage, Varney spoon-fed him a series of softball questions from his CEO pals—such as Jac Nasser of Ford, Michael Eisner of Disney, and Warren Buffett—that allowed him to dispense his well-worn pearls of management wisdom.

Then, Varney announced that it was time for the "truly tough part" of the evening and invited the students in the audience to ask questions. I'm not sure that Welch registered any of their questions as "tough," but their tone was a lot less sycophantic than Varney's, and some of them forced him to drop his mask and reveal his true management philosophy. Perhaps unsurprisingly, the most challenging of them did not make it into the broadcast, which I recently found on YouTube, but the student-run *Michigan Daily*'s coverage matches my memory.[2]

A student made his way down the steeply raked auditorium and stepped up to one of the microphones that had been placed at the end of the aisles. Why was GE refusing to clean up the million-plus pounds of carcinogenic polychlorinated biphenyls (PCBs) it had dumped into the Hudson River between 1947 and 1977? he asked. As a result of this dumping, the US Environmental Protection Agency (EPA) had classified 200 miles of the 315-mile Hudson as a Superfund site; dredging it would cost taxpayers billions. To make matters worse, in 1991, it was discovered that PCBs were still seeping into the river from GE's long-abandoned Hudson Falls mill.[3]

Welch looked like a bulldog ready to pounce. People need to be "realistic," he growled, respect all the work GE had done, and not hold the company responsible for further mitigation efforts. After a leak was discovered in 1991, GE spent $200 million on a groundwater pump and treatment system that reduced the flow of PCBs from five pounds to just three ounces a day.[4] Then he repeated GE's main talking point—a bald-faced lie—that "there is no credible evidence that PCBs cause cancer."[5] Only unreasonable environmental activists could expect the company to waste billions on irrational "greening" projects that would only have the "marginal benefit" of removing a flow of just a few ounces per day.

The contempt he showed the student still rankles me. Wasn't GE obliged to "fix what it broke"? Although I would spend the next two decades researching and writing about ways that businesses can be more environmentally and socially responsible, it wasn't until the events of the early 2020s—among them COVID-19, George Floyd's murder, and the Ukraine war—that the deeper implications of Welch's self-righteousness were brought home to me. He clearly believed his rationale was legitimate. But to me, there is something deeply wrong with a system that allowed him to evade such a fundamental responsibility—and that for a long time lionized him as one of the greatest business leaders ever.

While corporate leaders frequently talk about the sanctity of free market capitalism, what they really believe in is the privatization of profits and the socialization of costs. They intensively lobby governments to assume the various direct and indirect costs of their businesses, shamelessly misusing the concept of corporate personhood to gain legal rights—except when being a person would mean that they should take responsibility for their choices. Even more guilefully, they use a variety of strategies to remove such costs from their balance sheets and income statements and hide them from the public, including deliberate obfuscation, arcane accounting rules, and exploitation of the outmoded and fundamentally unfair ways that our society tabulates value.

This can be seen very clearly when you look at who benefited from and who paid for the inflationary spiral of the early 2020s. While the widely accepted narrative at first was that companies and consumers were both suffering, when the *Guardian* analyzed the financials and earnings calls of top corporations across a range of industries, it found that their quarterly profits had increased significantly in 2022. Data from the US Department of Commerce reveals a similar pattern: when inflation reached 8.5 percent in March 2022, corporate profits rose 35 percent.[6] This raises the question: Are corporations just making profits, or are they profiteering?

Profiteering is the exploitation of market imperfections to generate excessive and unfair levels of profits. At the height of the COVID-19 pandemic, some retailers took advantage of the high demand and temporary scarcity of essential goods like masks and sanitizers to charge exorbitant prices for them. Starting in 2021, Russia's threatened invasion of Ukraine led to disruptions in gas supplies. Energy companies exploited the fluctuations in prices to earn record profits. After Russia's invasion commenced in February 2022 and sanctions were imposed, oil and gas producers' income hit a new high of $4 trillion, according to the International Energy Agency, double the 2021 level. For the first six months of 2022, the top five oil companies—BP, Shell, ExxonMobil, Chevron, and Total—made adjusted profits of nearly $100 billion.[7]

While those are extreme and obvious examples of profiteering, such behaviors are pervasive, yet, because of how our systems are constructed, they are mostly hidden from sight. Over the past fifty-plus years, as corporations have overwhelmingly focused on delivering short-term value to shareholders, they have developed strategies and tactics that allow them to obscure and ignore the adverse consequences of the ways they produce and deliver their products and services. But someone has to pay these costs. For the most part, under the logic of today's economic system, it is society.

Another student at the Michigan event asked Welch a question about what we would now call DEI, or diversity, equity, and inclusion. It was well-known that the leading candidates to succeed Welch in the CEO role had been three white men: Jeffrey Immelt (who was ultimately chosen), James McNerney, and Robert Nardelli. As part of the selection process, members of GE's board had played golf with the candidates. Didn't that practice put women and people of color at a disadvantage, since so many golf clubs excluded them? The question was on point. Welch was a member of Augusta National Golf

Club, the site of the Masters, the United States' most prestigious professional golf tournament. Though the feminist icon Martha Burk launched a campaign to pressure the club into admitting women in 2003, it had held out for nearly a decade, until Condoleezza Rice and Darla Moore became its first female members in 2012.[8]

The question resonated with me because I had worked as a caddy at an exclusive golf club for ten years, starting at age thirteen, when I was old enough to get my working papers. Tramping through the beautiful, tree-lined landscape with a heavy bag of clubs over each shoulder, I would often hear golfers make racist and sexist remarks. Women were only allowed to play on Tuesdays ("ladies' day") and weekend afternoons—provided that they played with their husbands. The club's rules stipulated that all other tee times were reserved exclusively for male members and their male guests. While, to the best of my knowledge, that club did not formally exclude people of color from membership, I can't recall ever seeing a non-white golfer on its fairways.

Here, too, Welch pushed back: that's how business is done, he snapped. And the sad truth is, he was right. Golf is an important relationship-building activity, essential for developing the rapport with boards that CEOs need to be effective leaders. But Welch bristled at the implication that he might have benefited from his race or gender, or that anyone else might have been held back because of theirs. Earlier in the evening, in response to a lob from a CEO friend about his "most enduring success," Welch had reflected that it was the "meritocracy" he had created at GE. He might have sincerely believed that, but a host of well-known scholars, among them Thomas Piketty, Michael Sandel, and Robert Reich, have shown how un-meritocratic institutions like giant corporations really are.[9] Elites enthusiastically promote the idea of a meritocracy to hide the fact that upward mobility is constrained by institutional norms and practices that limit opportunities for women, minorities, and the less privileged.

Ironically—and appropriately—the term "meritocracy" was popularized by a 1958 book, *The Rise of the Meritocracy*, which used the term satirically.[10] The reality, its author Michael Young explained, is that "all manner of new ways for people to feather their own nests have been invented and exploited" by the already privileged, who nonetheless believe that their advancement is solely due to their merit.[11] As I discuss in more detail later, falling back on well-rehearsed discourse about "meritocracy" is a tactic to obscure the systemic nature of bias and discrimination in our world.

Behind a smoke screen of rhetoric about individual responsibility and personal choice, corporations and their leaders ruthlessly pursue their own interests, shifting the blame for the harms they cause onto society at large. People who want a share of the money and power these corporate titans control should "pull themselves up by their own bootstraps" like they supposedly did. As for the harms corporations create, it is up to us as individuals to avoid the unhealthy foods they produce, recycle the excess waste from their packaging, fact-check the social media sites they maintain to make certain they aren't feeding us disinformation, and so on.

Society has been led to believe that if enough people change their actions, we will change the world, and thus attention is turned away from the responsibility of corporations. Companies deflect attention from the problems they create by saying it is the government's responsibility to create solutions, or that these problems originate in their extended supply chains and are thus out of reach. These obfuscations deliberately promote a false view of reality in which it is up to us, the victims of their abuses, to resolve the problems they create.

Why should current and future citizens and taxpayers be on the hook for problems caused by corporations' shortsightedness and greed? It is a blatant theft of public resources. Worse still, the system has been deliberately designed to allow companies to maximize their selfishness. California businessman Paul Hawken, cofounder of the gardening retailer Smith & Hawken, put it this way: "We are stealing the future, selling it in the present, and calling it GDP."[12]

We are expected to believe that it is impossible for a great enterprise like GE to be sustainable, equitable, and profitable at the same time, but that it nonetheless should continue to chug forward, neither acknowledging nor being held accountable for the damage it does along the way. Economists talk about such unrecognized and unaccounted factors as the "external costs" or "externalities" of business: that is, the negative side effects of a company's operations and practices that are not factored into their profit and loss statements. These terms are just wonky enough to limit their full understanding to the accountants, sustainability experts, and activists who are trying to either hide or expose them.

But these hidden costs—which businesses intentionally obscure—don't just neutrally help corporations raise profits. Someone still has to pay for them, and the majority of the time, it is the public and the environment that foot the bill. The more of these costs that companies can push off of their ledgers, the higher their profits. The more devastating the environmental and societal consequences, the larger their reward for evading them.

Many corporations reap benefits from discriminatory behaviors. Denying loans to would-be homeowners in racially and ethnically segregated neighborhoods has been against the law since 1968, but it still shapes banks' lending practices today.[13] Because of the cultural expectation that women should be more involved than men in raising children, US companies have convinced us that childcare and parental leave are not their responsibility. Then, when schools were closed during the COVID pandemic, disproportionate numbers of women were forced to leave the workforce so they could take care of their homebound children. Companies save costs while women's careers are disproportionately derailed.

The hidden costs of fossil fuels are one of the most studied and explicitly quantified of these externalities. Harvard Business School professor Rebecca Henderson, author of *Reimagining Capitalism in a World on Fire*, arrays a substantial body of research to show that $10 worth of coal-fired electricity causes at least $8 worth of harm to human health and a minimum of $8 of environmental damage, so its real cost is more like $26.[14] But no one expects the power companies to pay for or in any way reimburse society for that $16.

Fossil fuel producers and users are obvious examples, but the externality problem is much more insidious and widely spread. Did you know that there is a good chance that the chocolate you eat was produced from cacao harvested by child and slave labor, and that its production has contributed to mass deforestation? Large chocolate companies depend on both to maintain their low prices and high margins.

How about financial services? These are frequently low-cost for the wealthy, while the economically disadvantaged are hit with high interest rates and fees. For instance, the average overdraft fee in 2020 was $33.47 (although it declined to $29.80 by the end of 2022).[15] Over the course of the COVID-19 pandemic, when millions of low-income workers were furloughed, America's top four banks reaped more than $4 billion in such fees. JPMorgan Chase alone pocketed $1.46 billion. Yet a report by the consulting firm McKinsey & Company indicated that fees for wealth management actually decreased during the same period.[16] In some cases, the financial industry is exploiting its own employees. A study from the UC Berkeley Labor Center reported a decade ago that, nationwide, fully one-third of bank tellers received some form of public assistance.[17] And that is just one of a host of shocking transfers of public resources, funds, and provisions to private corporations. In essence, the system has been set up so that the poor and governments subsidize the rich.

How about the plastic materials that are so ubiquitous in our world? The expectation that recycling is an individual responsibility has been ingrained in all of us. But what about the companies that produce all that plastic waste? I recently spoke with the CEO of a disposable drink-ware maker, who told me that when purchasing managers are given a choice between polypropylene or a biodegradable alternative that may cost twice as much, they inevitably choose the former. But how much is really being saved and by whom? Significant social and environmental costs are produced when discarded plastic packages, cups, and straws are deposited in landfills and the ocean, where they will remain for centuries. Those costs may not show up on the books of the companies that produced and purchased them, but humanity ultimately pays the bill.

The very air that we breathe is a free landfill for carbon emissions; the costs of climate change will number in the trillions of dollars. But the biggest emitters, the industries and countries that are the most responsible for the catastrophe, aren't required to pay more than a fraction of the cost, and most are fighting to avoid doing even that.

Because of the way our systems are set up, and how that shapes our cultural assumptions, the public does not recognize these negative effects as the responsibility of a company. So companies can simply ignore them, and the benefits flow right to the bottom line. Of course, if the value of something like clean air is not recognized and the damages to it are not tied to a responsible party, it gets abused.

This book aims to pull back the curtain on how business is engaging in profiteering by exploiting the public commons while convincing us that repair is our individual responsibility. As a result, this book shows in detail how the biggest crises of our day—climate change, inequality, and racism—are intimately connected to the same under-lying problem: the free lunch served to businesses every day of the year. While it is true that corporations didn't necessarily cause these problems, they perpetuate them and amplify their effects through their production, distribution, and marketing practices. Not only are companies passing off the associated costs, but they are actively sow-ing disinformation to convince us that they are right to do so.

———

How did we get here? Gary Gerstle, an American historian at the University of Cambridge, has argued that the last eighty years "can be understood in terms of the rise and fall of two political orders."[18] The first was the "New Deal order," which began in the 1930s when US president Franklin Delano Roosevelt established a social safety net that Americans eventually took for granted. The government safety net was supplemented by the generous benefit packages and pensions corporations gave employees through the 1940s, 1950s, and 1960s. While there was significant conflict between government and the corporate world, there was also a surprising amount of cooperation.

The second, which started in the 1960s and 1970s and picked up speed in the 1980s, is the "neoliberal order," in which free markets are sacrosanct and the government's main job is to get out of the way. The dominant view of the appropriate role of business took a 180-degree turn as well. Jack Welch, for example, was celebrated as "Neutron Jack" (after the neutron bomb, which would leave build-ings intact but kill the people) for the tens of thousands of layoffs, factory closings, and other cost-saving moves he orchestrated to deliver short-term value to shareholders during the early years of his tenure as CEO of GE.

More recently, however, the model Welch pioneered has under-gone a reappraisal. In 2022, for example, the *New York Times*'s David

Gelles published a systematic critique of Welch's management philosophy and the lasting impact it has had on business culture. The very title of the book pulls no punches: *The Man Who Broke Capitalism: How Jack Welch Gutted the Heartland and Crushed the Soul of Corporate America*. It is now clear, with some historical perspective, that the changes wrought by Welch were notable only due to their destructive nature.[19] But we need to go further in exposing the system that allowed such behaviors to be seen as a success.

Since 1980, when neoliberal principles took hold in our laws, markets, and cultures, the world's richest 1 percent have captured as much global income growth as the poorest half of the population. In the United States during this period, the income of the top 1 percent has grown five times faster than that of the bottom 90 percent.[20] The preponderance of temporary, contract, and gig workers in the twenty-first century has exacerbated wealth inequality and remains largely unaddressed. The *World Inequality Report* warns that in a "business as usual" future, global inequality will further intensify as climate change worsens in the Global South, which is more exposed to extreme temperatures.[21] Many of the people who live there will have to immigrate to safer places to survive.

The fundamental shift between the New Deal and neoliberal orders was dramatically illustrated in a 2020 essay in the *New York Times* by economist Robert Reich. In the 1950s, he wrote, Sears employees owned a quarter of the company, which allowed salesmen to retire with an average of $1 million in savings.[22] Compare that to Sears CEO Edward Lampert's complaints about the company's pension commitments in 2018, claiming they were a burden that hobbled the company's efforts to compete with other retailers, "many of which don't have large pension plans, and thus have not been required to allocate billions of dollars to these liabilities."[23] Think about Lampert's statement. Are employees who worked to build a business over decades simply liabilities? In our current economic operating model, that view is deemed correct.

Once companies were solely concerned with delivering short-term value, it no longer made sense to offer pensions or health-care benefits to employees, or to be conscientious about the environment. During the last five decades, the incentives and processes established to focus executives on share prices pushed them to exploit the very constituencies and resources that are essential for their success.

Gelles's examination of Jack Welch's disastrous legacy makes this clear. "For decades after World War II," he writes, "big American companies bent over backward to distribute their profits widely. In General Electric's 1953 annual report, the company proudly talked about how much it was paying its workers, how its suppliers were benefiting, and even how much it paid the government in taxes."[24] All this changed after Welch and his ilk took over the company. From 1981 until Welch stepped down in 2001, "G.E. unleashed a wave of mass layoffs and factory closures that other companies followed. The trend helped destabilize the American middle class. Profits began flowing not back to workers in the form of higher wages, but to big investors in the form of stock buybacks. And G.E. began doing everything it could to pay as little in taxes as possible."[25]

A key tenet of the neoliberal order that the Sears and GE cases illustrate is shareholder primacy, the idea that the corporation's sole object is the maximization of short-term profits for shareholders. The seeds for this idea were planted in an article by the free market economist Milton Friedman in the *New York Times Magazine* in 1970, in which he argued that corporations should only engage in activities that increase profits and, hence, shareholder returns.[26] According to this logic, companies should limit the responsibility they take for whatever factors can legally be considered external, like the air quality in the town where the factory is located or employees' medical expenses. And that is precisely what companies have done.

While there are some indications that corporate actors are beginning to acknowledge the need for a more expansive perspective, Gelles takes a cautious view. "With all the talk of stakeholder capitalism and ESG [environmental, social, and governance] and the 2019 Business Roundtable statement on the purpose of the corporation," he says, we are now "maybe at that point in a pendulum's arc when it pauses and starts to perhaps begin its trajectory back in the other direction." It was a generational project to implement the ideas of Friedman and Welch; it is likely to "take decades to rebalance things."[27]

To spur this generational project forward, it is important that we recognize how changes in underlying systems occur. Shareholder capitalism didn't become the dominant paradigm simply because Friedman articulated the idea; it was a product of many forces on many fronts. Two of the most significant were corporate governance practices, such as the development of stock options as a part of executive compensation packages, and legal changes regarding corporate responsibilities that explicitly defined the purpose of the corporation and its board in terms of shareholder service. Stock options have driven a huge wedge between executives and rank-and-file employees. As Figure 1 shows, back in 1970, the CEO-to-average-worker pay ratio was about twenty to one. Since the popularity of options took off, corporate inequality has skyrocketed; the ratio now stands at over three hundred to one.

Further, once executives were solely focused on delivering short-term value to shareholders, it no longer made sense to offer pension or health-care benefits to employees, to be conscientious about pollution, or even to worry about the long-term viability of the system after they had cashed in their shares. That is, this is a story

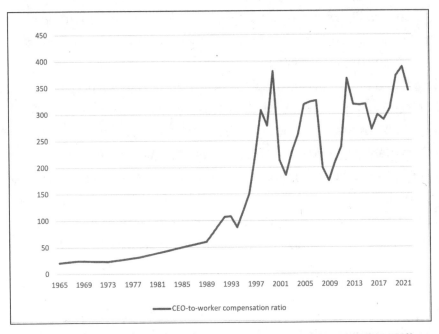

Figure I: CEO to average worker compensation ratio in the United States, 1965–2022[28]

not just about CEO's rising pay but as we will discuss in more detail later, also about systematic pressure to lower employees' compensation—a perverse incentive to treat coworkers worse.

To further see how systems change occurs, let's look at corporate governance related to stock options. The idea of stock options was developed in a series of academic papers building directly on the logic in Friedman's piece. Harvard financial economist Michael Jensen and his coauthors, in some of the most highly cited academic papers on firm ownership and control, discussed the natural conflict of interest that existed between shareholders—the owners of the firm—and the "agents" they hire to run the firm on their behalf (its executives).[29]

Since publicly traded firms can have hundreds of thousands or more shareholders, their power to monitor is dispersed, and so the agents can potentially misuse corporate assets for their own purposes. The solution, according to Jensen, is to financially align the interests of the shareholders and the agents via share-based compensation packages, which has led to spiraling executive compensation.

At the same time, another set of changes affected the market for corporate control. Companies and their boards were pushed to remove anti-takeover provisions. This was a way to keep executives in line with the threat of losing their job from a takeover. It also led to the era of corporate raiders, like Carl Icahn in the real world and Michael Douglas's Gordon Gekko in the movie *Wall Street*. Corporate raiders bought companies not to run them but to sell them off in pieces, dropping commitments to employees such as pensions and becoming rich in the process.

Crucial to this shift was a set of legal changes, particularly a well-known 1986 Delaware Supreme Court case involving the takeover of Revlon, which found that its board of directors was obligated to maximize stockholder value by accepting the highest bid. Directors could be sued or even ousted for not acting in the short-term interests of shareholders. The idea got stronger over time. In *eBay v. Craigslist*, in 2010, the Delaware Court of Chancery held that a corporate mission that "seeks not to maximize the economic value of a for-profit Delaware corporation for the benefit of its stockholders" is invalid, because it doesn't line up with the directors' fiduciary duties.[30] If additional missions are being pursued, the court found, they must also lead to an economic benefit.

But as is clear today, the consequences of these changes—intended and unintended—have been disastrous. In a 2020 documentary, Michael Jensen contritely accepted the blame for the negative effects his work has had on the world, admitting that he now knows that "maximizing shareholder value is a stupid idea" and that a sole focus on the stock price will lead to the unfair exploitation of labor.[31] Even Jack Welch, who was called the "poster boy for shareholder capitalism," ultimately acknowledged that "shareholder value is the dumbest idea in the world" when pursued exclusively, adding that "shareholder value is a result, not a strategy. . . . Your main constituencies are your employees, your customers and your products."[32] Better late than never, but once laws and corporate practices are in place, they are hard to change, and so we are still stuck with many of the practices their earlier activism created. Looking ahead, if we are to be able to reverse course, we should consider what we can learn from the playbook of this thirty-plus-year change effort.

———

Before we delve into solutions, let's look back and consider in more detail what the neoliberal model and shareholder-driven capitalism have led to over the last half century. Most of the gains they have produced have gone to the already wealthy. Between 1970, when shareholder primacy began taking hold, and 2018, the share of national income earned by middle-income households in the United States fell from 62 percent to 43 percent, while the share held by upper-income households increased from 29 percent to 48 percent.[33] The graph in Figure 2—known as an elephant graph for its shape, with a hump in the middle and long trunk extending skyward—illustrates the inexorable rise of inequality globally since 1995. Nearly all the substantial income and wealth gains in the global economy have gone to the top 1 percent, and mostly to the top 0.1 percent.

While this has been a boon for the rich, more attention needs to be paid to its costs, as the burdens of poverty and environmental degradation are increasingly borne by marginalized populations. As António Guterres, secretary-general of the United Nations, put it a few years ago, in today's world, a tiny number of people are sailing around on super yachts while countless more are clinging to inflatable lifeboats.[34] While his words are metaphorically apt, they miss

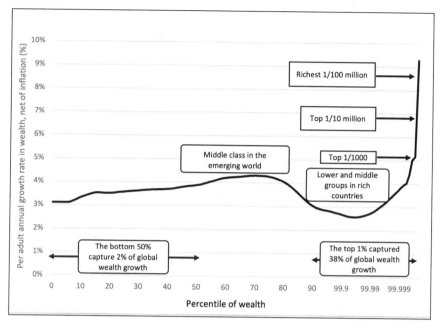

Figure 2: Average Annual Wealth Growth Rate, 1995–2021[35]

the causal connection. The rich are in yachts because they are systematically exploiting the people in the lifeboats, shifting their costs onto them to further increase their wealth.

A study of Organisation for Economic Co-operation and Development (OECD) countries, most of which have high average incomes, shows that a 1 percent increase in inequality lowers gross domestic product (GDP) by between 0.6 percent and 1.1 percent.[36] In other words, greater inequality results in an overall decline of national wealth. This reduces tax revenues and hence services like education and health care for the less well-off. All the while, the incomes of the rich continue to rise and they are increasingly able to buffer themselves from the situations faced by average citizens. It is a self-reinforcing dynamic, as French economist Thomas Piketty and others have shown.

Thus, counter to the common narrative that the savings and investments of the wealthy create a rising tide that lifts all boats, when wealth is concentrated the opposite occurs. In his book *Why Does Inequality Matter?*, for example, the Harvard moral philosopher Thomas Scanlon describes how the rich use their capital to exercise unacceptable forms of control over the lives of the less advantaged, increasing their own wealth and solidifying their positions and status. They do not allow resources to trickle down, as the wealthy would like us to believe.

Reams of social science studies have revealed the self-perpetuating cycles of privilege that define the lives of the wealthy and also the cycles of poverty and disadvantage that define the lives of most everyone else. Children born into wealthy families typically have access to better schools, more educational opportunities, and better health care, which can give them an unfair advantage in life. This contradicts the principle of equality of opportunity, a foundation of societies around the world—especially the United States—whereby, in theory, everyone should have an equal chance to succeed. Inequality exacerbates the resentments and social divisions that cause political instability.

Inequality also causes negative effects on the planet, as the richest 1 percent create twice the carbon emissions of the poorer half of humanity.[37] In 2021, the top 10 percent of global emitters (782 million people) accounted for about 48 percent of global CO_2 emissions, while the bottom 50 percent (3.8 billion people) accounted for only 7 percent.[38] So, over time, the inequality of conditions widens: the rich have better and better lives, while the poor endure more and more of the effects of climate change. North America is home to just 5 percent of the world's population but accounts for nearly 20 percent of the world's CO_2 emissions. Countries in the Global North have carbon footprints that are one hundred times greater than all the world's poorest countries combined.[39] Less-developed countries receive a smaller share of the benefits of fossil fuels while suffering more long-term damage.

It is important to look at these issues through a historical lens. Just as advantages are cumulative, so are damages; once in the atmosphere, carbon emissions take many centuries to dissipate. When assessing emissions, it is important to consider both the stock and the flows. Flows—such as how much the United States or China is emitting in a year—are frequently reported, but for climate change, the stock—or overall amount of carbon already released into the atmosphere—is more important. The factors creating global warming are mostly already in place, contributed by developed countries. Historically, the United States has contributed about 25 percent of global emissions, while Africa and Asia (excluding China) have contributed a very small amount.[40] Although Africa accounts for 16 percent of the global population, it emits just 4 percent of the world's CO_2.[41]

And who pays for the damage from climate change? A World Bank report estimates that ecological crises could push as many as 135 million people into poverty by 2030.[42] In a recent and compelling demonstration of this point, in 2022 nearly a third of the land area of Pakistan was underwater due to flooding. As the country's finance minister put it at the time, "Pakistan is bearing the brunt of the climate crisis despite its 'small carbon footprint.'"[43]

While policymakers around the world acknowledge these facts, countries in the Global North are reluctant to help the regions that suffer the most, even though the low wages in the Global South are what underwrite their lifestyles. The annual UN Conference of the Parties (COP) climate meetings draw attention to the issue, but decisive actions have not been forthcoming. At COP15 in Copenhagen in 2009, developed countries set a goal of spending $100 billion a year by 2020 to address the climate adaptation and mitigation needs of developing countries, but came nowhere close to meeting it. During the COP26 climate talks in November 2021, they further delayed the creation of this $100 billion-a-year fund.[44] In recent years, such as at COP28 in Dubai, which was led by the CEO of an oil company, many have argued fossil fuel interests have co-opted the COP process. So perhaps it is not surprising that public investments remain far below what was promised and what is needed.

Understanding the Conditions for Change

When considering the system and mechanisms for change, it is important to recognize that markets, profits, and capital are all historical and cultural constructions that depend on choices that we make. They shape our political, legal, social, and educational systems, which then reshape us in turn. We tend to take culture and norms for granted. They are not actively examined, much like the famous parable in which an older fish asks a younger fish, "How's the water?" and the younger fish replies, "What's water?" The point being, we are not aware of what surrounds us on a daily basis.

We have allowed businesses to define the assumptions that guide the lived realities of our economy and society in their favor, obscuring the fundamental inequalities that concentrate power and profits in the hands of a few. Piketty's 2020 book *Capital and Ideology* highlighted this point, describing the ideologies elites have developed throughout history to perpetuate their power.[45] In preindustrial times, heredity-based systems rested on norms of existing wealth and inheritance to define the legitimate source of social position, and privilege and mobility between social classes was limited if not entirely nonexistent.

Today, we're told that ostensibly just principles like meritocracy and entrepreneurship ensure that anyone who makes the right choices can rise up the ladder of success through hard work. But when we focus solely on individuals and the supposed opportunities they have, we ignore the structural and cognitive barriers that severely limit their options. This leads us to blame the poor for their lack of income mobility, instead of questioning the structures that hold them back.

We also reflexively blame big corporations for climate change and inequality. While they certainly make outsize contributions to these systemic issues (and so can also contribute to solving them), corporations, too, are products of a broken system that has long encouraged and rewarded their bad behavior. The crises surrounding the COVID pandemic shone a blinding light on just how broken it is, with extensive supply-chain disruptions, mass layoffs, and inadequate health care.

Employees of companies like Amazon and Costco exposed themselves to the contagion, working long hours and providing the essential services that allowed most Americans to enjoy the conveniences they take for granted. But in many cases, their employers were not paying them enough to cover their basic needs, such as food, housing, and health care. US Government Accountability Office research has shown that in 2020 the wages of many Walmart and McDonald's employees were so low that they qualified for Medicaid and food stamps. "In short," as *Bloomberg* put it in 2021, "corporate America is pawning off the cost of rock-bottom wages on taxpayers."[46]

It is not enough to blame and shame, or even just to reform the worst corporate actors; we need to rethink and transform the entire underlying system. As we will discuss in more detail below, the timing may be right for change, as the neoliberal paradigm that has reigned for more than forty years is fraying at its edges. But systemic change is challenging and cannot happen overnight. A good way to begin is by taking a second look at the Friedman article that was the watershed for shareholder primacy, and what came after it. While he did say that the business of business is to "make as much money as possible," what is often forgotten is that he qualified it by adding:

"While conforming to the basic rules of the society, both those embodied in law and those embodied in ethical custom."

Of course, when corporations violate the law, they need to be brought to account. But like Friedman and his intellectual followers did over decades in solidifying shareholder primacy, to effectively reverse course, we need to focus attention on changing the laws, norms, and customs that encourage their bad behavior. When laws fail to uphold our ethical standards, they need to be changed.

Maintaining the Status Quo

As frequently happens at the beginning of periods of dramatic upheaval, elites themselves are now calling for change. Often, they do so defensively, as a way to forestall governmental actions while making cosmetic changes that keep them in control. In late 2019, the Business Roundtable (BRT), an association of more than two hundred elite American CEOs, adopted a new "Statement on the Purpose of a Corporation," which declared that companies should deliver value not just to shareholders but also to stakeholders like employees and communities.[47] The theme of the 2020 World Economic Forum in Davos, Switzerland, was "Stakeholders for a Cohesive and Sustainable World." Leading investors like BlackRock's Larry Fink and government bodies such as the Securities and Exchange Commission (SEC) have challenged companies to take responsibility for their externalities.

But at a fundamental level, their pleas for corporate responsibility and stakeholder capitalism are more or less in line with what I heard from Jack Welch over two decades ago. The notions of "doing well by doing good" and finding a "win-win" that dominate discourse today are in keeping with the neoliberal idea that companies should always maximize their profits while maybe doing some good on the side. This shouldn't come as a surprise; those who benefit from the status quo have a strong interest in preserving it.

This, too, is typical of change projects throughout history: those in power begin by proposing solutions that deal with problems in a one-off fashion and that are frequently embedded within the paradigm they claim to want to change. They focus on symptoms instead of root causes. Today's "reformers" deny the fundamental conflict between caring for society and the environment on the one hand and optimizing shareholder value on the other. Believing that circle can be squared is a potent but dangerous fantasy that creates cognitive dissonance. American writer and activist Audre Lorde puts this powerfully with regard to discrimination: "The master's tools will never dismantle the master's house. They may allow us temporarily to beat him at his own game, but they will never enable us to bring about genuine change."[48] As we will discuss more later, pursuing change justified by the logic of the existing system will lead to "fixes that fail": solutions that seem plausible because they aim to address the symptoms but that leave the underlying systemic issues in place.

We need to view skeptically some of the calls for stakeholder capitalism and environmental, social, and governance accountability coming from corporate leaders, acknowledging that they may hide traps that even those with years of corporate sustainability experience can fall into. Consider, for example, Alan Murray's 2022 book on the promise of stakeholder capitalism, *Tomorrow's Capitalist*. A long-standing observer of large corporations, Murray, the CEO of *Fortune*, unquestioningly accepted the articulated view among corporate leaders that "in the long run, there is no tradeoff between purpose and profits."[49]

Murray has been rightly criticized for taking what his fellow CEOs say at face value, focusing on the bits of good they're doing that they want us to see, rather than the many bad things they're doing that they prefer to hide. One celebrated leader is JPMorgan Chase's CEO, Jamie Dimon, who helped draft the Business Roundtable's statement promoting stakeholder capitalism while sidestepping accountability for his own bank's failure to pay some of its employees a living wage and the billions in overdraft fees it charged its least-advantaged customers during the COVID pandemic.[50]

Insisting on a business case—that is, corporations doing good will lead to them doing well—for a just economic system precludes the governmental and private interventions that will also be needed to reknit our disintegrating social fabric and restore the planet. Recent research from Andrew King of Boston University and his collaborators has supported this point, arguing that, while the idea of a win-win may look compelling on the surface, it is often based on cherry-picked cases and motivated by a desire to make executives and customers feel good.[51]

There are literally thousands of studies on the financial benefit of doing good (for example, ESG or sustainability strategies), a number that in and of itself should raise questions. Why study the same idea over and over again? A few plausible reasons: One is because the researchers have an ideological commitment to the outcome, as King suggests. A related possibility is that it is just not possible to establish a firm relationship between "doing good" and "doing well," and so people keep trying. University of Warsaw professor Marc Orlitzky, coauthor of one of the most highly cited meta-analyses of the financial returns of ESG, supports this point, arguing "that the different measures and methods used by scholars make it impossible to form a meaningful synthesis."[52]

Even Harvard's George Serafeim—author of some of the most frequently cited academic studies connecting ESG factors with financial performance, as well as a recent book that pursues a win-win theme, *Purpose and Profit: How Business Can Lift Up the World*—concluded in a piece with his colleagues Michael Porter and Mark Kramer that "despite countless studies, there has never been conclusive evidence that socially responsible screens deliver alpha" (meaning they perform substantially better than their irresponsible peers).[53] In reality, much if not all of the academic evidence for the link between ESG and financial performance reflects the researchers' wishful thinking.

Part of what makes this line of argument seductive is that there are many examples where companies no doubt have profited by doing the right thing. We will even discuss some of these in this book. For instance, implementing energy-efficient measures, reducing waste, and improving materials-recycling practices can significantly lower utility and waste-disposal bills. Shifting to renewable energy sources may also result in long-term cost savings. And promoting the well-being and satisfaction of employees can lead to higher productivity and retention rates. But it is essential to recognize and acknowledge that, while there are many examples of doing well by doing good, to rely on this logic to substantially address our systemic problems is a fool's errand and misdirects attention from the structural problems to the conclusion that corporations will become sustainable because it is in their own self-interest.

A more arguable proposition is that the idea of ESG can be—and often is—used to gaslight the general public. As the authors of a long-form investigative piece on MCSI, the largest ESG rating agency, put it in *Bloomberg*, ESG is a "mirage," and sustainable investing is mostly about sustaining corporations' bottom lines, not the environment or society.[54] The idea that businesses' self-interest will solve the world's problems just offers false hope.

Companies trumpet their new focus on stakeholders as a way to obscure the underlying systemic issues. According to Sony Kapoor, managing director of the Nordic Institute for Finance, Technology, and Sustainability, "Most ESG investing is a ruse to launder reputations, maximize fees, and assuage guilt."[55] In fact, the focus on such investments creates false hope, oversells their capacity to outperform the market, and likely contributes to the delay of long-past-due regulatory actions.

So it is not surprising that, while many companies performed good works during the pandemic, a growing body of research suggests that most companies in the Business Roundtable are not following through on their avowed "fundamental commitment to all of [their] stakeholders." Scholars at London Business School and Columbia Business School found that many of the companies whose CEOs signed the BRT statement had higher carbon emissions than similar non-signatory firms and were cited for more environmental infractions.[56] Research from the Wharton School suggests that BRT signatories did less for their stakeholders than non-BRT companies while, not coincidentally, returning more money to their shareholders.[57] Some researchers have explained this as corporate "moral licensing," a phenomenon in which doing good in one realm gives an actor "permission" to ignore their responsibilities in another. An example of this is Marriott, a BRT signatory that soon after the pandemic struck was exposed by the *New York Times* to have increased dividends while lowering employee benefits.[58] For all the BRT's fine talk about stakeholder capitalism—whereby the group advocates that it is in business's long-term interests to serve society—it's also worth remembering that the BRT was a key player in the passage of the $1.5 trillion in business-friendly tax cuts during the Trump administration.[59]

The Business Roundtable's words are starting to look more like a public relations campaign to forestall greater governmental oversight than like a paradigm shift. After a detailed study of the policies and behaviors of BRT firms two years after the statement, scholars from Harvard concluded the statement was "mostly for show."[60] The disconnect between what BRT companies say and what they do is especially egregious when considering their dogged work to undermine environmental standards and accountability.

On the third anniversary of the BRT's announcement, the *Guardian* reported that, while the signatories generated "goodwill and positive PR by publishing bold climate goals," they have not been "held accountable or legally liable for" them. Further, the BRT has continued to spend "millions of dollars to lobby governments against meaningful climate action."[61] The group spent lavishly to stop the Biden administration's environmental agenda and is strongly opposed to important aspects of the SEC's proposals to require corporations to measure and report the greenhouse gas emissions generated in their supply chains, which is where the vast majority of their environmental impacts are.

Taking a page from the win-win of stakeholder capitalism, BlackRock CEO Larry Fink famously declared ESG to be an essential component of long-term value. As early as 2018, when being interviewed at the *New York Times*'s *DealBook* conference, he said, "Demand for ESG is going to transform all investing."[62] In other venues, Fink has argued that companies should report on their impacts on the environment and society, which will lower their long-term risks, lead to long-term value creation, and result in better management overall. Firms that do not take ESG factors into account, he warns, are more likely to face regulatory fines, lawsuits, and reputational damage.[63] As he puts it, ESG is "essential to long-term profitability."

But for all of Fink's full-throated defense of ESG, it is telling that in the face of "anti-woke" political pressure from pension funds in Florida and Texas, BlackRock announced in 2022 that it was scaling back support for environmental resolutions, backing only 24 percent of such resolutions compared to 43 percent the previous year, and that they "will continue to invest in and support fossil fuel companies."[64]

Even before this reversal, Tariq Fancy, who served as BlackRock's global chief investment officer for sustainable investing until 2019, said that BlackRock's approach to ESG created the illusion of progress while obscuring the fundamental challenges of climate change and other problems.[65] According to Fancy, BlackRock consistently chose profits over environmental responsibility, and he made the important distinction that assessing climate risk "isn't the same as fighting climate change." All BlackRock cares about is burnishing its own reputation by putting a coat of green paint on many not-so-green practices, and the investment firm's chief aim, Fancy said, was to get "money out before [climate change] hits."[66] All of which became blindingly obvious when Fink reversed course after the anti-ESG mob gained strength.

Is the Pendulum Swinging Back?

Columbia historian Adam Tooze, author of the 2021 book *Shutdown: How Covid Shook the World's Economy*, argues that the events of 2020 and 2021 provided the shock that was needed to end the era of neoliberalism and shift us into a new one.[67] Indian author Arundhati Roy provides further perspective. "Historically," she wrote in the *Financial Times*, "pandemics have forced humans to break with the past and imagine their world anew. This one is no different. It is a portal, a gateway between one world and the next."[68]

As the world struggled with COVID, it started to come to a new understanding of the existential challenge of climate change. The UN climate meetings in Glasgow in November 2021 concluded with the bleak projection that even if all existing climate commitments are met, temperatures will rise by 2.4 degrees Celsius by 2100, well above the 1.5-degree threshold for significant disasters such as dramatic sea level rise.[69] The finance minister of Tuvalu, an island nation in the Pacific, gave his address standing knee-deep in the sea to depict the likely fate of his country.

We need to better recognize that world-shattering crises tend to erupt relatively quickly. There is not a gradual on-ramp during which we can slowly change; the shocks occur in dramatic and discontinuous ways. When Mike Campbell, a character in Ernest Hemingway's 1926 novel *The Sun Also Rises,* is asked how he went bankrupt, he answers, "Two ways, gradually and then suddenly." This is how societal change occurs as well. It starts slowly. Little by little, things begin to shift as a new political party takes office and loosens environmental and business regulations. The norms around executives' fiduciary obligations start to change. Narratives around once-fringe cultural norms become socially acceptable. More floods occur. The changes may not appear to be negative or positive at first. But over time, they add up. And then, suddenly and seemingly without warning, comes a tipping point, when everything happens at once: war, famine, economic collapse. If we had been paying attention to how the changes were building up, we would have anticipated the big one. A number of the indicators mentioned above, and others I will discuss in this book, suggest that our world is on the precipice of such a massive change.

Human history has shown this again and again, from the abrupt collapse of Bronze Age civilizations in the Mediterranean in 1177 BCE, to the deforestation of Easter Island, to the end of the Anasazi and Mayan civilizations in the Americas. Ecological destruction played a huge role in all of these. Will our own future be any different? It is up to us, and our time is running short.

Although we face seemingly intractable divides and polarization, it is precisely during turbulent times that major societal reforms occur. As Piketty put it, during these times "ideology becomes increasingly fragile as the contradictions intensify," leading to paradigm shifts. Philosopher Thomas Kuhn identified such shifts in the sciences: when the dominant paradigm is no longer sustainable, it falls out of favor, leading to a new era that reflects a fundamental change in basic concepts, practices, and assumptions.

Considered from this perspective, while the virulence of the anti-ESG mob's rhetoric may cower actors like Fink, it is also a welcome sign of insecurity. The term "woke" was not even mentioned in the 2016 Republican debates, yet now it is commonly decried by many on the right as one of the most significant threats to America. ESG is now a toxic trio of letters that has come to encompass any kind of awareness of environmental threats or social inequality, despite there having been decades of ESG investing and vocal support of these causes for many years by influential financial market actors. People become more defensive when they know that the systems that have supported their privileges are crumbling.

Given climate-change-induced disasters, the rise of xenophobic populism, spiraling inequality, and racism, we are at one of those turning points between ideological eras. As the French author Victor Hugo once said: "There is nothing more powerful than an idea whose time has come."

Our current era has much in common with the Gilded Age in the nineteenth century, when leaps in industrial, communications, and transportation technology transformed the ways that people lived but also led to extreme income inequality and the rise of a new class of ultrarich entrepreneurs, such as John D. Rockefeller, Andrew Carnegie, Cornelius Vanderbilt, J. P. Morgan, and Jay Gould. There was political gridlock and a backlash against immigration, and in two national elections (1876 and 1888) the Electoral College delivered the presidency to candidates who did not win the popular vote. Our own epoch has seen the rise of billionaire technology entrepreneurs like Bill Gates, Elon Musk, Jeff Bezos, and Mark Zuckerberg, a hyper-partisan politics that is too gridlocked to deal effectively with health care, gun laws, and the climate crisis, and massive economic inequality.

Will this new Gilded Age be followed by another Progressive Era? It's hard to say for sure. While most people agree that it's wrong for companies to profiteer by carving out the most lucrative segments of the value chain while foisting the associated costs on society, we don't yet have an organizing framework to force companies to change. And while many people extol the power of stakeholder capitalism to reorient our systems, as discussed, this idea has been co-opted by those who benefit from the existing paradigm to forestall deeper change. A new organizing paradigm for society and the economy is hard to visualize, and, on the surface, there is no overarching logic to link issues like climate change, inequity, and racism together so they can be addressed and redressed comprehensively.

But perhaps we can. In the following pages, in addition to analyzing the problems that have developed over decades and that characterize our current economic system, I will also put forth a systems-change perspective to reverse course. There is not one simple solution, but this change will require multifaceted action directed at the root causes.

I don't underestimate our challenges. Such work has many parts that are interlinked and self-reinforcing and are more than what one company, group, or even government can do. But we have urgency on our side. It took decades for the neoliberal, shareholder-first ideology to become hardwired in our cultural and institutional systems, but, given climate change and global inequalities, we don't have decades to reverse the trend. However, we can take guidance from the post-Friedman revolution, as the success of the neoliberal project has left clues for how to tip the scales in the opposite direction.

———

The Profiteers is divided into three parts. Part I lays out what I see as the core problem with our economic system—the ways that businesses transfer their hidden costs onto society—exposing the systems that incentivize them to do so and the corporate gaslighting processes that distract the public from knowing who is responsible.

I thus aim to redirect the discussion about corporate accountability from a focus on how stakeholder capitalism and ESG are supposedly good for business to a deeper consideration of the impacts on society and the planet. The crucial question then becomes not how to reap the potential economic benefits of ESG, as is commonly argued, but who pays the costs for companies ignoring ESG?

A fundamental lesson I have aimed to impart to my students is the importance of focusing on the right questions. To me, the decades-long win-win dead end is an example of asking the wrong question. In the popular science-fiction novel *The Hitchhiker's Guide to the Galaxy*, when a supercomputer named Deep Thought was asked to provide the answer to the "Ultimate Question of Life, the Universe, and Everything," after 7.4 million years the machine replies, "42." Deep Thought then explains that, while it has found the answer, it was unclear what the actual "Ultimate Question" is, so the answer is meaningless.

Asking the wrong question can cause us to focus on wrong or even meaningless solutions and also miss the underlying causes of problems. Asking if doing well can lead to doing good is hardly the same thing as actually knowing how or why to deal with climate change and inequality.

But doing well by doing good is an easy pill for the public to swallow, and companies know this. So they have built up this idea to obscure the fact that huge shares of their profits depend on hiding externalities and maintaining the legal, economic, and social systems that allow them to skirt responsibility for those costs. These companies then further exploit—and in some cases, create—systemic gaps that leave society, the environment, and communities holding the bag.

Building off the critique in Part I, Part II of *The Profiteers* digs deeper into the problems of environmental sustainability and the fair treatment of labor throughout production systems and supply chains. Importantly, it also outlines a series of externality busters: emerging models of circularity, regeneration, and equity that are laying the foundation for virtuous cycles that can lead to systemic change.

While enhanced government regulation is clearly part of the answer, corporate innovation is equally essential. As the science fiction writer William Gibson famously wrote, "The future is already here—it's just not very evenly distributed."[70] Likewise, many of the new models I will explore are proven concepts but are neither well-known nor conceptually connected—yet. I articulate the ways a growing number of next-generation business leaders believe that they are responsible for their products from "end to end" and are creating an organizing framework for developing a new era of corporate responsibility. This is not built on the win-win logic of many so-called reformers today. Instead, these new leaders are rethinking the economic systems that underlie global business, taking novel actions to reimagine operations to minimize negative impacts, and creating new ways for business to properly absorb their hidden costs.

Grove Collaborative, for example, was founded in 2014 to help people find home products—soap, skin care, pet food, and more—that use sustainable ingredients and packaging. It has since grown into a successful online subscription service with annual revenues of about $400 million and a valuation of over $1.5 billion; in 2022, it went public.[71] One of its focuses is the problem of plastic waste. "I can make more money selling virgin plastic that the world has to deal with down the road," cofounder and CEO Stuart Landesberg told me. "That's it, that's my incentive—it's in my shareholders' mandate." As for recycling, it's "a wonderful distraction that allows consumers to distance themselves from the negative impact of the single-use product that they're consuming."

But, Landesberg continued, "it's a false choice to say that the options are between today's insane and unconscionable use of virgin plastic or just increasing plastic recycling. Of course, it's better to be recycling, but that's not actually the choice that we, as an industry, have." As he articulates, the responsibility of industry should be to stop using a material that is environmentally destructive, further reduce the overall amount of packaging, and choose materials that can be as close to a closed loop in recycling as possible—such as aluminum and paper, which, once used, can be almost entirely recycled to create new products. Grove Collaborative is putting its money where its mouth is. Recognizing that its biggest externality is plastic, the company priced plastic packaging and put it on the balance sheet, effectively taxing itself and the brands it sells to incentivize the use of more sustainable materials.

The shoe and apparel company Allbirds has developed an in-depth carbon accounting system, and the personal care company Dr. Bronner's is working to create a "regenerative organic standard." Other pioneers in this space include Greyston Bakery, the maker of the brownie bits in Ben & Jerry's ice cream, which developed an "open hiring" model to overcome biased employment practices. Financial services to scale these models are essential elements of any new system. The insurance company Lemonade is pioneering an innovative and responsible way to insure peoples' homes and lives. Financial technology company PayActiv has created an electronic payments system that allows employees to access their wages before payday, without the high interest rates of costly payday loans and with the added benefit of building savings and financial stability.

While many of these companies are in North America, this is a global movement, and there are important innovators in Europe, Asia, and South America as well. Germany's Ecosia, for example, is the largest search engine based in Europe. It attracts users with a unique proposition: every search helps reforestation efforts around the world. Tony's Chocolonely is a Dutch chocolate company that was founded with the goal of eliminating slavery and child labor from the cacao industry. Nativa, an Italian consulting company, led efforts to introduce a new corporate structure into Italian law, the *società benefit*, or benefit corporation. Brazilian health and beauty giant Natura &Co has pioneered activism around the world.

The leaders of these companies—in industries ranging from finance, tech, and consulting to food, home goods, and apparel—are radically rethinking our economic systems and taking novel actions to reimagine business operations in responsible ways. But if their efforts are to succeed, we need to appreciate the scale and scope of the problem—and learn to see through the smoke screen of disinformation and lies that the system uses to protect itself from scrutiny.

While Part II examines specific problems that stem from externalities, in Part III of this book, I open the aperture to consider a number of broader groups and systems that can hold companies accountable for their end-to-end responsibilities. I unpack the need for action across governmental, market, business, and consumer sectors to spur change toward an economic system that prioritizes and reinforces regenerative practices that lead to positive externalities.

While there is no shortage of examples of bad actors in our global economic system, there are many others who are demanding fairer and more sustainable practices and working to create new paradigms in which profits and prosperity are shared, businesses make positive contributions to society, production processes become less environmentally destructive, and everyone has a shot at success.

During World War II, Allied supreme commander Dwight D. Eisenhower coordinated the largest military undertaking ever with the 1944 D-Day invasion of Normandy. He not only managed huge sea, air, and land forces but also accounted for unpredictable weather as well as the mercurial political wills of Franklin Delano Roosevelt, Winston Churchill, and Charles de Gaulle. When asked about his principles of success, Eisenhower said, "Whenever I run into a problem I can't solve, I always make it bigger. I can never solve it by trying to make it smaller, but if I make it big enough, I can begin to see the outlines of a solution."

There is incredible truth to this adage when considering today's huge, systemic problems like climate change and inequality. If we try to solve our tough problems by making them smaller—for example, by just focusing on certain aspects or specific companies—we can only see the same constraints we have become accustomed to. This familiarity masks our vision and prevents us from finding new insights. However, by making the problem bigger, a new context can be seen, bringing aspects of the larger system into consideration. This allows us to look at things with a fresh set of eyes, opening the way to new thinking and new avenues of creativity.

If we are to create a new paradigm for business that is regenerative at its core—that is, one that shifts the logic of business from a linear "take, make, waste" orientation to one where virtuous cycles drive positive change—we need to see the overarching system and delineate the multi-sector and coordinated action that is necessary for reform.

Taking pages from the playbook of the post-Friedman intellectuals and activists that created today's neoliberal system, I highlight the importance of cross-sector work—joining governmental response, changes in investment markets, and reorientation of corporate priorities that form the elements of a paradigm built on new corporate governance standards and mechanisms and the reconceptualization of finance and ownership. I also show how mobilized corporations and individuals can collectively push for change.

Thus, while I expose the bad behavior of corporations and the bankruptcy of the neoliberal regime that encourages them, my goal is not simply to critique but also to lay the groundwork for a better understanding of how individuals, businesses, and governments can work together to recreate our economic system and pave the way for a more equitable, sustainable, and ultimately regenerative future.

PART I

HOW AND WHY WE ALL PAY FOR BUSINESS'S FREE LUNCH

1

Business's Free Lunch

Recognizing the Hidden Costs

The classic 1967 film *The Graduate* contains a famous piece of career advice that Benjamin, the lead character played by Dustin Hoffman, receives from a middle-aged family friend. "I just want to say one word to you," he says. "*Plastics.*" He adds, "There's a great future in plastics."

The scene evokes the generational divide. To a 1960s college graduate, a staid career in something as sterile as plastics is anathema. But fifty-plus years later, the link between "plastics" and a "great future" is painfully ironic. Plastic lasts forever, yet it is overwhelmingly manufactured for single-use, throwaway applications.

Discarded plastic is piling up everywhere, and there is no end in sight. Much of it is being dumped into the oceans, where circulating currents have formed five gigantic patches of plastic waste made up of everything from soft drink bottles and abandoned fishing nets to clouds of microplastics (particles that range between several micrometers and five millimeters in size). These patches extend all the way to the ocean floor.[1] All five are far from any country's coastline, which means that they are out of sight and out of mind.

But they have significant effects on the environment. They are killing marine life, choking entire ecosystems, and, perhaps shockingly to many, contaminating our own food. Most of the fish we eat contain measurable amounts of microplastics. As plastic breaks down, it leaches toxic additives, which enter the food chain through the soil and drinking water. By one estimate, a typical American eats, drinks, and breathes some seventy-four thousand microplastic particles every year, which comes out to about five grams per week, enough to make a credit card.[2]

A recent study in the journal *Science* suggests that, at current rates, "the scale of plastic entering the world's oceans will triple by 2040, to an average of 29 million metric tons of waste, per year."[3] Waste plastic is as grotesquely visible an example of an economic externality—in layman's terms, the adverse societal and economic effects that spill over from companies' production—as anyone could possibly think of.

While the problem with plastic is highly visible, it is just the tip of the externality iceberg. To understand the extent to which companies systematically off-load their costs onto society while trying to convince us that they are doing the opposite, let's consider Amazon. Amazon flourished during the pandemic, growing its fulfillment infrastructure by 50 percent, adding more than 250,000 employees, and seeing its profits soar by more than 200 percent.[4] As one of the creators of the "Climate Pledge," which encourages large companies to declare their carbon neutrality goals, Amazon has been lauded for its work on climate change.[5] Amazon committed to being carbon-neutral by 2040, ten years ahead of the UN Paris Agreement goal.

But in fact, as we will discuss in more detail, this is mainly greenwash. Amazon is a prime example of a company that pushes the costs of its success onto society. First, let's consider how the company shirks paying the taxes that support the infrastructure and services it uses. In 2021, Amazon reported record profits of more than $35 billion (75 percent higher than its 2020 record haul) but paid just 6 percent of those profits in federal corporate income taxes in the United States.[6] In 2021 and 2022, it paid no corporation tax at all in the United Kingdom.[7] Fair Tax Mark, a group that exposes corporate tax avoidance, labeled Amazon the "most aggressive" company when it comes to tax avoidance, noting that its accounting is so opaque that it is impossible to figure out what they owed.

Yet Amazon extensively uses the public goods and services that are funded by the taxes that are mostly paid for by others. The company depends on US transportation infrastructure—from roads to runways—to deliver products. Its facilities rely on locally shared services in education, hospitals and health care, and police and fire departments, on top of all the other infrastructure required to move energy, water, waste, and people around and to keep the peace. Although what Amazon is doing is technically legal, it is ethically wrong to contribute so little toward public goods while reaping such huge advantages.

Individuals and small businesses can't afford to hire teams of elite accountants and lawyers to help them evade their tax liabilities, so their earnings are significantly lower. That is also the case with other large businesses that choose to pay their fair share and contribute to society. Amazon undercuts them and pockets the profits, while society foots the bill.

Amazon has been praised for paying its workers a minimum of $15 per hour. But it has fervently resisted unionization, which would give its employees the ability to negotiate not just for fairer pay but for better working conditions. And Amazon's working conditions could be a lot better than they are. Workers liken their jobs to being human robots; they are expected to meet daily "pick" rates, which for many are impossibly high. Rina Cummings, who worked at a New York warehouse, reported that the constant pressure to meet the daily rate led to injuries on the job and unexpected stresses. For instance, if a package burst while being packed, she was required to clean up the mess and was still expected to hit her hourly rate. Cummings had been disciplined when such situations led her to not be able to do so.[8]

Workers at Amazon fulfillment centers have reported that their twelve-hour shifts allow for only one eighteen-minute break to get water and use the washroom, in addition to their thirty-minute unpaid lunch break, despite their having to walk as far as fifteen miles a day. Approximately 40 percent of workers at Amazon's warehouses are considered "seasonal," a situation dramatized in the Academy Award–winning film *Nomadland*. Amazon does this because labor laws do not require the company to provide workers categorized as temporary with benefits or job security. This type of employment isn't really temporary, yet companies can avoid paying benefits by categorizing it as such, thus creating externalities. Who ends up paying for those workers' health care when they become seriously ill?

What's more, many former workers have said that Amazon's strict monitoring of employees creates a culture of fear. If you work too slowly, or don't complete enough tasks in a day, you are at risk of being fired. Amazon is also notorious for its lax safety regulations. Injury rates for Amazon warehouse workers are, on average, close to twice as high as the company's competitors, and in one case five times higher.[9] The National Council for Occupational Safety and Health has included Amazon in its "Dirty Dozen" list of "companies that needlessly expose workers to preventable hazards, leading to preventable illnesses, injuries and fatalities" five years in a row.[10]

There have been reports of racist practices at Amazon as well. According to a *New York Times* investigation, in 2019 Black associates at a New York City warehouse were 50 percent more likely to be fired than their white peers. Employees at an overwhelmingly Black Alabama plant that attempted to unionize in 2021 spoke of a hostile work environment and "egregious and blatantly illegal" anti-union activities.[11] At other Amazon warehouses, Black employees made complaints to management about racist images in the workplace and even receiving death threats, all of which they claim were ignored by the company.[12]

Not surprisingly, Amazon quickly cycled through employees in the pandemic year of 2020, even as it grew. The *New York Times* reported that Amazon's leaders had an "almost palpable fear of running out of workers."[13] The issue was not just that working conditions were unbearable; the company's employment model is deliberately designed to offer very little upward mobility and includes mechanisms that encourage employees to leave after a few years. While one may suggest that at least Amazon is contributing to the economy by providing jobs, this argument is untenable because these jobs are more like parts of a machine that are quickly worn out and then discarded. This saves Amazon the expense of cost-of-living raises while reducing the risk that workers will organize. It also follows from what executives report to be a major tenet in company founder Jeff Bezos's philosophy: that people are lazy and, like literal cogs in a machine, should be replaced when they are no longer of use.[14]

Going one step further in our quest to understand who pays for Amazon's success, let's consider its core business model: shipping products to purchasers' homes and offices. While companies including Amazon put out statements that they are endeavoring to lower the amount of paper and plastic in their packaging, is this a real priority? What Amazon emphasizes the most is speed, so it ignores the potential environmental savings that could be realized by being more proactive in offering people different shipping options to reduce carbon costs or prompting them to make environmental choices, such as lower plastic consumption.

Of course, Jeff Bezos would reply that Amazon is simply giving its customers what they want. But given its scale, Amazon has a real opportunity to innovate in ways that could improve our planet. If it were a truly responsible citizen, it would focus on that and not just on avoiding taxes. Instead, it gaslights the public while delivering profits to its investors, including Bezos himself. Of course Bezos's own wealth ballooned during the pandemic, allowing him to travel to space in his own rocket. As of early 2022, Bezos could have *personally* provided a $105,000 one-time bonus to each of his 876,000 employees and still be as rich as he was when COVID hit.[15]

Amazon and other technology companies' business models are also problematic. Amazon claims that the services it offers to third parties are neutral technologies, providing marketplaces in which buyers and sellers can connect. In reality, Amazon draws on its customer search and sales data to design and sell its own generic look-alike products, undercutting the smaller businesses that use its platform. Facebook and Twitter also frame themselves as neutral platforms so they can sidestep responsibility for the disinformation that is published on their sites and the negative externalities of their services.

Amazon may be an extreme case, but once you start looking at how some of our biggest and most successful companies do business, the fundamental unfairness that underlies our economic system becomes more apparent. The irony is that not only is Amazon not called out for its exploitation of the public commons, but unbelievably it frequently tops annual lists of best companies, such as *Fortune*'s "World's Most Admired Companies."[16]

But, reminiscent of the recent reevaluation of the late twentieth-century lionization of GE and Jack Welch, my bet is, decades in the future, Bezos's model will be reconsidered and the destructive consequences of his management philosophy laid bare.

We Keep Repeating the Tragedy of the Commons

The pollution in our air, the plastic waste in our oceans and landfills, and companies' exploitation of labor and infrastructure without paying their fair share are all variations on the classic tragedy of the commons that many of us learned about in elementary school. In 1833, the British economist William Forster Lloyd published a pamphlet that included a hypothetical example of the excessive use of public resources: Dairy farmers shared a common piece of pasture, which each of them had the right to graze their cows on. If any of them raised more livestock than what was informally allocated, it would lead to overgrazing. The farmer would gain additional benefits, but the damage from overgrazing would be borne by the community. If every herder made the same self-interested economic decision, everyone's long-term interests would suffer.

The story of the Grand Banks fisheries provides us with a modern example. For centuries, the Grand Banks fisheries near Newfoundland were known for their abundant supply of cod, attracting fishers from all over the world. Twentieth-century technologies allowed fishing boats to catch more cod than ever, leading to many years of record hauls. But as a result, the population was pushed past the point where it could naturally sustain itself and suffered irreparable damage; by the early 1990s the cod population had collapsed to 1 percent of what is once was, and may never recover.[17]

In the modern context, the term "commons" refers to any shared resource, such as air, water, and even labor and supply chains. Though everyone loses eventually, the over-grazers and the over-fishers benefit handsomely at first. In many ways, the abuse of the commons is the logic of unbridled capitalism, which demands expansion and growth, no matter the consequences. Typically, the abuses of the system are not recognized until it is too late.

A well-known example of how overusing common resources can lead to devastating consequences is the case of the St. Matthew Island reindeer. In 1944, twenty-nine reindeer were introduced to a small, desolate island in the Bering Sea that had long lacked herbivores, so it had accumulated a large supply of lichens, a traditional food of reindeer. There were no natural predators on the island, so this small population of reindeer boomed. By 1957, a return visit by scientists found that the population had climbed to about 1,350 animals. By 1963, the population had risen to 6,000, despite estimates that the carrying capacity—the steady-state natural-resource limit for the population—was only about 1,600 to 2,300 reindeer. They were overusing the resources and eventually exhausted the island's food. Mass starvation ensued and the population rapidly crashed. By 1966, only forty-two reindeer remained alive.[18]

The process underlying such dramatic consequences is known as overshoot. There is a time lag in understanding and naturally responding to potentially negative consequences from resource overuse, so resources end up continuing to be overconsumed beyond a sustainable level and then all of a sudden rapidly disappear. Since the 1970s, the international research organization Global Footprint Network has been calculating and publicizing Earth Overshoot Day, "when humanity has exhausted nature's budget for the year," illustrating that, for the rest of the year, humanity runs an "ecological deficit by drawing down local resource stocks and accumulating carbon dioxide in the atmosphere." In the early 1970s, there was limited overshoot, while in 2023, Earth Overshoot Day fell on August 2. So, for almost five-twelfths of the year, humanity is not unlike the reindeer on St. Matthew Island after reaching carrying capacity.[19]

The historian Peter Linebaugh warned, "The commons is invisible, until it is lost."[20] Every year we are in overshoot, moving closer to the inevitable collapse, although on a day-to-day basis we are not aware of what is to come. In the 1968 essay in *Science* that identified the tragedy of the commons problem, the biologist Garrett Hardin summed up the inevitable outcome: "Ruin," he wrote, "is the destination toward which all men rush, each pursuing his own best interest in a society that believes in the freedom of the commons."[21]

But Nobel laureate Elinor Ostrom showed the tragedy of the commons is not a foregone conclusion. Overturning conventional beliefs, her research demonstrated that communities can effectively manage and sustain shared resources. In addition to a better understanding of costs, benefits, and what is valued, her work points to the importance of many topics we take up in Part III of *The Profiteers*, including collective action, monitoring, and accountability. These are key elements not just to systemically recognize and effectively manage negative externalities, but also to lay the foundations for an economic system that promotes positive externalities.

———

Throughout this book we will explore a number of questions related to how unrecognized costs should be addressed, such as: What should businesses' responsibility for the commons be? How much should we pay for companies' hidden costs? How much should our children and grandchildren pay? And, at a fundamental level, how should economic value and the associated responsibility be accounted for in the twenty-first century? Ultimately, the issue is what we value—that is, what we consider to be a part of the economic calculus and what we don't. In the plastics case, for example, the economic costs of waste to society, public health, and the environment are not calculated, while the cost for companies to use virgin versus recycled plastic is. These are questions that are rarely considered, but, if we are to change the underlying systems to build a sustainable and equitable society, they must be.

In her book *The Value of Everything*, the influential economist Mariana Mazzucato pointed out that distortions in the way we tabulate value allow certain players to portray themselves as value creators, even when they are just transferring existing value to themselves or, even worse, destroying it.[22] To illustrate her point, she shows how standard economic metrics systematically undervalue government investment. Companies in industries ranging from pharmaceuticals to aerospace to computer technology have prospered thanks to basic research that was funded and conducted by governments. While we all enjoy the technologies of GPS, touch screens, the Internet, and the mRNA vaccines that defeated COVID-19, the government's inputs into their creation are not valued economically. So, when companies use these technologies to create products, the government's efforts are not recognized as a being a core part of the economic value the companies create. Conversely, what does an investment bank actually produce? The "value" they are said to create is mainly derived from transaction fees they levy for other companies' financing, which do get recognized and counted but arguably do not add much true value to society.

A parallel critique is offered by Raj Patel, a research professor at the Lyndon B. Johnson School of Public Affairs at the University of

Texas, Austin. Economic history, he writes in his book *The Value of Nothing*, records an inexorable march toward commodification, in which "we seem unable to see or value our world except through the faulty prism of markets."[23] The book's title comes from an apt Oscar Wilde aphorism: "Nowadays people know the price of everything and the value of nothing."

Thinking about the external costs—those that fall outside of traditional financial accounting systems—shines a light on the idea that more and more value is being extracted from our world by increasingly larger and wealthier private actors. In other words, the rich are abusing the commons to build up their fortunes and, as GDP and other measures of growth increase, we consider this "development" and call it "progress."

This may sound hyperbolic, but historically elites have frequently used their power to seize public resources. In the United Kingdom, the enclosure laws enacted in the seventeenth and eighteenth centuries literally took common land that farmers had used for generations—and had a legal right to—and made it the private property of local landowners. In *The Making of the English Working Class*, the historian E. P. Thompson says that enclosure was "a plain enough case of class robbery, played according to fair rules of property and law laid down by a parliament of property-owners and lawyers."[24]

Thomas Piketty calls the dominant business ideology of our day "proprietarianism" or "the ownership society." It is not a surprise that property rights and ownership are respected while the commons are abused. In traditional accounting, the contributions of nature or human and societal welfare to private wealth, and private wealth's depreciation of public wealth, go unrecognized. It is a distortion, deeply rooted in the system, to treat wealth entirely as value produced through exchange. In such a system, only goods sold on the market are counted.

External goods (water, air, living beings) that are "used" but are outside the exchange system are regarded in this calculus as basically free gifts. So, while environmental degradation is a result of production, our accounting systems do not disincentivize or even account for it. But it does disincentivize any efforts to repair that degradation. To understand the true value of the externalities that corporations off-load onto the public, we must begin by counting public wealth (such as clean air and water) in the same way that we do private wealth (such as individual incomes or GDP). But given the very short time horizons that our current economic system uses to calculate profits and the very long time horizons of nature, the system "cannot function under conditions that require accounting for the reproduction of nature," as the sociologist John Bellamy Foster writes.[25]

In *The Value of Everything*, Mazzucato traces how we, as a society, decide what *value* means. Mercantilists in the seventeenth century believed that value came from precious metals, and that the accumulation of gold and silver was the route to national power and prosperity. Physiocrats in the eighteenth century regarded land as the only source of value and farmers as the only productive force in society. Adam Smith and Karl Marx agreed that value derived from the costs of production, principally labor. Twentieth-century technologies changed the ways that production and distribution are organized, planting the seeds for the twenty-first century, in which our focus is less on the forces of production per se and more on subjective factors, such as the preference for leisure over earning a higher amount of money. These factors especially reflect the interests of the biggest players (businesses, elites, capitalists), who aim to tilt the system in their favor.[26]

The tension between public and private wealth was recognized as far back as 1804 by a Scottish thinker and politician, James Maitland, the eighth Earl of Lauderdale. In his *Inquiry into the Nature and Origin of Public Wealth and into the Means and Causes of Its*

Increase, he argued that an inverse relationship exists between public and private wealth: an increase in one can only come at the expense of another.[27] This is now known as the Lauderdale paradox. Maitland defined public wealth as "everything that humans desire, benefit [or are pleased by]"—including abundant commodities such as water, wild nature, and air—which, since they cannot be bought and sold, are considered to have no value under capitalism. But when resources are extracted from nature and turned into economic commodities, public wealth becomes private wealth. The resource gains an exchange value due to its scarcity and privatization. In the words of the late economist Paul Sweezy, since profit is the top priority of capitalism, the natural environment becomes "a means to the paramount ends of profit-making and still more capital accumulation."[28]

Lauderdale's paradox recognizes that natural resources, and hence public wealth, diminish as they are converted into private wealth. As such, one wonders about the logic of the win-win view, in which businesses' gains inevitably lead to society's welfare. The equation captures the gains but not the losses. When only private wealth is counted, people wrongly assume that a rising GDP by definition means their country is becoming richer, but in actuality it is the rich getting richer at the cost of the rest of society.

Considering the True Value (and Costs) of Business

How, then, do we reconcile the differences between private wealth and public wealth? How can we ensure that the pursuit of wealth by individuals and corporations does not inevitably lead to the destruction of the commons? Understanding and recognizing the externalities is the first step.

Arthur C. Pigou, an English economist and professor at the University of Cambridge in the early 1900s, formalized the idea of externalities as the side effects of industrial or commercial activities that are not reflected in the costs of the goods produced via those activities.[29] The OECD defines externalities as "situations when the effect of production or consumption of goods and services imposes costs or benefits on others which are not reflected in the prices charged for the goods and services being provided."[30]

As is evident from these definitions, externalities can be positive or negative. Positive externalities, for example, include infrastructure that can enhance economic productivity and improve overall quality of life in a region: a new road that opens an area for commercial development; high-speed Internet access that enables information sharing, online education, e-commerce, and telecommuting; and public transportation that reduces traffic congestion and air pollution and makes it easier for people to access job opportunities, education, and services. Positive societal spillovers accompany investment in common goods like infrastructure and education.

A canonical example of positive externalities is found in Silicon Valley, where entrepreneurs and investors greatly benefited from the private and government-funded research that was being undertaken at local universities like Stanford and the University of California, Berkeley. The universities attracted leading talent in fields such as computer science, engineering, and entrepreneurship. They and their students often collaborated with local companies on projects, leading to the transfer of knowledge and expertise. This attracted venture capitalists, who invested in promising start-ups, creating a virtuous cycle that further encouraged innovation and entrepreneurship in the region.

Negative externalities, on the other hand, create hidden costs that companies can avoid and pass on to society and the environment while basically enjoying a free lunch for themselves. Since today's model of capitalism incentivizes corporations to operate with solely one target in mind—profit maximization—society's interests (or "public wealth," as discussed above) are routinely sacrificed to maximize the accumulation of "private wealth"—the financial value in the market—for companies. That is, if there is not a price on something to be exchanged, the associated societal costs are ignored, buttressing companies' profits.

Externalities are endemic, and while some, like plastics in our ocean and smog in the air, can be highly visible, others are less visible and thus intractable. Corporations and the powerful frequently work to keep the existence and impact of these externalities below the radar. The PCBs GE dumped into the Hudson River were not visible to the naked eye, but they harmed aquatic life and made the water unsafe for human use, despite Jack Welch's well-rehearsed lines.

Societal externalities can be even less obvious. As discussed, poverty and inequality have become more and more endemic in recent years. Who pays for this? Certainly, those subjected to inferior life conditions do, but the effects of poverty and inequality extend beyond the individuals experiencing them and impact society as a whole. Yet, companies pocket the benefit from lower wages. Likewise, poor support of employee health care reduces costs, yet inadequate access to health care and nutrition lead to higher incidences of illnesses and chronic conditions that impose burdens on public health systems. And as noted previously, excessive inequality slows economic growth.

Inequality exacerbates discrimination, which worsens social tensions and conflicts. Discrimination stifles diversity in various fields, including science, technology, and the arts, causing societies to miss out on the unique perspectives and contributions that might have led to greater innovation and creativity. We will discuss more of these less-visible externalities in later chapters.

A key theme of this book is that, to better account for the true costs of production, these societal costs need to be recognized in some way by business, so the price of a good reflects its true cost. This could be done voluntarily. Of course, a commonly discussed idea is government taxes or regulations to limit externalities. But we should not discount the complexity of how to account for externalities and that in some cases—as we will discuss more later, such as for systemic risks that have widespread consequences—pricing mechanisms are not enough. But as a first step, it is useful to try to account for the societal and environmental costs from such behaviors.

Such actions have a long history. For instance, sin taxes are an example of how externalities can be factored into the prices of goods and services. While many object to carbon taxes as a violation of free market ideals, they fail to recognize that, as far back as 1776, the pioneering thinker of free market capitalism Adam Smith wrote that taxes on tobacco, rum, and sugar were appropriate.[31] Smoking, excessive drinking, and the consumption of sugary beverages are associated with a host of diseases like type 2 diabetes, emphysema, and lung cancer. Society pays in the form of higher insurance costs and reduced productivity. Unlike carbon taxes, taxes on these goods are already part of our underlying culture and so are not actively discussed or questioned.

Environmentalists and those on the left also look askance on carbon taxes, as they in effect "license pollution" and turn irreplaceable natural resources into commodities. In *The Value of Nothing*, Raj Patel describes "cap and trade" as "a market-based approach that effectively turns the atmosphere into something you can foul for a fee."[32] While it is important to recognize this critique, the utility of such approaches, at least in exposing what society pays, cannot be denied. Powerful corporations have been hiding the true costs of their free lunches for so long that we cannot afford to be too fastidious.

What justifies sin taxes is the fact that individuals who consume those products incur costs for nonusers. Nonsmokers are harmed by secondhand tobacco smoke. Innocent people are hurt and killed in alcohol-related traffic accidents and violence. Smoking and drinking during pregnancy are associated with fetal weight loss, premature birth, congenital malformations, stillbirths, fetal alcohol syndrome, and sudden infant death syndrome.[33] Gambling, which is also heavily taxed, can destroy families when done compulsively.

A growing body of research shows that taxes on such products can reduce their consumption and hence their adverse consequences. For example, when the US federal government raised cigarette taxes by $0.62 per pack in 2009, the youth smoking rate dropped by 10 percent, and total cigarette sales dropped by 8.3 percent. Between 2005 and 2015, the overall percentage of smokers dropped from 21 percent to 15 percent.[34] It's been found that a 10 percent tax on cigarettes will reduce demand from adults by 4 percent and by youths between the ages of twelve and seventeen by 11.9 percent.[35] While it is not perfect and also has some potential downsides, which we discuss later, pricing and taxing externalities clearly has an important role to play.

For instance, consider carbon emissions. Looking at just the one hundred biggest environmental risks created by companies, the environmental data-collection firm Trucost estimated their total cost to humanity at $4.7 trillion a year.[36] The most significant impacts emerge from greenhouse gas emissions and water and land use. The sectors causing the most damage are coal power generation in East Asia and North America and agriculture, particularly in areas of water scarcity. The environmental and societal costs in those sectors far outweigh overall revenue. They are negative externalities that all of us are paying for, while the companies enjoy the profit.

To bring this idea more to life, consider the externalities of a McDonald's Big Mac. In *The Value of Nothing*, Patel itemizes them, everything from the "environmental damage and climate induced crises, which lead to resource depletion, and health related factors such as obesity and high blood pressure." He also shares data from a report by the Centre for Science and Environment in India that showed how "a burger grown from beef raised on clear-cut forest should really cost about two hundred dollars."[37]

Leah Garcés is the CEO and president of Mercy for Animals and the author of the 2019 book *Grilled: Turning Adversaries into Allies to Change the Chicken Industry.*[38] In it, she documents the real costs of raising seventy billion chickens a year in industrial conditions. The chickens are kept indoors in crowded cages and fed antibiotics to prevent infections. This contributes to rising antimicrobial resistance (AMR) in humans, which, as we will discuss in more detail, could cost society from $300 billion to more than $1 trillion annually by 2050.[39] It is quite possible that at some point in the near future people will once again die as a result of a simple cut or a toothache because antibiotics no longer work. This is a pretty steep price for our cheap chicken patties and hamburgers.

In addition to the type of food we eat and the problems that result, the vehicles we use are another example of a free lunch. Gas-guzzling SUVs are more profitable for—and so extensively promoted by—car companies, but they create tremendous negative effects on society and the environment. For instance, a 2007 study from the research group Resources for the Future showed that if you add up all the mileage-related externalities—namely, congestion, accidents, and local air pollution—the cost of gasoline would be a whopping extra $2.10 per gallon.[40] A more recent study that just considered climate change effects estimated that a gallon of gas leads to $0.72 of negative external costs.[41] If we captured the externalities, we should be paying a lot more at the pump. But this would lead people to be less likely to buy the cars that are the most profitable for auto companies, and so they and fossil fuel companies lobby extensively to keep gas taxes down to underwrite a solid profit stream of SUVs. This is opposed to Europe, where companies have less lobbying power and so roads are filled with the smaller, more efficient cars that are more appealing to the public due to the higher fuel costs.

While these approaches all seem relatively straightforward (although, as we will discuss in more detail below, they are not), these are in many ways the "easiest" externalities to identify. But if we are to fully account for the free lunch business serves itself, this recognition is a first step for us to be much more comprehensive and systematic.

Looking Deep into Supply Chains

Identifying externalities is not for the faint of heart, especially when we look into supply chains. Michel Scholte, a social entrepreneur in the Netherlands, cofounded True Price, an organization that aims to reduce food insecurity and shape a sustainable global economy through a pricing system that identifies and incorporates the costs of negative social and environmental impacts.[42] The challenge is doing so in a way that is fair and sustainable, rather than simply passing the costs on to consumers. When there is transparency about the true price of products, he said, we can "design markets in a way in which basic sustainable and healthy goods such as food, housing, transportation, stay accessible and affordable for all."

When Scholte was studying sociology in college, he came to the conclusion that the Global North keeps "commodity countries in subservient positions" so as to exploit their natural resources and labor for the benefit of consumers in the developed world. Since producers in the developing world are not fairly compensated, they lack the capital they need to economically advance.

Human-rights-related factors are an important externality that is difficult to price. True Price relies on the United Nations Guiding Principles on Business and Human Rights, and as a baseline requires companies to have systems and practices that ensure that human rights are respected throughout their supply chains. Those principles "include having a house, having food, having access to water," Scholte said. On the environmental side, it means being free from deadly toxins and other factors.

While pricing externalities can be an effective tool to raise awareness of just how much of a free lunch businesses are getting, Scholte emphasizes that initially the benefit is informational and that externalities should be factored into the costs of production in a progressive way, with the wealthy, or companies, paying proportionally more. Scholte notes, "We say, you, the consumer, must have the ability to voluntarily pay the true price," and True Price is working with supermarkets in the Netherlands to post the cost of externalities on the goods they sell, giving consumers the opportunity to pay them voluntarily. The excess is then returned to the smallholder farmers in the Global South who produced the products.

———

Of course, it is important to recognize that such systems are hard to create and will never be perfect. Even carbon, perhaps the externality easiest to quantify, is exceedingly difficult to price. Because of the uncertainties (and, of course, politics), its value varies widely across the hundreds of studies and position papers that have examined the issue. The Trump administration, for instance, priced the cost of carbon emissions at between $1 and $7 per metric ton, while the Obama administration had set a price of $43 per metric ton. Nobel laureate William Nordhaus estimates the price at about $40 per ton, but economists Nicholas Stern and another Nobel Prize winner, Joseph

Stiglitz, think this is far too low and estimate it at $100 per ton. Sweden introduced a carbon tax in 1991 and has gradually increased it. As of 2022, it was set at more than $125 per ton.

Many critics rightly point out that calculating prices for many externalities is a fool's errand. In an article entitled "Heroic Accounting," Andrew King and Kenneth Pucker use the example of fluoride, a chemical added to drinking water and toothpaste to prevent cavities, to illustrate the challenges. Fluoride is harmful to some aquatic organisms. To arrive at the correct price for fluoride emissions, accountants would require information on where and how fluoride is used and what organisms are involved, then they would have to balance that against the good of less tooth decay. Beyond fluoride, there are thousands of other pollutants whose costs need to be calculated.

Furthermore, in many cases, effects cannot be easily isolated to just one company or community. Systemic risks transcend individual sectors or regions and affect multiple interconnected systems simultaneously, creating the potential for extreme disruption or failure of an entire system. The failure of a large bank could cause other banks to fail and so have broader effects on the entire financial system. Managing and mitigating systemic risks requires multifaceted and coordinated efforts, so the proposed solution to just price the externality would fall short. Following the 2008 financial crisis, the US government and other actors engaged in many different types of interventions involving multiple government agencies, from the Federal Reserve to the Treasury Department, and a variety of economic policy levers, from increased spending to infusing equity into troubled institutions.

Climate change is now a relatively well-known systemic risk, but it took decades and significant acts of planetary destruction to bring it to our attention. The challenges of systemic risks can be seen when contrasting the struggle over international agreements on climate change with the 1990 amendments to the US Clean Air Act and similar regulations in Europe that successfully reduced the emissions that cause acid rain. The key difference was that the effects of acid rain are more immediate and local than the effects of climate change. Damaged forests and acidified lakes were visible and directly attributable to the sulfur dioxide and nitrogen oxides being emitted by upwind plants. That meant specific solutions could be more easily identified and implemented, such as installing scrubbers on smokestacks, switching to low-sulfur fuels, and enforcing existing regulations.

Climate change impacts, in contrast, are a problem of the global commons; they are distributed unevenly and often most affect those who contributed the least to the problem. That makes it more challenging to identify the various causes and build consensus for action.

Other important systemic risks are biodiversity loss and antimicrobial resistance. Clearing forests for agricultural purposes and the widespread use of pesticides, and the associated contamination of soil and water sources, reduce habitats, leading to significant biodiversity loss. This leads, in turn, to reduced crop yields and increased health-care expenses due to environmental degradation and disease. It can also lead to the loss of livelihoods in sectors dependent on natural resources, such as fisheries and tourism.

Biodiversity loss is systemic because it affects the stability and functioning of whole ecosystems, with far-reaching consequences for human well-being and the economy. For instance, it increases the risk of zoonotic diseases like Ebola, SARS, and COVID-19, which jump from animals to humans. When natural habitats are destroyed or fragmented, humans come into closer contact with wildlife, increasing the likelihood of infection.

Additionally, routine overuse of antibiotics in food production has spurred the development of antibiotic-resistant bacteria, which may not be immediately noticeable but is a ticking time bomb that will lead to significant challenges in the future.

Because these systemic effects reach beyond any company or country, we need to recognize that the neoliberal tactic of simply saying the government should address externalities through taxes or other pricing mechanisms is nothing more than a way to avoid responsibility. Systemic effects are bigger than any one company or country can manage, and, to make matters worse, many companies use their financial resources and social capital to lobby against regulatory solutions. So while a detailed understanding of externalities costs is necessary, it is not sufficient. We need to find new approaches to holding companies accountable for the damage they create that also look at whole systems.

But as the work of True Price shows, even imperfect information can be of use to start to help companies take action. Many companies have added internal carbon fees as a "shadow price" to prepare for the time when carbon pricing becomes the norm. A decade ago, German athletic brand Puma, which was owned by French luxury conglomerate Kering, created an environmental profit-and-loss calculation. This placed a monetary value on the natural capital—the effects on air, water, soil, and biodiversity—that the company relied on. Had it paid for the natural capital across its value chain, Puma estimated it would have cost roughly $100 million per year, which is a large proportion of the company's profits.[43] Other examples include Microsoft, which charges its divisions $15 per metric ton of carbon, which it then invests in energy efficiency and clean tech.[44] French food corporation Danone has begun releasing carbon-adjusted earnings per share to show how much of its profits depend on the lack of carbon pricing.[45]

But as of 2023, only 34 percent of the world's top two thousand public and private companies had plans or targets to reduce carbon at anything like the pace in the Paris Agreement.[46] And as we will see in subsequent chapters, an even smaller percentage have set that goal for their entire value chains (what's called "Scope 3" emissions).

Carbon is just a start; we need a much more comprehensive understanding of companies' overall environmental and societal impacts. While government action is certainly a big part of the solution, we also need business innovation: companies like Danone, Microsoft, and Puma, which are working to expose their own externalities and develop forward-looking ways to address them. It's not surprising that so few companies are jumping at the chance to account for their negative externalities and in fact are actively distracting us from being aware of such responsibilities. This is the subject of our next chapter.

To rebalance society and the economy, it will no doubt take a multifaceted and multi-stakeholder approach—one that involves not only the voluntary efforts of a handful of pioneering companies but forceful government action and pressure from investors and the general public to flip priorities from negative to positive externalities and prioritize virtuous versus destructive cycles. We will examine these levers and more in Part III.

2

Society Pays the Bill

How We Are Tricked into Covering Business's Hidden Costs

f you were alive in the 1970s and living in the United States, you're likely familiar with the "Crying Indian" ad. One of the best-known television commercials of my childhood, it features a white American actor of Italian heritage dressed in a Native American costume. He lands his canoe on a riverbank strewn with plastic and other trash. The camera pans to his face as a single tear runs down his cheek. In an ominous tone, the voice-over says, "People start pollution, people can stop it." Decades later, I was astonished to learn that the group that put out that public service announcement, the innocuously named Keep America Beautiful, was founded in 1953 by the American Can Company and later joined by Coca-Cola, Dixie Cup Corporation, and a number of other companies that rely on the production of single-use plastics. All of them actively opposed environmental initiatives that cut into their business.

Plastic producers and the packaging industry also coined the term "litterbug" as part of their efforts to remove state laws that mandated the use of returnable glass bottles. Their hope was that people would direct their energies to their individual garbage disposal habits as opposed to considering the root cause of the problem: the companies that create and distribute all those packing materials that end up as waste.

The power of these messages is that they are, in part, on-target. It is unquestionably true that we should not throw trash out of our cars, and we should make every effort to ensure our waste is disposed of in the proper places. We should also bring our own bags to the grocery store, responsibly carry metal straws, and drink water from non-disposable bottles. But at a deeper level, are these messages really about how individuals can save our waste-strewn world, or are they an effort to deflect responsibility from the corporations that produced the waste to the consumers? The terrible truth is that we have been gaslighted.

Many in the Global North buy into foundational assumptions about the power of markets and Adam Smith's "invisible hand," whereby the pursuit of individual self-interest creates desirable outcomes for society without any need for central planning or government intervention. On one level, this idea makes sense. If markets really were completely open and frictionless, prices and outputs would converge at optimal levels. Consumers would be well served and employees fairly compensated. But as baked into our culture as this idea is, the world is significantly more complicated than what Smith envisioned and many economists and public commentators still believe. In fact, corporations, the wealthy, and the power they have play a significant role in markets, politics, and society.

Alfred Chandler, an influential business historian at Harvard, argued that in the late nineteenth and early twentieth centuries, the rise of large corporations created a "visible hand" that led to centralization of market decision-making and management, allowing managers to shape markets through the firms they run.[1] While the analogy is apt, Chandler has been criticized for focusing too much on the efficiencies created by managers, neglecting the influence of social and political factors. Sociologist William Roy, alternatively, argued that the corporation is not a natural and inevitable step in the evolution of business as technology developed but represents "socialized capital," whereby powerful actors work to protect their social positions and economic standing.[2] So, an even more apt analogy for understanding the role of corporate power in shaping ideas and markets may be "unseen hands," recognizing that these powerful actors can work behind the scenes to buttress their interests and power, subtly shaping societal values, behaviors, and cultural norms but without revealing their influence.

As we delve more into the complex world of corporate influence, it will become evident that the privatization of profits and socialization of costs is not an isolated phenomenon; it is a systemic issue that permeates our economies and societies. Corporate actions manipulate public opinion, consumption patterns, and societal beliefs. Governments dance to the tune of corporate interests, and the scales of justice are tipped in their favor.

Overall, there are many strategies by which externalities are passed on to society through omitted information and misdirection. Using creative PR, distorted accounting, and intensive lobbying, companies exploit the gaps in laws and regulations that allow them to stick society and governments with their costs while they collect the profits. The time has come to shed light on these unseen hands shaping our world.

———

Returning to culpability for plastic waste, the plot thickens when one considers that the Keep America Beautiful companies knew that plastic products would end up in landfills and not be recycled. All the way back in 1974, an industry insider wrote in a speech that "there is serious doubt that [recycling plastic] can ever be made viable on an economic basis."[3] Yet what these companies have done since is spend millions of dollars to air public service announcements that place the onus for the plastic crisis at the feet of individuals. In an interview with NPR, Larry Thomas, the former president of the powerful trade group the Society of the Plastics Industry (today the Plastics Industry Association), said, "If the public thinks that recycling is working, then they are not going to be as concerned about the environment."[4]

The recyclability of plastics is in fact a "big lie" that has been decades in the making, deliberately propagated and maintained by industry trade groups. Thanks to their efforts, it is now commonly accepted that once a product leaves its manufacturer's possession, it is solely the responsibility of the buyer to dispose of it properly. The recycling symbol of three "chasing arrows" is ubiquitous on plastic packaging; recycling bins are everywhere. Isn't it up to us to use them?

Industry documents dating back to 1989 show how executives from oil and plastics companies lobbied US states to require the recycling symbol to appear on all plastic containers and packages, even when they knew there was no way to recycle them. The plastics industry trade group even uses the numerical resin codes that appear inside the symbols to promote a sustainable image—which in many cases is completely illusory—by including them prominently in many of their own advertisements. Says Finis Dunaway, professor of American environmental history at Trent University in Canada, "It telegraphs to the consumer that this is something that is recyclable, and maybe perhaps even has been recycled before."[5] Jennie Romer, a former EPA official, says this symbol is "deceptive and misleading" regarding whether the plastic will be recycled.[6]

Many of these facts came to light through a lawsuit filed by the Earth Island Institute that seeks compensation from corporations for the damage plastic pollution has done to the planet. The lawsuit also demands that those companies stop misleading the public by advertising the "recyclability" of products that are never recycled. "These companies should bear the responsibility for choking our ecosystem with plastic," said David Phillips, executive director of Earth Island Institute. "They know very well that this stuff is not being recycled, even though they are telling people on the labels that it is recyclable and making [them] feel like it's being taken care of."[7]

The fact is, most plastics are not being recycled, even when conscientious individuals do the "the right thing." For instance, Garten, a recycling facility in Oregon, sends most of the plastic it receives to landfills. Workers at the Rogue Disposal and Recycling center in southern Oregon buried all the plastics that came through their facility, except soda bottles and milk jugs.[8] All the while, companies like ExxonMobil, Chevron, and Dow Chemical have been spending millions of dollars on ads that urge individuals to recycle—money that could have been invested in improving and expanding the ability to recycle.[9] Is it any surprise that only an estimated 5 to 6 percent of plastic is recycled in the United States? While the figure used to be closer to 10 percent, it has fallen dramatically since China stopped accepting shipments of US trash.[10] Over 90 percent of the plastic trash we believe is being recycled is actually incinerated or dumped in landfills or the ocean.[11]

Given the scope of the problem, we can see why companies are trying to distract us instead of taking responsibility for the waste their products create. While Coca-Cola, PepsiCo, and Nestlé have sustainable development activities that they actively trumpet, they also remain the biggest contributors to plastic pollution worldwide.[12] In 2022, the nongovernmental organization (NGO) Break Free from Plastic led a global audit on plastic pollution that gives us a concrete idea of just how much that is. Between 2018 and 2022, a total of 206,895 volunteers collected more than 2,125,414 pieces of plastic waste in places like beaches, city streets, and waterways all over the world: 85,035 were from Coca-Cola products, which made it the leading contributor.[13]

PepsiCo, which produces and sells over a billion products with single-use plastic packaging daily, came in second.[14] The maker of such well-known brands as Pepsi, Mountain Dew, Lay's, Gatorade, Tropicana, 7 Up, Doritos, Brisk, Quaker Oats, and Cheetos, it is one of the most successful food, snack, and beverage corporations in the world. As of 2022, PepsiCo employed some 315,000 people in more than two hundred countries and regions. According to a 2022 report by the Ellen MacArthur Foundation and the UN Environment Programme, the company creates 2.5 million tons of plastic products per year, of which only 7 percent is produced from recycled material.[15] The report also found that while brands like PepsiCo, Coca-Cola, and Mars made plans to reduce the proportion of virgin plastics in their products, the absolute amount of virgin plastics they use actually grew due to increases in overall production, which means they are falling far short of their own sustainability goals. Other companies on the list of biggest plastic polluters included well-known names like Nestlé, Unilever, Procter & Gamble, and Philip Morris.

Misleading us about the recyclability of plastic is only one example of how big business gaslights us, one part of a nefarious plot that has caught most of the world unawares. For years, Exxon ran ads in the *New York Times* that questioned the scientific research on global warming.[16] Shell and other fossil fuel companies, as well as General

Motors, Ford, and other automakers, having privately calculated the damage they were causing the environment in the 1980s, chose to downplay the threat in public.[17] And gig-economy companies like Instacart and Uber extol the freedom and flexibility of working without attachment to an organization, downplaying the lack of benefits and rights in such arrangements.

We should all be looking for ways to help keep our planet healthy and our society equitable, but shouldn't the burden rest mostly on the big corporations that create these problems in the first place?

Corporate Gaslighting Tactics

The question of responsibility is one that companies really don't want us to ask. And they have successfully distracted us from doing so for decades, in the same way that elites always have: by using their power to shape how we experience reality through political lobbying and PR campaigns. Another word for that is "gaslighting."

The term originated in a 1938 play by Patrick Hamilton about a man who manipulates his wife into believing she is crazy. He does this by secretly dimming and brightening the gaslights in their home, causing them to flicker and change in intensity. When she notices these changes, he insists that nothing is wrong, leading her to question her perception of reality. George Cukor adapted it into a movie in 1944, and over time the word has been used to refer to more general patterns of manipulation and deception. The *New York Times*, for example, has written about "medical gaslighting," when physicians mislead patients about the severity of their symptoms. Multiple writers on CNN have used the term to describe former president Donald Trump's self-serving statements, especially about the 2020 election and the Capitol riot on January 6, 2021. Gaslighting is not just a favorite tactic of abusers but of politicians, CEOs, managers, and other authority figures. It is sadly ironic that a significant source of gaslighting about fossil fuels, plastics, climate change, and environmental impacts has been the fossil fuel industry, which produces the gas that would go in such lights. The term has become so common that Merriam-Webster chose it as its word of the year in 2022.[18]

As I define it, corporate gaslighting is presenting a false view of reality with the aim of convincing the "victim" (i.e., us) that they are responsible for a wrong that the gaslighter committed. This can occur in myriad ways and through different corporate strategies. As with the "Crying Indian" advertisement, companies can create fake citizens' groups to make us feel responsible through ostensibly public pressure, while we don't realize we are essentially being tricked by the companies.

This is how a dominant ideology is formed, how we come to take certain ways of operating for granted. In *Capital and Ideology*, for example, Thomas Piketty shows how the discourse on meritocracy and entrepreneurship "often seems to serve primarily as a way for the winners in today's economy to justify any level of inequality whatsoever."[19]

Because this discourse elides the systemic causes of problems like racism, poverty, and climate change, we are gaslighted into believing that it is up to us and only us to change the world. And if it doesn't change? Well, it's our own fault for not pulling ourselves up by our bootstraps and working harder. We have become convinced we can achieve anything through hard work and grit, whether that is our own success or the solution to societal problems. Sometimes the gaslighters deny that the problems even exist. In short, we are being hoodwinked.

Astroturfing

A common strategy of corporate gaslighting is astroturfing: the sponsors of an organization, product, event, or advertisement hide their real identity—as with the "Crying Indian" commercial—to make it appear as though it was a grassroots initiative.

The Western States Petroleum Association (WSPA)—which includes Chevron, Shell, ExxonMobil, and others—is expert in astro-turfing and has been doing it for years. In 2014, a leaked presentation revealed that the WSPA had fabricated grassroots organizations to stoke the fires of climate-science denial, leading to the failure of legislation that would have aided in the fight against climate change.[20] In 1998, the American Petroleum Institute created the "Global Climate Science Communications Plan," a step-by-step road map for misleading the public about the effects of climate change by casting doubt on the science. The plan was specifically devised to keep the United States out of the Kyoto Protocol, the first global mandate focused on reducing greenhouse gas emissions. According to the plan, it would be considered a "victory" if "average citizens 'understand' (recognize) uncertainties in climate science" and "those promoting the Kyoto treaty on the basis of extant science appear to be out of touch with reality."[21] The trade group engaged in this plan while publicly pretending to be on board with the need to reduce greenhouse gas emissions.

ExxonMobil was connected to a putatively grassroots movement called Santa Barbara for Safe & Local Transport. The organization's promotional materials suggested that it was focused on the environment; in fact, it was designed to promote offshore drilling. Its campaigns and ads on social media feature racially diverse students and families and suggest that offshore drilling is essential for school funding and student achievement.[22] Similarly, in 2019, the Alliance of Western Energy Consumers boasted that they had "defeated all carbon pricing bills" in Oregon.[23] BP and Shell had claimed to support carbon pricing, yet their employees were recipients of the boastful email, suggesting that both companies supported the alliance's efforts. Both companies are also public members of the Consumer Energy Alliance. Though this sounds like a pro-environment group, it lobbies against emission limits and clean fuel programs. When questioned, the group replied that emission limits don't achieve significant environmental outcomes.

Astroturfing doesn't just occur in the energy and oil industries; it's rampant everywhere. Recently, the Massachusetts Coalition for Independent Work emerged, ostensibly to fight for gig workers' right to be recognized as independent contractors. Uber, Lyft, DoorDash, and Instacart were the companies behind this group. The reason, of course, that they refuse to label their workers as employees is because they would then have to meet specific labor standards and would be unable to profiteer from overworking and underpaying them. To give you a sense of what is at stake, these companies spent $200 million to campaign for Proposition 22 in California, which exempted them from a bill that would have required their workers to be classified as employees. The companies could have used that $200 million to increase their workers' wages.[24]

Selective (and False) Presentation

While the above examples are about masking advocates' true identities, another gaslighting strategy is a company or group masking its behavior by selectively emphasizing its seemingly positive works. With greenwashing, for example, companies present a "green" image while continuing to operate in the same dirty way they always have. The term goes back to the 1960s, when the hotel industry began placing notices in hotel rooms asking guests to reuse their towels to save the environment. Guests dutifully complied and still do. Hotels, meanwhile, saved a fortune on labor and reduced water use and were able to keep their towels longer. While saving water is a positive, the term stuck, as it represented the disconnect between the industry's real motivations and what they communicated.

Such "washing" imagery has also spread beyond environmental contexts. Pinkwashing, for instance, uses support for breast cancer awareness, which is symbolized by a pink ribbon, as a marketing ploy without genuine commitment to the cause. And bluewashing occurs when organizations attempt to present themselves as socially responsible or ethical, frequently aligned with the United Nations' blue logo or other international initiatives, but they may not meet those standards in reality.

There are countless examples of such behaviors. BP changed its corporate logo from a shield to a green starburst and pushed a new corporate acronym, "Beyond Petroleum," suggesting that the company was transitioning to green energy. It worked until the Deepwater Horizon disaster revealed its lack of environmental standards and oversight.[25]

Or take Keurig. For years, the company assured Canadians that its single-use plastic coffee pods were recyclable once the coffee grounds were removed. While this may be technically true, most Canadian provinces do not actually accept Keurig pods in their recycling centers. So while these communications made the company look good, in that country their statement was de facto false. The damage this caused was significant: in one year alone, the city of Toronto had to remove ninety tons of Keurig pods from recycling bins.[26] The fast-fashion giant H&M peppers its marketing materials with buzzwords like "conscious" and "sustainable"; however, a report by a watchdog group recently deemed that 96 percent of the company's sustainability claims were "unsubstantiated or misleading."[27]

Companies and wealthy individuals use philanthropy in much the same way. Nineteenth-century industrialists like Andrew Carnegie and John D. Rockefeller, who ruthlessly crushed labor movements and formed monopolies to quash their competitors, washed their reputations by sponsoring lavish projects for the public good, like libraries, concert halls, and universities. A more modern example was described in a 2021 *New York Times* article about Marc

Benioff, the founder and CEO of Salesforce, a cloud-computing company that thrived in the pandemic.[28] While some of Benioff's actions—such as his efforts to secure protective gear for hospitals during COVID, his philanthropic initiatives on behalf of San Francisco's homeless, and his support for a 2018 California ballot initiative that would have resulted in about $10 million in new taxes for Salesforce—are laudable, they are significantly overshadowed by his other efforts to undermine the public interest. For instance, the *New York Times* reported that in 2018 his company recorded over $13 billion in revenue while paying no federal taxes by deploying "accounting hocus-pocus that made its taxable income vanish." Then Salesforce repeated the zero-tax trick in 2020, despite recording $2.6 billion in profit.[29]

Ultra-wealthy entrepreneurs like Benioff, Mark Zuckerberg, and Bill Gates benefit from public goods financed by taxpayers—the country's infrastructure, its schools, its networks—while avoiding paying taxes themselves. This type of thinking is just another example of selective presentation of positive information to launder a reputation, directing attention away from the bigger picture where the work of their companies in fact harms societies. And let's not forget that there is a causal link. These companies and individuals can afford the philanthropic giving they boast about because they've foisted so many of their costs onto the public.

Tilting the Cost-Benefit Equation

Costs and benefits are more subjective than the presentation of hard numbers may suggest, as they require individuals to make judgments about what to optimize and what a good or bad outcome is. Companies can selectively present the costs and benefits of their actions to sway the public or to convince the government not to regulate them. Overall, the increasing use of economic analyses to undergird policy decisions has gone hand in hand with the rise of the neoliberal paradigm that underlies many of the issues I discuss.

"It costs too much." Thanks to decades of neoliberal indoctrination into the primacy of shareholder value, most of us have been conditioned to focus on the costs of fixing a problem, rather than the costs of inaction.[30] The fossil fuel industry, for example, has long insisted that climate action is so expensive that it would wreak havoc on our economy. The American Petroleum Institute has produced reams of research that emphasizes the high costs of proposed climate legislation and promoted it through astroturfed public interest groups. But climate inaction is much more expensive. It is becoming clearer by the day that it will lead not just to economic failure but potentially civilizational-level crisis.

In her book *Thinking Like an Economist: How Efficiency Replaced Equality in U.S. Public Policy*, the University of Michigan sociologist Elizabeth Popp Berman noted that the turn toward "the economic style of reasoning" has had devastating consequences for the implementation of public policies.[31] Bottom-line assessments of public-goods issues may seem scientific, but they elide moral and social considerations that weigh just as heavily. Many deploy mathematical models disingenuously to confer legitimacy on arguments that are simply self-serving. The crucial fact is that economic models rest on assumptions, and frequently those assumptions are politically influenced. Often, the data that is plugged into them is poor or inappropriate.

Setting politics aside, most externalities are quite difficult to price. As discussed above, there is controversy about the "social" cost of carbon. The Obama administration undertook a detailed study of the effects of carbon emissions all the way out to 2300, using a 3 percent rate to adjust the potential value of future events to their worth in today's terms, taking into account factors such as the time value of money and potential risks.

In this model, as noted, each additional ton of carbon dioxide emissions costs society $43.[32] While the number sounds quite precise, it is important to recognize that the model underlying it includes a number of factors, such as rising temperatures, possible effects from extreme weather, associated agricultural losses, and trends in human population growth. All of them could be adjusted in ways that move the cost up or down.

Arguments about those assumptions may reflect legitimate disagreements, but they are frequently motivated by self-interested considerations. The fossil fuel industry hires its own economists to create models that inflate predicted costs while ignoring benefits; these economists then present their results to the public as independent and disinterested. So when Trump administration experts followed these assumptions and changed the discount rate in the Obama administration's model to 7 percent, the social cost of carbon was cut to about $1 per ton in a single stroke.[33]

Benjamin Franta, a Stanford historian who focuses on climate disinformation, recently commented that this "tendency to focus on the cost of action and not the cost of inaction" has "played a key role in undermining numerous major climate policy initiatives in the U.S. over a span of decades."[34]

"The opportunities are incredible." The other side of the cost-benefit coin is when positives are hyped up to the exclusion of negatives. This also shows up in the climate debate and other types of win-win arguments about stakeholder capitalism. Companies will gain such substantial returns from their sustainability activities, the reasoning goes, that the government needn't regulate them; they will be more than motivated to act on their own. While such arguments may be in the service of greenwashing, often the companies that make them are not fooling us so much as they are fooling themselves. Psychologists have documented an "optimism bias," in which people over-weight an action's odds of success and the positive outcomes associated with it and under-weight its potential for failure or negative repercussions.

Hundreds of companies have set long-term goals focused on being "net-zero." These promises, especially in the early days, sounded amazing; it felt as though real change was going to happen. But many of them were just PR gambits, to be trotted out whenever companies were looking to avoid short-term accountability. It is easy enough to say you are going to run a marathon in 2050 (a common net-zero target date), but without a plan and a training regimen, it is just an empty aspiration.

There is a similar phenomenon with investors. Powerhouse investment firm BlackRock got significant media attention in early 2021 when Larry Fink stated that he expected all the businesses BlackRock invests in to be carbon-neutral by 2050.[35] But without an action plan or more details, such pronouncements are meaningless. ExxonMobil and Chevron, which have both announced plans to become carbon-neutral, are among the 1,600 "laggards" that don't disclose environmental information to the Carbon Disclosure Project, which should raise significant questions about their compliance.[36] Many of the companies that do disclose, including Amazon and BP, only do so selectively. As of 2023, a mere 0.4 percent of companies issued disclosures that met all the key indicators for a credible climate transition plan.[37] Most companies' strategies revolve around the purchase of offsets to bring them to net-zero, when what is needed is a transformation of their entire business.

The achievement of net-zero may not be possible, let alone absolute zero, where companies achieve carbon neutrality without using carbon credits to offset their remaining emissions. As we will later discuss in more detail, improved energy efficiency can lead to an increase in energy consumption as prices get cheaper. The phenomenon is known as a "rebound effect."

History shows that as new energy sources emerged and we moved from burning wood to coal, and then from coal to oil, new technologies did not immediately replace the old. In the eighteenth century, coal-fired furnaces began to be widely used, but coal accounted for less than half the world's energy use until as late as 1900. It took decades until oil became the world's most consumed energy source, but during the same period, the global consumption of coal almost tripled.[38] In fact, looking historically, there has only ever been one true energy transition: from wood to coal. As new types of energy were tapped, they led to energy additions, which raises questions about whether the potential of an "energy transition" from fossil fuels to renewables is actually possible.

With the expansion of renewables, one wonders what will happen to the existing infrastructure of oil, coal, and gas. Will they really be abandoned, or will the increasingly cheap solar and wind energy just add to our overall energy consumption and not displace fossil fuels at all? The graph in Figure 3 of energy usage over the past two hundred years supports the latter proposition. While there is much discussion of the expansion of green technologies like solar and wind, coal and oil still dominate our energy supplies, and few talk about scaling that down or how renewables can actually replace fossil fuels.

Another form of optimism bias occurs when companies refuse to acknowledge the underlying structural issues that cause a problem—for instance, poverty or discrimination—focusing instead on superficial fixes that often amount to window dressing. There are many such instances, including the myth of meritocracy—the idea that anyone can achieve social mobility through hard work and grit—that is threaded through the discourse in much of the Global North and particularly in the United States, where the American Dream remains a powerful fantasy. By continuing to invest in the idea that individuals need to pull themselves up by the bootstraps,

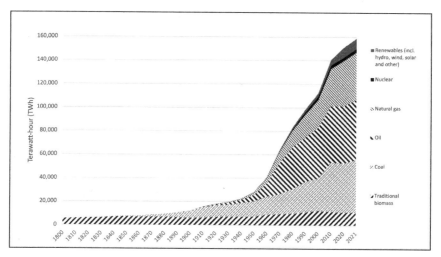

Figure 3: Global Primary Energy Consumption by Source[39]

companies convince the general public that there is nothing wrong with a system that allows them to exploit lower-cost labor to the benefit of their shareholders. Those who are not able to move forward are blamed for not investing enough in their education or not working hard enough. Seen in that light, "meritocracy" is a lose-lose system for the disadvantaged and a fig leaf for the privileged.

"Not my responsibility." This is another method of avoidance that companies engage in. Under the traditional retail model, the "customer is always right" may not have been a better way to do business, but it did mean that companies shouldered some responsibility for their customers' satisfaction. But in today's direct-to-consumer market, "it's not my problem" is a common cop-out. The *New York Times* shared the shocking story of the Gartner-McMillan family, who bought a remote control from Amazon with a broken battery cover. Their nineteen-month-old daughter swallowed a battery, suffering permanent damage to her esophagus. Though Amazon had listed, warehoused, and delivered the product, it maintained it wasn't liable for it, because it was sold by a third party, a position the Supreme

Court of Texas supported. That third party's listed address was in China; neither the courts nor Amazon were able to reach them.[40]

University of California, Los Angeles, professor Miriam Posner explained that the supply chains that drive global capitalism depend on "partial sight."[41] Companies are able to get customers so many things so cheaply and quickly because they only know what they have to. When it comes to anything else—say, the supplier's labor practices, its trustworthiness, or the quality of its goods—they turn a blind eye. The fact that Amazon itself could not reach the third-party merchant of the remote control is a straightforward consequence of its business plan. While Amazon may quickly offer refunds to satisfy consumers, when bigger issues occur, the company has no incentive to do better for its customers; it makes its money off quick delivery and convenience. Consumers must let their concerns about product safety and workers' conditions slide if they want to keep getting cheap goods within that one-to-two-day Prime delivery window.

Since Web 2.0 exploded, the information industry—whether news sources or social media platforms—has consistently evaded responsibility for the rampant misinformation and embedded biases in posted content. During the 2016 US presidential election, for example, anti-Semitic posts, often from no-name accounts and bots, ran rampant on Twitter and Facebook. Once elected, Donald Trump used Twitter as his main mouthpiece, further amplifying the flow of weaponized misinformation, whether about his policies, COVID, or his political enemies.

But social media companies have tried to gaslight us into believing that they are just neutral platforms. It's not their responsibility; it is up to us to fact-check what we see on their platforms. But they are the ones who sell our data and are constantly fighting for our clicks and mindshare. The platforms' decisions to maximize user engagement, monetize relevant data, and base decisions on analytics mean they see their users as so many data points and dollar signs. Hate speech and disinformation generate lucrative engagement, and that is the reason why social media companies are so reluctant to deal with it.

This leads to a winner-take-all mentality in which the focus is on grabbing as many "eyeballs" as possible, rather than providing sound information. Facebook, for example, offers a "boost" option, which allows businesses to pay for their ads to be targeted toward certain demographics.[42] The more money a business pays, the more attention the product gets. This means that profits on Facebook and other platforms are directly related to the time people spend online and the content that is shown to them. To maximize our attention, they make their sites as addictive as possible. Editors, the gatekeepers of traditional media, are replaced by integrated recommendations systems, boosted/paid/targeted advertising systems, and proprietary algorithms. The algorithms that create virality are opaque. Even if we want to view and share only objective information, the algorithms curate what we see in our news feeds based on our past clicks, our demography, and whatever other inputs they consider.

We now know that disinformation campaigns—some led by hostile foreign governments—play roles in elections in the United States and around the globe. All of the social media platforms are vulnerable to them, especially Facebook and Instagram. The wholesale buying and selling of personal data has led to a digital landscape that is filled with dubious claims, polarizing rhetoric, and weaponized fake news that is explicitly designed to weaken our sense of community. Following an investigation Facebook conducted in 2021, the platform acknowledged that Russian agents had purposefully sowed lies, misinformation, and confusion on the site to serve their own geopolitical purposes.[43] But the report was too little too late, as Facebook had knowingly allowed those Russian agencies free rein on the site during the presidential elections of 2016 and 2020. Foreign governments are not the only culprits. Anyone can use these tools to reap money and power. With lockdowns and work-at-home orders during the COVID-19 pandemic, people spent more time online than ever before. Misinformation about the virus spread widely and, with a total disregard for the age-old tradition of fact-checking, was further disseminated across mainstream media channels.

Corporations have weaponized social media as well. In 2020, the *Guardian* revealed that social media conversations about the climate crisis were being shaped by automated Twitter bots, which accounted for fully 38 percent of tweets about "fake science" and a quarter of climate-related tweets each day.[44]

With the advent of powerful artificial intelligence (AI) tools, these problems will only worsen. Understanding how AI algorithms make decisions, particularly in critical areas like health care and finance, is difficult, leading to a host of further concerns about externalities and unintended consequences. AI poses profound threats to privacy as well, as, in addition to being biased, facial recognition technologies and predictive analytics infringe on our civil liberties.

But social media and technology-based companies continue to vigorously stand behind section 230 of the Communications Decency Act of 1996, passed when the Internet was in its infancy. In 2023, the US Supreme Court upheld the act, which states that "no provider or user of an interactive computer service shall be treated as the publisher or speaker of any information provided by another information content provider" and thus protects platforms from liability for third-party content. The companies claim that this provision is absolutely critical to the success of their business and that it is beneficial for all. In reality, section 230 is being used more broadly than was originally intended; platforms were also expected to remove "obscene, lewd, lascivious, filthy, excessively violent, harassing, or otherwise objectionable" material from their sites, "whether or not such material is constitutionally protected."

Manufactured Cultural Wedge Issues

The labeling of Democratic Party policies, LGBT and trans people, civil rights activists, and more as "woke" and "socialist" is a long-standing way to misdirect society's attention from the root causes of systemic problems. In conservative circles, those terms carry the same baggage that "political correctness" once did.

Once a pejorative for performative righteousness and empty virtue signaling, "wokeness" has been blown up by Republicans into a mortal threat to both capitalism and democracy. Republican presidential hopeful Vivek Ramaswamy, a former entrepreneur in the health-care and technology sectors, is the author of *Woke, Inc.: Inside Corporate America's Social Justice Scam*, which argues that ESG investing and other corporate efforts to address externalities and societal problems are not only ineffective and cynical but subversive and economically ruinous. As he explains it, ESG programs let the private sector "do through the back door what our government couldn't directly get done through the front door." Liberal states like California and New York, he claims, have pressured "the BlackRocks of the world into using everyone else's money to also advance" ESG objectives.[45] Ultimately this left-wing, woke agenda is being forced on America in violation of business leaders' "fiduciary duties."[46]

But looking deeper, this obsession with opposing supposed woke cultural influence seems more like reactionary overreach by corporations and investors that are looking to protect their vested interests in environmentally and socially devastating practices. Tariq Fancy, the former BlackRock executive, astutely points out that while Ramaswamy claims that it is government, not corporations, that should fight climate change, he conveniently fails to acknowledge that not only are companies by far the biggest emitters but also many have vested interests in environmentally detrimental practices and spend lavishly to prevent the government from regulating them.

Billionaires like the Koch brothers and their allies in the fossil fuel industry have successfully lobbied Republican-controlled states, such as Texas and West Virginia, to pass anti-ESG legislation. Fancy finds it ironic that Ramaswamy targeted BlackRock for its asset managers' supposed penchant for putting their radically woke environmental values above investors' returns. As Fancy puts it, "They're not violating [their] fiduciary duty." They're just putting "green paint on what they're already doing," and the critics' mistake is to believe that "this green paint is actually real."

It is clear which actors are putting their ideology above economic reality, and it is not the woke supporters of ESG, as Ramaswamy, Florida governor Ron DeSantis, former vice president Mike Pence, billionaire Elon Musk, and others suggest. Fossil fuel companies and their investors are benefiting, while local populations foot the bill. Daniel Garrett, an assistant professor of finance at Wharton, and Ivan Ivanov, a senior economist with the Federal Reserve Bank of Chicago, found that anti-ESG legislation of the sort Ramaswamy advocates hurts states' economic performance. Five banks in Texas paused their underwriting of municipal bonds after the state passed anti-ESG laws in September 2021, causing between $300 million and $500 million higher costs to the state over the next eight months.[47]

———

While I have come to consider externalities as a corporate theft of public resources, I came across a more apt characterization in a recent essay by Julianne Zimmerman, managing director of Reinventure Capital, a women-owned and -operated venture capital firm. She opened the piece by identifying externalities as "systematized grift."[48] The Cambridge English Dictionary defines grift as "ways of getting money dishonestly that involve tricking someone," which I think is a more apt description of what underlies corporate action on externalities, as I have tried to communicate in this chapter.[49] Externalities are not a neutral assessment of costs and benefits, as economists back to Pigou would have us believe. Particularly in the neoliberal era of shareholder primacy, companies now employ many tricks to hide information and misdirect our attention in order to socialize their costs while privatizing their profit.

When considering the culpability of corporate leaders like Jack Welch, Jeff Bezos, and Elon Musk in creating today's crises, I am reminded of the prescience of Ray Anderson, the late founder and CEO of Interface, a pioneering producer of sustainable commercial flooring. After examining the ecologically destructive nature of the products his company produced, he set the company on a path to fully eliminate its environmental footprint. In reflecting on the damage his company had done to nature in the past, his conclusion was that he should have been "convicted as a plunderer of the earth." In a 2009 TED Talk, he assessed that "theft is a crime. And the theft of our children's future [will] someday be considered a crime." "In the future," he declared, "people like me will go to jail."[50]

Anderson's statements may seem extreme, but given the recent reassessment of Welch's destructive model, it is clear the tide seems to be turning in holding companies and their leaders accountable, and, more and more, the plunders' and grifters' true colors are being exposed. Fossil fuel companies are now defendants in dozens of lawsuits in the United States that accuse them of deception over climate change, and so are responsible for the subsequent damages to the tune of billions of dollars. To cite just one example, communities in Puerto Rico, an island that has already suffered massive consequences from climate change, recently launched a lawsuit to hold

ExxonMobil, Shell, BP, and Rio Tinto accountable for their cynical use of trade associations, think tanks, and scientists to disseminate misinformation about the links between greenhouse gas emissions and extreme weather. As former US vice president Al Gore described when discussing this audacious PR plot through which fossil fuel companies seeded doubt about climate change: "I think it's the moral equivalent of a war crime. . . . It is, in many ways, the most serious crime of the post–World War Two era, anywhere in the world. The consequences of what they've done are just almost unimaginable."[51]

This might be the first attempt to seek legal redress for corporate gaslighting, but it will certainly not be the last. Jeff Goodell, a climate change writer for *Rolling Stone* and the author of the 2023 bestseller *The Heat Will Kill You First: Life and Death on a Scorched Planet*, reflected on the coming culpability of fossil fuel companies for their decades of rampant pollution and systemically hiding their externalities: "I would not have said this even five years ago, but I have really come to see this now as a crime story. This is a kind of looting of the atmosphere of the Earth, siphoning off resources and grossly profiting off of that at the expense of many other people—billions of people—on this planet. And I understand that's a big thing to say, but I think it's just pretty obviously true."

While the future may be one where companies will be held accountable for how they have gaslighted us to bolster their profits, we first need to better identify how they are purposely avoiding paying the costs of their actions. In the next section of the book, we will take a closer look at the ways that companies avoid paying for their environmental and social externalities through such gaslighting and other tactics. We'll also consider some companies that are working to find solutions that attack those problems at their roots.

PART II

BROKEN SYSTEMS AND INNOVATIVE SOLUTIONS

3

Who Pays for Carbon Emissions?

The belief that digitization and energy efficiency go together is pervasive. We are thrilled to rid ourselves of physical materials when tech innovations allow us to. The shift to streaming music and video, for example, reduced the need for CDs, DVDs, packaging, and transport. This "dematerialization" seems like a huge benefit to the environment, and it has, in fact, by some calculations helped reduce carbon dioxide emissions intensity by more than 40 percent.[1] Progress in telecommunications similarly allows us to attend meetings via videoconferencing, rather than driving or flying, and the rise of remote work means less energy spent on commuting and keeping the lights on in office buildings. The twenty-first century's technology boom has ushered in a more environmentally friendly way of living. Or so it seems.

Companies that live primarily in online spaces tout their green image in marketing and public relations campaigns. In its 2022 *Environmental Social Governance Report*, for example, Zoom promoted the significant environmental savings that can be realized from online as opposed to in-person conferences.[2]

But the truth is that digital technologies, and specifically streaming media content, result in significant pollution because of the overall electricity they require. According to Maxime Efoui-Hess, an energy and environmental expert for the Paris-based think tank the Shift Project, streaming a half-hour show has an emissions cost of 1.6 kilograms of carbon dioxide, which is equivalent to driving 3.9 miles (6.28 kilometers).[3] In fact, the digital world is becoming one of the leading culprits of greenhouse gas emissions. The Shift Project's study "Climate Crisis: The Unsustainable Use of Online Video" found that digital technology accounts for 4 percent of greenhouse gas emissions and that energy use is growing at a rate of 9 percent every year. With the advent of powerful AI tools like ChatGPT, it is projected that the power needs, and so emissions, of data centers will dramatically increase in coming years.[4]

For one person, it may be just a photo or a few minutes of video, but, overall, our collective Internet traffic through these individual daily decisions has made a huge negative contribution to climate change.[5] So while there may be efficiency in the delivery of content online, it leads to much greater consumption and an overall increase in the use of energy. The online world now exceeds the emissions of the aerospace industry, whose climate impacts are much more front and center in the public consciousness, although estimated to only be about 2.5 percent of world totals.[6]

The technology giant Cisco has estimated that about two-thirds of the global population is online.[7] The fastest growing share of Internet use is video: 80 percent of all data transmitted online is video data, 60 percent of which is streamed.[8] Viewers may think these videos reside in an intangible "cloud," but in reality they are stored on servers that use huge amounts of electricity when they are idle and even more when their content is streamed to individual users. A recent study found that the carbon generated from Netflix's ten most popular movies and series in the twenty-eight days after their release was the equivalent of driving 1.8 billion kilometers.[9]

Netflix acknowledges its environmental impact but is less forthcoming about how it will address it. When Netflix published its early sustainability reports, the company's energy use was portrayed as a two-headed beast, direct and indirect. Indirect energy use emanating from its partners and along its supply chain accounted for about four times as much energy as its own operations.[10] But the company's more recent disclosures have become more selective and focused only on direct emissions from its hardware infrastructure, corporate offices, production studios, billboards, and delivery network. In 2021, this accounted for approximately 156,555 megawatt-hours (MWhs), up from 51,000 in 2018 (1 MWh can power the average home for 1.2 months, so 150,000 MWhs hours could power some sixteen thousand houses for a year).[11] Like many companies, Netflix announced a goal of being net-zero by 2022.[12] But as of October 2023, it had yet to disclose whether it had reached its target.

Even if Netflix had reached net-zero by its targeted date, a closer look at how the company accounts for this would reveal significant omissions, such as exempting itself from responsibility for the energy used by transmitting video streams. Netflix accounts for a significant share of total global Internet traffic—about 15 percent in 2023—and, as a result, a major proportion of the electricity that its customers' televisions, computers, phones, tablets, and Wi-Fi transponders consume.[13] In Netflix's own words, Internet service providers and device manufacturers should "ideally account for those emissions themselves."[14] In other words, according to Netflix, these emissions should not be its concern.

But according to the University of Bristol's Daniel Schien, whose carbon modeling tool has been used by Netflix and other large organizations, "The calculation of carbon footprint should include user devices as that is where the digital services are being consumed."[15] Not doing so is a bit like claiming that a bacon, lettuce, and tomato sandwich is low in calories if you only count the lettuce.

The gaps between what companies like Netflix claim about their environmental emissions and what they should be held accountable for can be huge. For instance, as we will discuss in more detail below, companies systematically exclude much of the emissions from their value chains through selective accounting and the use of offsets. In this way, their net-zero goals often amount to smoke and mirrors. Another important distraction we will discuss is how many companies tout their energy efficiency, which in principle makes sense but can be misleading, as efficiency frequently leads to lower costs and hence more use, and as a result more overall emissions.

But in addition to documenting the accounting and PR tricks that many companies are using, I provide a number of examples of companies that are taking responsibility for emissions through their entire value chain, from end to end, which is an important principle if we are to hold companies accountable for their environmental impacts. From detailed net-zero plans to well-executed, nature-based solutions, to rigorous carbon labeling, in this chapter we also explore how some companies are working to authentically consider their climate impacts.

What Is a Company's Environmental Footprint?

The Paris Agreement, a 2015 international treaty on climate change organized by the United Nations, called for the public and private sectors to achieve net-zero emissions by 2050 at the latest. But when companies like Netflix crow about becoming net-zero, it is important to ask what exactly they are accounting for. As we have seen, Netflix currently draws the line at its own direct operations. Even companies that consider indirect costs seldom consider their responsibilities end to end—meaning after the usable life of the product, when it is disposed of or recycled—or the additional energy expenditures that its use entails. Carbon neutrality or net-zero is still just a dream. For many companies, it is just a marketing gimmick.

An egregious example is ExxonMobil, which has committed to being net-zero by 2050. How is it possible for a fossil fuel company to be net-zero? In 2022 alone, ExxonMobil was responsible for 762 million tons of greenhouse gas emissions, equivalent to the entire country of Germany, according to the *New York Times*.[16] Absurdly, the company's net-zero pledge did not include the carbon emissions from the oil it sells, which is about 85 percent of its carbon footprint.

Understanding carbon emissions stemming from production—both for virtual and physical goods and services—is complex and requires considering the entire process of production from the extraction of raw materials through the end use by consumers. To fully understand what should be included in a company's emissions calculations, we need to consider the three main groups, or "scopes," of emissions that should be accounted for. Scope 1 emissions are those from activities directly under the company's control (for example, the carbon that comes out of its own smokestacks). Scope 2 emissions are those that result from purchased electricity, steam, heat, or cooling.

Scope 3 emissions, many of which originate in a company's value chain, are trickier to calculate; they tend to be at once a company's largest sources of emissions and the ones it is least likely to account for. These include emissions related to the extraction and production of purchased materials; business travel, including employees' commutes; waste disposal; and consumers' use of the products.[17]

According to McKinsey, 90 percent of an average consumer company's total environmental impact occurs in its supply chain.[18] Many companies have shifted their manufacturing operations to low-cost "pollution havens" like China, Pakistan, and India that have minimal environmental regulations and rely on coal-fired power plants. The finished products are then transported on ships and airplanes that burn diesel and jet fuel. But the companies may not account for any of that as they report on their progress toward sustainability.

If we really want to understand the total emissions of online video, shouldn't Netflix consider how much energy is expended by the viewers' computers, phones, and tablets? These devices are estimated to be the largest contributors to streaming-related emissions.[19] Netflix actually has some control over these sources of emissions. Changes in its compression algorithms could reduce the amount of computer resources that are required to view streamed videos, or files could be optimized for less-polluting devices. While this would not be a silver bullet, it illustrates the importance of thinking end to end.

Unless a company takes responsibility for acknowledging emissions of its whole value chain, it will likely use accounting tricks to only examine certain parts. That increasingly pushes emissions into places where they are not counted as within the company's purview and responsibility. When announcing Amazon's "Climate Pledge" in 2019, Jeff Bezos said, "We want to use our scale and our scope to lead the way."[20] Since then, Amazon has claimed to have made huge strides toward meeting its goal of net-zero by 2040. But that goal is within reach because the company only accounts for the climate impacts of products that bear the Amazon brand label. Unbelievably, these only make up about 1 percent of its online sales.[21]

Amazon is not alone. A report by the NewClimate Institute and Carbon Market Watch found that of the twenty-five largest companies in the world, only one, the Danish shipping company Maersk, had a net-zero pledge with "reasonable integrity" and was one of only three companies (the other two were Vodafone and Deutsche Telekom) that included "full value chain emissions" in their plans. Amazon, Google, IKEA, and Walmart, to name a few, achieved particularly low scores in this report.[22]

Environmental Savings Does Not Equal Diminished Emissions

Many companies report on their carbon emissions "intensity"—emissions on a per product or service basis—instead of overall emissions. Energy efficiency is important, but frequently it is directly connected to *increased* total emissions. As Netflix moved from the distribution of DVDs to streaming, its customer base expanded and so did emissions, a point reflected in the economic principle known as the Jevons paradox. As the steam engine fostered the industrial revolution in Britain in the 1800s, many were concerned about the sustainability of England's coal supplies. Some thought the solution was to develop more efficient engines. But as the economist William Stanley Jevons noted in his 1865 book *The Coal Question*, the "rebound effect" of those more efficient engines led to an increase in coal consumption. "It is a confusion of ideas to suppose that the economical use of fuel is equivalent to diminished consumption," he wrote. "The very contrary is the truth."[23]

Some economists thus believe that the only way to save the environment is to reduce economic growth in general and hence consumption. "Degrowth" is a political and economic theory, first formulated in 1972 by the Austrian French social philosopher André Gorz, that advocates shrinking economies. To that end, it argues that nations should stop using GDP as a measure of economic progress.[24] The philosophy certainly flies in the face of the key orienting assumption of capitalism, which has an overwhelming focus on growth.

To be clear, I am not arguing that the world should fully embrace such a strategy, if only because it would tend to freeze countries at their current level of economic development, perpetuating the vast disparities in wealth between Europe and North America and less developed countries in the Global South. Economic growth is necessary to bring benefits to many countries in Asia and Africa, lifting their populations out of poverty and improving their quality of life.

But the underlying premises of degrowth orient us to the important idea that an increased focus on energy efficiency is likely a mirage and that continuing growth using current approaches will inevitably increase aggregate pollution, although perhaps at a smaller per-unit rate than before.

Without such an acknowledgment, we will continue to hold companies accountable in the wrong way, and reporting smaller per-unit rates provides a useful tool for gaslighters. For example, Netflix funded research that showed that its switch to video streaming has made its business "increasingly carbon efficient and dematerialized." But regarding net-zero, this is misleading, as Netflix's own data shows that its carbon footprint is in fact increasing: a very substantial 50 percent between 2020 and 2021. This, Netflix said, was "as expected," because of the post-pandemic rush to return to TV and film production, but the company assured the public that it was "finding new ways" to meet its reduction goals.[25]

A 2023 investigation of major food companies' climate reports and filings by the *New York Times* illustrated that such disconnects on emissions performance are pervasive. Despite committing to being net-zero by 2050, in 2022, Starbucks reported a 12 percent increase in its total emissions compared to 2019. But during this time, the company's revenues increased 23 percent, so Beth Nervig, a spokeswoman for Starbucks, concluded that rising emissions was a natural process, in part since the company "saw our business grow." Fast-casual Mexican restaurant Chipotle reported a 26 percent increase in supply-chain and other emissions in 2022, despite having set a goal of halving its emissions by 2030. And other companies with similar contradictory actions include McDonald's, which has pledged to be net-zero by 2050, yet the company's emissions in 2021 were 12 percent higher than its 2015 baseline. Of the twenty large food and restaurant companies examined, the report concluded that more than half have not made any progress on their emissions reduction goals or have reported rising emissions levels.[26]

Fortunately, some companies are starting to recognize the fundamental challenges with net-zero commitments and are drawing our attention to them. Starting in 2018, Seventh Generation, the iconic home and personal care product company, committed to a 90 percent reduction of its Scope 1 and Scope 2 emissions by 2030 and an equal reduction in Scope 3 emissions from consumers' use, including the end of a product's life.[27]

Importantly, Seventh Generation recognizes the salience of Jevons paradox. "To date, we have been unable to fully decouple our product sales growth from our total greenhouse gas (GHG) emissions," the company admitted in a release, "which means that as we sell more products, our GHG footprint goes up, instead of down as our science-based climate target demands. With higher product sales, our 2020 absolute, or total, emissions increased 140% compared to our 2012 baseline. All of our carbon footprint is attributable to purchase of materials and ingredients and the making, distribution, and use of our products (Scope 3 emissions). These emissions increased in 2020, as they have annually since 2012."[28]

The process of accounting for and then reducing emissions is complex and convoluted. While many companies have taken advantage of this to obscure the public's understanding, others are engaging with the challenge in authentic ways by being transparent. Acknowledging the true situation, as Seventh Generation has done, helps focus attention on developing ways to actually address the underlying issues.

Importance of Avoided Emissions

Tim Frick is the founder of Mightybytes, a digital marketing agency that helps organizations meet their business and marketing goals through planet-friendly IT practices. When I was talking with him about Jevons paradox, I thought of Albert Einstein's famous quote: "A clever person solves a problem. A wise person avoids it." That is, we should from the beginning incorporate sustainability into the design and conception of a product and try to avoid the need to emit in the first place, as opposed to reducing or offsetting emissions later, as is the common strategy today.

Frick emphasizes that, as you consider "the entire life cycle of a digital product or service, you begin to see how design and technology choices contribute, often unintentionally, to the Internet's massive environmental impact." Choices around shipping options, data privacy, and accessibility can impact the ways that users engage with a product or service and have unintended consequences. Decisions about how servers are powered or whether digital workers are paid a living wage may not directly impact how end users engage with a product, but they clearly have consequences for equity and sustainability.

Most companies should start by considering their use of infrastructure as a fixed emissions cost. So for Netflix, just thinking about the efficiency of streaming is not a good way to consider environmental impacts, because the company's underlying networks and data centers operate 24-7 whether or not people are streaming.

A good analogy here is with an airline. The carbon impact of an airline results from the planes flying and is not significantly affected by how many passengers are on the planes. Netflix's reporting approach focuses on the passengers, not the plane. Calculating emissions using an orientation like this mainly results in net-zero being an accounting exercise—moving the numbers on a report to achieve a goal—as opposed to an operational program focused on reducing carbon in the value chain.

Building on the typology of Scope 1, 2, and 3 emissions, the idea of avoided emissions is increasingly being talked about as "Scope 4."[29] Using power from renewable sources, like solar or wind, is an obvious way to avoid emissions. But it is also important to think more fundamentally about a company's products and services and how they can be reengineered or redesigned. For instance, Riccardo Bellini, the CEO of haute couture fashion brand Chloé, told me that 80 percent of Chloé's sustainability challenges can be "solved at the design table." Bellini attributed 58 percent of Chloé's emissions to its raw materials. After better understanding emissions, designers were able to shift from cotton toward lower-impact materials such as linen and hemp in their designs. By 2025, 90 percent of the fabrics Chloé uses will be low impact, dramatically lowering the company's carbon emissions.

Seventh Generation CEO Joey Bergstein also emphasized to me how essential it is to start with design to avoid emissions. A key focus of his company's research and development team when creating new products is the end-to-end environmental impact. He told me that when the designers determine product attributes, they carefully consider "what alternative materials and ingredients we can use that still meet our standards." For example, to get rid of plastics altogether, products need to be reinvented to remove water, and the company has active research efforts to create effective waterless products for laundry, dish cleaning, counter cleaning, and handwashing. That is, due to its environmental commitments, Seventh Generation is developing effective cleaning products in powder or tablet forms that are packaged in easily recycled materials like aluminum or cardboard. Like the example of Chloé, this is an important recognition about the need for a fundamental reinvention of production processes from the ground up.

The Mirage of Offsets

Instead of improving their processes and materials to avoid emissions, many companies simply buy carbon offsets, delaying the hard decisions they will need to make in the future.

Furthermore, most offsets today are mainly just an "an accounting maneuver that allows more greenhouse gas to enter the atmosphere."[30] After examining 190 million tons of carbon offsets purchased in more than fifty thousand transactions in 2021, a *Bloomberg* investigation concluded that too many companies make "bold climate claims justified by cheap renewable-energy offsets that don't counteract global warming."[31] Many offsets that are tied to solar or wind projects are "largely bogus," the investigation concluded, for reasons we will discuss more below, although they sound good to the general public and allow companies to claim they are net-zero or on a path to being so. Credit Suisse Group AG was particularly singled out; *Bloomberg* assessed that the company's claims to be carbon-neutral are "based on purchases of low-quality carbon offsets that experts rate as useless."

Similarly, an in-depth analysis by the *Guardian* found that the most used offset programs "are likely to be 'phantom credits' and do not represent genuine carbon reductions."[32] The nonprofit Verra runs one of the world's most widely used greenhouse gas crediting programs. The *Guardian* found that 94 percent of Verra's rainforest offset credits had no benefit to the climate, and that the threats to forests that the offsets supposedly addressed had been overstated by about 400 percent on average for Verra projects. The carbon offsets "used by Disney, Shell, Gucci and other big corporations are largely worthless and could make global heating worse," the author concluded.

An underlying issue is that companies typically assess carbon crediting systems based on cost as opposed to the effectiveness or credibility of the offset program. Research on carbon accounting suggests that four key issues must be considered when assessing the validity of offsets: additionality, permanence/durability, buffer pool, and leakage. While somewhat technical, these ideas are crucial for understanding why most offsetting schemes are so misleading. As more and more companies' carbon claims are scrutinized, these ideas will likely become more widely known, especially in corporate leadership suites.

The concept of additionality focuses attention on the fact that a good carbon offset leads to reductions "in addition" to what would have happened anyway. For example, when assessing the offset potential of a forested area, one should not use the embodied carbon in the entire forest in the offset amount but how much carbon would be saved over and above what would be expected based on natural conditions. If it is unlikely the forest would be logged or cut down for any reason, then that forest offers no true offset potential. It is only by saving forested land that would have otherwise been cleared that an offset is realized.

Delta Air Lines for instance, was recently sued over its claim that it is "the world's first carbon-neutral airline."[33] As it turns out, about half of the offsets Delta used to make its carbon-neutral claim came from renewables, but since solar and wind power are now the cheapest sources of energy in many locations, using them does not actually offset power plants fueled by coal or natural gas. That is, these sources would have been chosen based on cost, and their installation did not require the closing of any fossil fuel plants. An expert review of Delta's largest single source of renewable offsets, the Los Cocos II wind farm in the Dominican Republic, determined that it almost certainly didn't offer additional carbon offset support.[34] Though these offsets were cheap to acquire, they did not lead to a reduction in fossil fuel power sources, and so they are not a valid way of reducing Delta's carbon footprint.

Another example of a lack of additionality is an offset project that distributes low-energy lightbulbs in a developing country, which would presumably lead to reduced energy consumption in the years ahead. But it's hard to prove additionality with absolute certainty because nobody can predict the future or determine what would have occurred without the project. For instance, the local government might decide to distribute low-energy bulbs independently to ease the strain on the electricity grid. In such a case, the bulbs provided by the offset company would no longer be considered additional since the energy savings would have occurred without the offset project's intervention.

Permanence or durability of an offset refers to the length of time that it will actually reduce carbon. Ideally, it will be for decades or centuries, as carbon emissions are very long-lived. Reports show that around 25 percent of carbon remains in the atmosphere for hundreds to thousands of years.[35] To compensate for this, offset credits must be associated with reductions that are similarly long-lasting. If the reductions are later reversed, meaning they are emitted back into the atmosphere, then the offset loses its compensatory purpose.

Say a farm owner offsets her carbon use. When the farmer dies and her grandkids sell the farm to a developer, the carbon is released. If a forest is used as an offset and a fire later burns down the project's trees, some or all of the carbon may be reemitted. Similarly, when planting trees, we can't know what the long-term life of that tree might be, and so we can't know how long its positive net effect will last. The benefits of tree planting depend on the species of tree, the region it's planted in, and the extent to which it will be protected.

To address the risk of carbon reductions being reversed, most carbon-offset programs have established "buffer pools." These are additional credits a company (or individual) purchases to account for future events, such as wildfires, as an insurance mechanism. If a reversal occurs, credits are retired or canceled from the buffer pool on behalf of the project's buyers.

Though this idea makes sense in principle, the methodologies used to calculate the needed buffer are typically suspect because they usually don't take account of climate change. The 2020 and 2021 wildfire seasons in California caused losses that are likely to fully deplete the credits set aside in the state's buffer pool, burning through protections meant to last a century in less than a decade. There are calculations that show that the California buffer pool is already "effectively insolvent."[36]

Even with the best intentions, it's hard to accurately predict the outcomes of offset projects and ensure that buffer pools are appropriately sized and managed. Buffer pools are intended to address uncertainties, but they may not be accurately calibrated to account for all possible variations in emission outcomes. If the buffer pool is too small or inadequately designed, it could lead to an over-allocation of carbon credits.

Finally, leakage is when the negative consequences of carbon emissions are merely shifted from one region or area to another. For instance, emission reduction efforts might lead to the relocation of carbon-intensive industries to areas or countries with weaker or no carbon pricing regulations. Or a carbon offset protects one forest but leads to an increase in logging in another. Under these scenarios, the emissions are just moving from one place to another so should not be considered offsets.

Consider the example of renewable energy projects. A wind farm may replace fossil-fuel-based power generation in an area, reducing local emissions. But if the overall demand for electricity increases, perhaps due to lower prices, other regions or power plants outside the scope of the offset program might rely more on fossil fuels, leading to emissions leakage.

For carbon offsets to be more than publicity gimmicks and window dressing, all of these features must be explicitly included and addressed as part of the offset calculation and creation process.

Nature-Based Solutions: Going Beyond the Hype

Projects that aim to protect or restore nature, particularly tree-planting initiatives, are used by many companies for offsets and to promote a green image. Unfortunately, most such programs are implemented ineffectively, and so are mostly greenwash.

On the surface, tree planting seems like a great way to reduce CO_2 and help combat climate change. Trees absorb CO_2 during photosynthesis and store it in their biomass (trunk, branches, leaves, and roots) and in the soil, and so can play a crucial role in carbon sequestration—the capture and long-term storage of atmospheric carbon dioxide. Tree-planting initiatives have the additional positive benefit of engaging people in an actionable way in a nature-based solution. The idea clearly resonates; reports from the *Guardian* and CBS News about how tree planting can reverse climate change have gone viral.[37] Even then president Trump promised US support for the World Economic Forum's One Trillion Trees Initiative.[38]

But when we focus too much on the trees, we tend to miss the forest. Tree planting has been overhyped, and many efforts are mostly greenwashing. Many experts in the space refer to such offsets as "trash," "garbage," or other saltier expletives. The problem is that, first, most projects are not planting grown trees that offer immediate benefits. Too often, seedlings that are not sturdy enough to thrive on their own or produce benefits are planted. Many are left to die; one large-scale study found that only about half of replanted trees actually survive.[39] Further, because of the transportation and planting efforts, tree-planting programs can even add more carbon to the atmosphere. What's needed is rigor and a systematic approach.

Christian Kroll, the founder and CEO of Ecosia, a search engine focused on sustainability that has planted more than 130 million trees since 2009, told me that while we should not discount or underestimate the importance of nature-based solutions in favor of new and shiny technologies, the details very much matter. "There are a lot of organizations that are talking about planting billions of trees," he said. "The problem is that you need to actually do it. Commitments are very easy, and even planting trees is easy, but then doing that successfully so the trees actually grow and survive and really benefit the communities and biodiversity, that is the difficult part."

Kroll wanted to create a business that could help address the environmental degradation he saw during his time living in Nepal and Latin America. The founder of a comparison website for financial products, he realized that most of his money was going to Google for advertisements connected to searches and grasped what a strong business model Google has. So he founded Ecosia with the mission to divert cash flows from search ads and devote them to environmental projects instead.

To ensure the trees it plants actually deliver environmental benefits, Ecosia has a dedicated tree team and a chief tree-planting officer, whose specific job it is to find the right tree-planting partners and follow up to see if they have delivered. The monitoring tools the company uses include satellite imaging and site visits, which are updated into a monitoring database of the more than fifteen thousand different locations where Ecosia has planted trees.[40]

Kroll sees hope in advanced technologies like carbon capture but believes they can only provide half a solution. "The other 50 percent," he said, "is nature. . . . I would say if we don't manage to plant at least a trillion trees in the next two decades, then we probably will not be able to solve climate change."

For all the abuses of tree-planting initiatives, Ecosia's work reminds us that we should not throw the baby out with the bathwater. Similarly, for all my critiques of offsets, I believe they should not be fully abandoned but rather be better constructed and monitored, and that companies should be held accountable if they're not. While the first priority of companies needs to be reducing and eliminating the emissions in their operations, rigorous ways of offsetting will have a place in our net-zero transition for the foreseeable future. For instance, Native, a Vermont-based company that partners with businesses looking to mitigate their climate impacts, creates offsets that were rated as the best overall carbon offset by *Investopedia* in 2023. Native provides information and best practices to assesses additionality, leakage, and durability and does rigorous on-site monitoring.[41]

To change the system, we must use many different approaches and strategies. What's key is that they are rigorous and science based, and, to not be misled by gaslighters, we need to demand well-defined accountability systems to ensure compliance over time.

Working Backward Versus Working Forward

The meatpacking giant JBS slaughters almost ninety thousand animals every day. Between the methane from cows and the diesel fuel it burns to power its operations, the company's environmental impacts are enormous. But it still announced it would be net-zero by 2040, despite the fact that its emissions had increased by 50 percent in just the last five years. The analogy used in a 2022 *New York Times* opinion video is that this is akin to promising your doctor now that you will quit smoking in sixteen years.[42] In July 2023, the US National Advertising Review Board found that JBS had not yet formulated nor started implementing a credible net-zero plan, so it recommended that the company discontinue publicizing its 2040 net-zero emissions goal because such claims lead consumers to believe that JBS is actively engaged in such plans.[43]

While JBS is an easy target, its approach is more the rule than the exception. Alberto Carrillo Pineda, the founder of the Science-Based Targets Initiative, the largest voluntary climate mitigation program for businesses, points out that while many sustainability reports tout goals, little is said in them about the steps being taken and the processes used to ensure those goals are being worked toward.[44]

In contrast, the shoe and apparel company Allbirds demonstrates a deeper approach to accounting for and achieving carbon neutrality. Its shoes are made from sustainable sources such as wool, tree fibers, sugarcane, recycled plastic bottles, and castor oil. Even its cardboard packaging is more than 90 percent recycled. The company is also pioneering a new way to account for its carbon.[45] Hana Kajimura, Allbirds' head of sustainability, told me that in setting its 2025 and 2030 emissions targets, the company "took the cradle-to-grave approach to our footprint, encompassing product use, end of life, and corporate emissions. We think we should be accountable to the impact of our product even after it leaves our door." For example, the company designs for longer life and less need for cleaning. It also includes the waste created when its shoes are discarded in its calculations, a rarity today.

She emphasized that most companies set empty goals. While the pronouncements of many companies are in line with the science-based targets that are needed to keep warming below 1.5 or 2 degrees Celsius, their roadmap is blank and they "work backward on how to get there," Kajimura said. "That takes a long time; you put the target out there and it takes years to figure out how you are actually going to achieve it. It leaves you with this big question mark—an innovation gap." That is, the company needs to find new, innovative processes or procedures to achieve the goal. Extending the map analogy, it is like you are planning a journey starting with the ultimate destination, with no idea how to get there, but you hope some new transportation technology or route will appear that will make it possible.

As we discussed above regarding Netflix and Amazon, this gap is frequently filled with innovative and selective accounting—such as limiting what parts of the business "count" toward climate targets and using ineffective offsets—as opposed to operational change.

Allbirds, alternatively, began its journey from where it is now, working forward from its current emissions, looking at each product's carbon footprint and then setting out to reduce it immediately. "We just started shaving that down by looking at all the inputs and saying: 'What if our wool was all from regenerative agriculture?' 'What if our factories ran on 100 percent renewables?' 'What if our customers were washing and drying our product less often?' How much would each of those things contribute to a reduction in our carbon footprint?" Beginning in this fashion allowed Allbirds to gain an accurate understanding of the carbon emissions of each aspect in its value chain and also the levers it could pull to reduce it.

The contrast with Netflix, for example, is clear. A company needs to start with its value chain and rigorously account for emissions throughout it. Changes in one part of the value chain can have big effects in others.

Along with an empty map with no understanding of the route to the goal, companies setting distant time horizons is another issue.

For instance, some companies may set a net-zero goal for 2050, which sounds logical, as that is the same as the Paris Agreement. But that time horizon is beyond the scope of any one sustainability person's career or the public's attention span. As Kajimura expressed, "Those goals are important to set that long-term ambition, but so is near-term accountability, and that's why we have 2025 as the focus."

As a result of its bottom-up analysis, Allbirds announced it will meet ten quantitative commitments for its materials and practices by 2025 and expand to a near-zero per-unit carbon footprint by 2030. These commitments include getting 100 percent of its wool from regenerative sources, reducing the use of raw materials by 25 percent, and sourcing 100 percent renewable energy at facilities it owns and operates, as well as educating consumers on lower-impact ways to clean footwear and apparel. Taken together, this amounts to a science-based target to reduce absolute Scope 1, 2, and 3 emissions by 42 percent by 2030.

Having a deep environmental focus can also spur innovation. For instance, wanting to reduce the carbon footprint of a shoe sole, Allbirds dedicated significant research attention to the effort. In 2018, the company introduced SweetFoam, the first carbon-negative polymer for shoe soles on the planet. Derived from sugarcane, it fits the contours of a customer's foot, bringing elasticity and comfort and vastly improving on existing nonpetroleum-based options.[46] The sugar is grown in southern Brazil without irrigation and using a minimum of fertilizer; it is a fully renewable resource that grows rapidly, removing carbon from the atmosphere in the process. Its biomass is used to generate the electricity that powers the mill and also to fertilize the next batch of crops.[47]

More importantly, SweetFoam is not patented; other shoe companies are free to use it and integrate it into their own shoes. Allbirds CEO Joseph Zwillinger told me that while the open sourcing of SweetFoam "sounds super altruistic," it's also pragmatic. Due to economies of scale, as more companies use it, it becomes less expensive.[48]

Cost, it goes without saying, is a serious concern for every business. It is also where much of the discourse about how companies will engage in win-win sustainable behavior falls short. "Sustainability is an expensive investment," Kajimura admits. But while there may not be a "green premium" to offset all investments in using recycled or natural materials, she told me that other sustainability initiatives—like shipping predominantly via ships instead of airplanes, using fewer materials, and minimizing waste—save so much money that the strategy ultimately does save Allbirds money on a per-product basis. But had the company not been committed to being a sustainable organization and thought through these processes end to end, those savings would have never been found.

Zwillinger told me that Allbirds was founded with a specific intent: "We've chosen an industry that has an enormous environmental impact on the world. Over twenty billion pairs of shoes are made every year, close to 2.5 billion in the US alone. It's a huge industry, and brands are not able to invest in materials quite as much because they're getting squeezed by the sales and distribution model. We just haven't seen any leadership from the footwear industry, in terms of focusing on sustainable sourcing of materials. So we have this overarching goal: we want to make a shoe like a tree."

Collective impact and changing overall industry structures, which we will discuss in detail in Part III, is crucial to systems change. In 2020, Allbirds partnered with its competitor Adidas to create the lowest carbon footprint sneaker ever. Adidas had launched its own sustainability initiatives via its Parley for the Oceans program (sneakers made from upcycled plastic waste collected on beaches). At a meeting in 2019, it seemed like a no-brainer to both companies to partner up. The Adizero x Allbirds 2.94 kilogram CO_2 shoe was introduced in 2022. Since the carbon output of an average sports shoe is closer to fourteen kilograms, the reduction of carbon emissions per unit by almost 80 percent is a remarkable feat.[49] And as of the spring of 2024, Allbirds will begin selling its M0.0NSHOT shoe, the world's first net-zero-carbon shoe, and the company is committed to achieving this milestone without use of offsets.

Carbon Footprint Is the New Calorie Count

An important starting point for Allbirds was labeling every one of its products with a carbon footprint tag covering all areas: product development, design, manufacturing, distribution, logistics, use, disposal, and even discontinued products. Kajimura explained: "We have really anchored the message and storytelling around that per-product footprint, because it aligns with that label you see on our product. What that means quite practically is that in 2030 that label on our product will be less than one kilogram of CO_2 per product."

As they step up efforts to address the climate crisis and shrink their carbon footprints, companies are sharing information about the steps they're taking and their effectiveness. They do so not just to prove that they're not greenwashing, but to educate consumers on the impacts of their purchases and hopefully reshape their choices. As the general public becomes more knowledgeable about carbon footprints and sustainability, it will be harder for consumers to be gaslighted about the topic.

Another company that is working to give consumers visibility into the carbon footprint of its products is Numi Organic Tea. Founded in Oakland, California, in 1999 by siblings Ahmed Rahim and Reem Hassani, the company sells ethically sourced teas inspired by the traditional desert-lime tea they drank as children in Iraq. Its packaging includes a carbon footprint label that accounts for emissions in four categories: ingredients, packaging, transport, and preparation. Hassani told me that "the biggest sources of our greenhouse gas emissions are transportation and product use. Simply boiling water can consume double the amount of energy that it takes to get that tea in the bag and to your doorstep, depending on your energy source." Numi is doing exactly the kind of emissions accounting that companies like Netflix avoid, and it is important because only by understanding emissions throughout the value chain can appropriate change strategies be devised.

The number on the packaging—0.038 kilograms CO_2 per bag—may not mean anything to most people, but as Jane Franch, Numi's vice president of sustainability, explained, it's all about promoting carbon literacy. Including this information "opens the door to conversations around energy policy. For many of us, this concept is still quite abstract and feels so far away. It's something they're talking about in Washington, but how does it impact me? By bringing it straight to your cup of tea, you have energy policy, right there in your cup."

Just Salad, a chain of fast-casual restaurants, introduced a carbon-labeled menu a few years ago.[50] "Before the '90s," noted Sandra Noonan, Just Salad's head of sustainability, "you didn't have standardized calories and vitamin and mineral counts on food packaging. So we said, 'What if the new calorie label is the carbon footprint label?' Obviously, it's not a perfect analogy, but why can't there be consumer literacy around carbon?" Just Salad CEO Nick Kenner also told me that assessing carbon emissions for each product allowed the company to specifically denote some menu items as "climatarian," after which sales of those items increased by 10 percent. As Numi Organic Tea's Franch put it, "It's not about whether everybody knows what a gram of carbon is; it's about developing that cultural competency and literacy around carbon in a similar way to how we developed it around calories."

———

Labeling is not a panacea, of course, and in the wrong hands it can become another gaslighting strategy. The term "ecological footprint" was first coined in 1992 but only entered the vernacular when the oil giant BP co-opted it, even creating in 2004 an online carbon footprint calculator for consumers to use.[51] It was a subtle act of misdirection. Suddenly, carbon emissions became the responsibility of each of us, rather than of BP. Tom Greenwood of the digital marketing company Wholegrain Digital described the slippery slope: "My concern with carbon footprinting is not that it isn't a useful tool, but that it's become dogma and the cult leaders are the fossil fuel companies themselves." Greenwood also reflects that focusing too much on it as the key solution "blinds us to the bigger picture, including the wider range of stakeholders involved, the more radical solutions that might be needed and the broader ecological crisis that is about more than just carbon emissions."[52]

Policy as an Externality Buster

While voluntary corporate action and investment are certainly important levers for change, as discussed in Chapter 1, externalities throughout history have traditionally been addressed though government action such as taxes, credits, and regulations—and governments are already playing a major role in the reduction of emissions.

For instance, there is an increasing use of carbon taxes and emissions trading schemes to encourage businesses and individuals to reduce their carbon footprints. As of 2022, about 30 percent of global emissions were under such programs.[53] In the European Union, these taxes covered about 40 percent of emissions, and prices ranged from close to $100 per ton in Nordic states to about $1 in Poland.[54]

Importantly, the European Union also recently passed a carbon border adjustment mechanism, which would function like a carbon tax on goods imported into the region if the producer was not under an existing carbon tax program, and so limit the ability of firms to avoid carbon taxes by producing in so-called pollution havens.

Many national programs use markets to price carbon, and the price fluctuates. A starting point for considering the optimal carbon tax rate is the marginal social damage from greenhouse gas emissions expressed in dollars per metric ton of carbon dioxide equivalent. Because carbon dioxide includes oxygen atoms, a molecule of CO_2 is almost four times heavier than a molecule of carbon. So, one ton of carbon corresponds to 3.67 tons of carbon dioxide when burned. That's one side of the equation, and relatively straightforward.

But as we have seen, calculating the other side—the social damage—is a slippery slope of assumptions that can be politically abused by governmental and other interested actors. In addition to the slipperiness of the price, if the carbon polluters simply transfer the cost to consumers, then the burden will fall hardest on the poor. To ensure the cooperation of all industries (including the investment world), governments should use a variety of approaches. For instance, the Biden administration's 2022 Inflation Reduction Act focused more on "carrots" to incentivize green production and encourage companies to decarbonize (like tax credits and loans), rather than "sticks": policies meant to punish them for using fossil fuels or taxing carbon emissions.

———

Most of us have known for decades about the damage that the fossil fuel industry wreaks on our environment. What's surprising is the extent to which we have been gaslighted into allowing fossil fuel companies and others to socialize their harms. Empty promises and flawed accounting that allow a company to claim net-zero are not enough; bad actors must be held fully accountable for their harms and forced to change their practices. We as a society need to place responsibility where it truly belongs and refuse to blame ourselves for the problems created by the fossil fuel industry and the biggest corporations that are straitjacketed by a short-term, profits-first mentality. While clearly we should all be aiming to be as responsible as we can for our individual energy use, we also need to shift attention to the companies whose emissions are at the root of climate change.

Over time it is essential to understand what end to end means in corporate emissions accountability. Companies should not be responsible for just their direct emissions from operations (Scope 1) but also indirect emissions from energy use (Scope 2) and what occurs in their value chains (Scope 3), including upstream with suppliers and downstream through consumers and end of use.

On the frontier are also historical emissions, which are recognized at the country level at UN COP meetings and other intergovernmental gatherings, but much less so for companies. It can be convenient to ignore that the effects of carbon emissions are cumulative; pollution pumped into the air has staying power. So, beyond the issues illustrated above, an additional issue is that much of the discussion about net-zero pledges and emission reduction assumes there is an annual blank slate and that all countries, and hence companies, should be focused on reduction. As of this writing, Microsoft is the only company that has committed to offsetting all of its emissions since its founding in 1975 by 2050. The plans for doing so are still evolving. Initially Microsoft focused on direct air capture, in which machines pull carbon out of the air; more recently the company has been considering other technologies. The lack of discussion about historical emissions is remarkably unfair to still-underdeveloped countries and will likely continue to rise on global policy agendas. So Microsoft's commitment and the investments it ultimately makes in these technologies will likely have far-reaching benefits, not only for the world but also for the company's position in the future.[55]

We need to be better educated in environmental issues if we're not to be tricked by companies like Netflix and Amazon, who use creative accounting to claim they are net-zero. Holding bad actors accountable is important. What is not acceptable is doing nothing. From detailed net-zero plans to nature-based solutions to carbon labeling, this chapter has shown that some companies are working hard to account for their emissions and reduce them. Allbirds, Ecosia, and Numi Organic Tea are just a few examples of what innovative entrepreneurs can do.

While corporate innovation is essential to find new ways to address our emissions challenges, such voluntary initiatives are not enough to overcome the problem of climate change. Governmental carrots and sticks are essential to spur action from companies in ways that just asking them to do the right thing won't. But as we will see in the next chapter, some of the underlying systems that encourage bad behavior are too broken to be repaired. Ultimately, they will have to be uprooted and replaced.

4

Who Pays for Damage to the Earth?

R obyn O'Brien began her career in a traditional way: with an MBA from a top school and then a job at a leading investment firm. But when her one-year-old daughter had a life-threatening allergic reaction to something she ate, O'Brien's life turned in a different direction. Applying the skills she had honed as a financial analyst, she dove into the data behind the rise in food allergies among US children. The information she uncovered was shocking. "Our own American food companies," she told me, "formulate products with cheaper ingredients that tend to be artificial" but make them with natural ingredients for other countries, because those countries have higher standards.

In her book *The Unhealthy Truth* and a TEDx talk about our food system, she asked whether children are allergic to certain foods or to what is done to them: the genetic alterations that make animals grow faster and bigger, the pesticides that increase farmers' yields, and the cheap but toxic chemical additives that extend a food's shelf life.[1]

What frustrated O'Brien was how successful the business model of agrochemical powerhouses like Bayer (which owns the former Monsanto), Syngenta, and Dow has been, even as our collective health has deteriorated.

In this chapter, we will examine the structure of agricultural production, looking at its effects on the planet, on agricultural workers and their communities, and of course on consumers. While agriculture makes up only about 5 percent of US GDP and has receded into the background of life in the Global North, it has a pervasive impact on us daily. From the food we eat to the fibers in our clothing and ingredients for many other consumer products, our reliance on the natural world is much greater than most of us appreciate.

Farming and especially animal husbandry are some of the biggest drivers of climate change and biodiversity loss. By some estimates, today's large-scale agricultural model makes up 25 percent of global greenhouse gas emissions and is a major contributor to deforestation.[2] Farm machinery and the trucks that transport crops to market use large quantities of fossil fuels. Industrial agriculture also creates significant threats to biodiversity worldwide by altering habitats, affecting species' distributions, and increasing the risks of extinction for many plants and animals.

So, the answer to the question this chapter's title asks is obvious. The global agriculture system is a prime example of profiteering. The astronomical profits that gigantic international companies earn are literally built on the backs of farmers around the world while also causing significant long-term risks for life on the planet more generally. Farmers carry extensive levels of debt, obesity and health issues plague humanity, and all the while agricultural companies' profits reach new heights. We are also undermining our future. As a 2023 UN report documented, pollution, deforestation, and unsustainable land use practices combined with climate change and the spread of invasive species have put about one million animal and plant species at risk of extinction, many within decades.[3]

But many entrepreneurs and companies are aiming to change these systems, including Robyn O'Brien. In 2018, O'Brien cofounded rePlant Capital, a financial services firm that invests in agricultural solutions that prioritize regeneration. In doing so, she joined a movement that is directing billions of dollars toward the transition of farmland from "agrochemical" practices to "soil to shelf" agriculture, as she described it. Regenerative practices not only eliminate the current debt-ridden financing model that makes it so hard for small-scale farmers to survive. They also reduce the potential health effects from chemicals and genetically modified organisms (GMOs) that affect us all, while benefiting the soil by restoring nutrient density, increasing carbon drawdown, and reducing chemical runoff into waterways.

As the world population has grown, chemical fertilizers have enabled larger yields, saving many from hunger. But our knowledge of plant biology and soil ecology has progressed in recent decades, and the time has come to shift to ways to increase agriculture productivity that don't have the negative effects of today's dominant agrochemical model.

Focusing on regeneration is the flip side of the externalities coin: it shows how spillovers from companies' production can also land on the positive side of the ledger, creating virtuous cycles. A large body of research now argues that regenerative agriculture can lead to long-term productivity growth. Further, while much of the focus on sustainability has resulted in the rebound effects discussed in Chapter 3—in which emissions savings are offset by people consuming more—regenerative production, alternatively, can restore and improve natural systems, social capital, and economic value.

Standing in the way are the large companies whose business models are based on chemicals and the farmers they have trapped in a vicious cycle of debt. So there is still a David and Goliath aspect to the rise of farms and businesses that adopt regenerative practices. Agribusinesses have scale and power, but as we will discuss in more detail below, upstarts are exposing their vulnerabilities.

Negative Spillovers of Today's Agricultural Systems

The traditional model of agriculture began to change in earnest in the 1980s, when new laws and court rulings made it easier for food and chemical giants to apply for patents for agricultural inputs.[4] Large chemical companies like Monsanto and DuPont developed a host of genetically modified seeds, which they own the exclusive rights to. In the quest for large-scale efficiency, modern agribusiness promotes the cultivation of a few high-yielding seeds, causing traditional and native crop varieties to be neglected or replaced. Genetically modified crops with pest-resistant traits may inadvertently harm nontarget species, causing significant impacts on biodiversity. As forests, wetlands, and grasslands are converted into monocultures, diverse ecosystems and the species that depend on them are lost. Absent diversity, plants cannot evolve to become more adaptable and resilient.

Many of the monoculture crops that now dominate world food production are already on the brink of collapse in many places. The increasing lack of biodiversity has far-reaching implications for human well-being and the world economy. A 2023 report, for instance, finds that 85 percent of the S&P Global 1,200 companies significantly depend on nature and biodiversity across their direct operations.[5]

Take coffee. Most of us enjoy our morning brew, but few realize how vulnerable many coffee crops are, particularly those of the arabica species, which makes up over 70 percent of the global coffee trade. As global temperatures rise due to climate change, the suitable geographic range for coffee cultivation is expected to shrink by 50 percent by 2050, with the highest impacts being felt at low latitudes and altitudes. The world's dominant production regions in Brazil and Vietnam are expected to experience substantial reductions in areas suitable for coffee growing, impacting the livelihoods of millions of smallholder farmers and significantly raising prices for consumers.[6]

Beyond its negative effects on the land, agribusiness harms humans as well. Leah Garcés, author of *Grilled*, reports that, just for chickens, there is $5.2 billion worth of farmers' debt in the United States and that large companies benefit and profit while individual family farmers are "held hostage."[7] O'Brien similarly told me that "US farmers carry over $426 billion in debt, and that is primarily to finance the agrochemical model." Farmers are trapped in these systems because "they have to purchase patented seeds every year or they're in violation of their contracts. Then they have to purchase the chemicals that are required to treat and grow those genetically engineered seeds or they're in violation of their contracts." Furthermore, farmers are contractually prohibited from reserving some of their harvest and replanting it the following year, as they did for millennia, so every year they need to buy the expensive seeds.[8] The result is a closed loop—a monopoly, essentially—which is good for the monopolist but bad for everyone else.

Climate change is exacerbated by the production of many of these products, which further weakens the farmers' position. Unpredictable weather events—droughts and more frequent heavy rain—are affecting their yields and hence their incomes. In India, wild animals like elephants are coming out of the jungles and stomping through farms in search of water and food that are scarce due to habitat destruction and climate change.[9] In Africa, rising temperatures are increasing food and water insecurity, leading to the wholesale displacement of populations. Sub-Saharan Africa has experienced the most frequent and intense climate extremes over the past few decades. African regions within fifteen degrees of the equator are expected to experience ever longer and more frequent heatwaves. According to the UN's Intergovernmental Panel on Climate Change (IPCC) forecasts, droughts will be significant in the Sahel, the vast semiarid region between the Sahara Desert and the tropical savannas in the south of Africa.[10]

One vivid recent example of how the excesses of our current agricultural production model can spill over to communities is hog farms in the United States, where animal waste is first collected in cesspools and then, when they are full, is sprayed onto fields as fertilizer. Some of it is then carried by the wind into nearby houses, causing respiratory infections. For that reason, these farms are almost always located in low-income areas where residents have little power. According to Garcés's reporting, "When you look at a map . . . they've set up in places where people have less agency to fight against these externalities being put upon them. . . . If hog waste was being sprayed on the state capital, it would stop in a day."[11] This is also one of the biggest examples of environmental racism, when environmental hazards disproportionately affect marginalized communities.

Governments around the world spend billions to subsidize animal farms—to the tune of about $500 billion per year—even though they are one of the most ecologically destructive industries. Tellingly, hardly any programs include incentives for farms to become more ecologically sustainable. During COVID, the US government supplied livestock producers with $270 million in assistance. Meanwhile, livestock production across the planet threatens to swallow up as much land as the entire subcontinent of India within the next thirty-five years.[12] The effects of agribusiness are not just felt on the land. For instance, coral loss is closely associated with beef production in Australia.[13]

As people become more aware of the problems with industrial agriculture, we are seeing some initial attempts at reform. Among them is the development of certification processes like fair trade and organic production systems that aim to help producers in developing countries achieve better trading conditions and more sustainability. These certifications are focused mainly on products that are exported from developing to developed countries, such as coffee, cocoa, sugar, tea, and cotton. Fairtrade International is one of the most recognized fair trade certifications; its blue and green emblem can be found on many products around the world.

While many people do not want products that contribute to environmental degradation, pesticide pollution, and the use of exploitative labor practices, some systems that have been designed to overcome these issues have also been compromised by corporate interests. Consider cotton. In 2021, the *New York Times* published an exposé that showed that a large majority of cotton from India that is labeled as organic is not organic at all.[14] There is widespread deception around other supposedly organic products as well. Vik Giri, founder and CEO of Gallant International, a Los Angeles–based company that supplies products made with organic cotton to businesses, told me that part of the reason fraud is so rampant is that buyers don't have deep relationships with their suppliers. "Companies need to go further than certifications," he said. "We need to build a transparent supply chain so we can feel good about where our cotton comes from. That starts with investing in farmers who are making the transition to organic and connecting with them."

Sustainable Development Is a Bridge. Regeneration Is the Destination.

We are all used to hearing about sustainable development, for example the UN's well-known Sustainable Development Goals, based on seventeen critical needs. But while the word "sustain" implies that we can repair our system, what it actually needs is a gut renovation. The word "sustain" suggests that it's possible to achieve a balance between economic, social, and environmental factors by subtracting negative externalities. "Regeneration" is about much more than the mitigation of harm; its goal is to make systems better, replenish resources, restore and improve ecosystems and communities, and foster long-term resilience.

"If you think of sustainability, it's like keeping things as they are," Garcés said. "We don't want that. Things are terrible. We want to regenerate. We want to create topsoil, create healthy soil so we can have food for the future." Along these lines, one farmer told me, "organic is about doing less harm. Regenerative is about making the world better." Thus, the focus can no longer be on maintaining or scaling back our current situation. Nor can it just be on organic farming, as important as that is. We clearly need to focus on not just breaking even but delivering positive externalities.

Vik Giri from Gallant International also contrasts organic with regenerative. He acknowledged that growing organic foods and fiber is important, because GMOs, fossil-fuel-based fertilizers, pesticides, and herbicides are all banned from organic farming practices. But the issue, he said, is that "the standard organic certification doesn't even begin to dive into the specific farming practices that protect and build soil health, promote biodiversity, conserve fresh water, or ensure the welfare of animals." Gallant takes its farming practices much further on the sustainability spectrum and looks at the system holistically. Its products meet standards in what he called the "holy grail of farm sustainability: soil health, animal welfare, and social fairness."

As we will discuss, regeneration is a general idea that can be applied to many industries to create virtuous cycles, but it is most visible and advanced today in agricultural practices that concentrate on natural methods of soil enrichment that improve the water cycle, support biodiversity, and enhance adaptability to climate change.[15] For example, the hooves of grazing animals loosen soil and compact inedible plants, accelerating the formation of organic materials. Cover crops like mustard, alfalfa, and clover act as a kind of living mulch, protecting the soil from wind and water erosion while feeding its microbes.[16] No-till techniques are also crucial, as mechanical disturbances have negative impacts on microbial communities in the soil and accelerate erosion.[17]

Traditional agrochemical practices revolve around growing the same crops year after year, which depletes carbon and vital nutrients from the soil. About a third of the world's topsoil is already severely degraded. If current land-use patterns continue, the United Nations estimates that all of Earth's topsoil will be degraded within sixty years.[18]

Through regenerative practices, soil organic matter is produced when plant or animal tissue decays. Although most soils contain only 2 to 10 percent organic matter, it plays a vital role in soil health. For every 1 percent increase in its organic matter, an acre of soil can hold an additional twenty thousand gallons of water. Increased water-storage capacity means that crops are better able to withstand droughts and heavy rain. Soil organic matter also reduces nutrient loss and erosion by maintaining surface residues, roots, and pore structures. When plants have the nutrients and root systems they need to grow, they synthesize compounds to fight pests and diseases. There is also increasing evidence that foods grown in soil that is rich in bacteria, fungi, and nematodes is healthier.[19]

Regenerative agricultural practices also promote biodiversity by creating habitat diversity and providing food and shelter for pollinators, beneficial insects, birds, and other wildlife species. This contributes to ecosystem resilience and supports ecological balance.

In all these ways, regenerative agriculture produces positive externalities that are beneficial to society and the environment. The goal of returning agriculture to its regenerative roots is beginning to gain traction. In 2021, President Joe Biden touted a regenerative practice in a speech to Congress, praising "farmers planting cover crops so they can reduce the carbon dioxide in the air and get paid for doing it."[20] Our generation has inherited a massive environmental crisis, but if you flip the script, there is also a massive opportunity to drive change.

Illycaffè, the global coffee producer, is increasingly focused on just these issues. "Drought, floods, high temperatures—many different climatic kinds of disasters are impacting production," third-generation owner Andrea Illy told me. Illy is a chemist, so he took a yearlong sabbatical to study insetting (ways to keep more carbon in the soil) and emerged with a plan. "The IPCC," he said, "recommends always pursuing a double benefit. If you have a healthier soil thanks to regenerative agriculture then you probably have a healthier plant and a healthier food and a healthier consumer."

Illy told me that the company is taking a three-stage approach to the pursuit of soil and human health with its farmers: "We determined that what is needed first is improvements in agronomic practices; second, developing new cultivars and varieties that are more resilient to the effects of climate change; and third, migrating coffee plantations to higher latitudes or higher altitudes." The company is starting to pilot carbon-free plantations and spreading its practices broadly. "The net-zero agronomic practices that we develop in those pilot plantations will be taught to all the company's farmers to help scale up net-zero coffee agriculture."

Generating Systems Change in Agriculture

To change intractable systems, we need action on multiple fronts. Robyn O'Brien reflected that she was "frustrated by how slowly the industry was tackling some of these systemic issues." The bottleneck, she said, was the supply chain, and the key lever to changing it was the farmers themselves. McCain, the world's largest producer of frozen french fries, recently committed to having 100 percent of its supply chain regenerative by 2030. But as we will see, changing farmers is not just about flipping a switch or convincing them of a business case. As with so many of the systems-change examples we explore in this book, it requires a few key elements, including a change in mindsets, the introduction of new practices, and collective action in areas such as finance.

O'Brien recalled asking McCain's leaders, "Who are your most forward-thinking farmers who understand that we need to move away from this agrochemical model toward this regenerative, restorative way of farming?" That way, the company could start the transition with people who had already bought into the idea and then use those early successes to convince more traditionally minded farmers. O'Brien emphasized that regenerative farming isn't new. It has been practiced for generations by many farmers of color who didn't have access to financing for pesticides and other modern-day developments because of discriminatory lending practices. But for farmers who adopted the agrochemical model, the shift requires them to embrace practices that their grandparents or great-grandparents used, while incorporating newer technologies such as drones and water sensors.

As with any system-wide change, it is a collective issue, and all of the key players must be involved. This is why O'Brien works with major corporations like McCain. In 2022, rePlant announced a partnership with the food and beverage giant Danone North America to help its dairy farmers finance biodigesters that capture methane gas and use it to generate electricity, powering their farms and nearby communities.[21] rePlant will invest up to $20 million to support Danone's North American farming partners as they transition.[22]

The first loan went to the McCarty Family Farm in Kansas, a fourth-generation dairy farm.

Given these up-front cost issues, O'Brien emphasized the importance of finance. As she explained, you can't fix a broken food system with a broken financial system: "One farmer I met at an event in Kansas said, 'I've been in debt since I was thirteen years old, and I'm tired of being in debt. I've had this relationship with my lenders for thirty years. Why should we switch over to you?' I said, 'You were just up there talking about your debt. That lender is so happy to keep you in debt. rePlant is successful when you don't need us anymore.' They're just so conditioned to that system. We have an extractive agricultural system because the financial system is enormously extractive of our farmers."

Some practices of regenerative agriculture—such as letting soil sit fallow for a period—can be costly to implement, but the system ultimately requires fewer input costs, so farmers can break out of debt and start to earn profits. A farmer in Indiana who worked with rePlant to transition his seven thousand acres from genetically engineered corn and soy saved half a million dollars in his first year. Those savings speak for themselves, which is important because the politics around GMOs, agribusiness, and pesticides are so fraught. "When you're talking about climate or you're talking about the environment, it can be a polarizing political conversation," O'Brien explained. "But when you simply make it about the math for the farmer, that this is the smartest financial decision that they can make, that's really where our team shows its strength."

Furthermore, focusing on the soil and regeneration can even lead to new sources of revenue. Sustainability consultancy Native is developing unique financing mechanisms to promote regenerative practices. A project in Montana, for instance, uses detailed grazing-management plans to ensure that cattle graze smaller plots of grasses for shorter periods, allowing longer periods of rest and regrowth for each plot before it is grazed again. This also allows for a lot more trampling of grasses and manure into the soil. After a few seasons, so much carbon has been returned to the soil that it can be sold as legitimate offsets (as opposed to the greenwash ones discussed in the last chapter).

Jennifer Cooper, the company's vice president of client strategy, told me that Native cofounder Tom Stoddard's mantra is "Soil is the new wind," as soil regeneration can help sequester the high levels of CO_2 from our atmosphere and creates benefits for farms, ranches, and our food system that can also be monetized.

But, as noted, the challenge is the entrenched traditional systems. Farmers need access to capital to escape the trap. "The costs occur at the outset," Cooper explained, "while the carbon and soil health benefits occur over decades. We, collectively, should not be asking first-mover farms and ranches to take on all the costs and risks of figuring out which practices work for their farm."

Supply Chains Built Around Regenerative Agriculture and Certification

Michael Bronner first became involved in environmental efforts in 1998, when he and his brother David took over their father's company, Dr. Bronner's, a family-owned maker of organic soap and personal care products. The company has a unique history that dates back to 1948, when Emanuel Bronner, a minister and third-generation master soap maker, used the labels on his ecological soaps to spread the moral and religious ideas he publicly preached, that we must realize our unity across religious and ethnic divides or perish: "We Are All-One or None!"

After Emanuel's death in 1997, the family continued to run the company and maintain his vision. Today, Dr. Bronner's is renowned not only for its high-quality, multiuse soaps but also for its mission of social responsibility and environmental sustainability. The company is committed to making socially and environmentally responsible products of the highest quality while dedicating profits to help make a better world. They champion fair trade, organic farming practices, wage equality, and animal advocacy, truly embodying their motto of "All-One!"

While the company has always had an unconventional approach to business and strong commitment to social and environmental causes, under the Bronner brothers' leadership, Dr. Bronner's has become a model of a company that does not just aim to do no harm but actively seeks to do good. Michael Bronner has championed a number of progressive causes, such as regenerative organic farming, wage equality, and drug policy reform.

Dr. Bronner's products already used natural ingredients, and the new leadership led the company to achieve organic and fair-trade certifications. In doing so, they formed international relationships—in Sri Lanka for coconut oil, in Ghana for palm oil, in India for mint oil—and, in doing so, really came to know the farmers and their products "from the root to the fruit," as Michael Bronner put it. And the company ensured that "everybody was being paid well along the way."

Over time, Michael realized that, even with these certifications, there was not enough focus on giving back to the land and farmer. In 2017, Dr. Bronner's, Patagonia, the Rodale Institute, and a number of other companies and farmers established the Regenerative Organic Alliance (ROA) to create certification standards for animal welfare, social equity, and organic sustainability. The resulting Regenerative Organic certification, Michael explained, "is kind of like the maxim from *Lord of the Rings*: 'one ring to rule them all.'"[23]

Tablas Creek Vineyard, for instance, is working with the ROA to further consumer understanding and acceptance of this certification.[24] "We're a speck on the fingernail of agriculture as a whole," said Jordan Lonborg, the vineyard's viniculturalist, but from a visibility perspective they have an outsize impact. He explained that "corn farmers aren't getting media coverage. You don't have powerful people visit a corn farm, but you have people from all walks of life coming to California and drinking wine."

Since regenerative agriculture involves a closed-loop philosophy that limits the use of external products, Tablas Creek generates its fertilizer on-site. "That's basically what regenerative farming is," said Lonborg. "It's nothing new, but it's a way people have been farming for hundreds and hundreds and hundreds of years, although like with other certifications, it forces you to look at your property a bit differently."

Emphasizing the cognitive shift that is needed, he said that when people think of vineyards, they just see grapevines. But if you're "going to start farming regeneratively," he continued, "you need to hit that reset button and reevaluate what you think a healthy vineyard should look like. There shouldn't just be grapevines. It should be as far from a monoculture as possible. That could mean planting fruit trees throughout your property or vegetable gardens or perennials . . . doing whatever you can do to create more of a biodiverse ecosystem."

———

Most food products must travel a long road before arriving at our table. Not everyone benefits equally along the way. Large businesses use their privileged positions in the supply chain to exploit farmers, who are on the front line of production. The farmers' use of chemicals and other practices then causes harm to communities and consumers.

But these issues are something that every company should be considering. As we saw in the last chapter, responsibility for emissions is increasingly focused on Scope 3, and for many companies, that includes inputs from the natural world. Given climate change and the risks from biodiversity loss, those supplies are more vulnerable than ever. At the same time, companies are increasingly accountable for their impacts.

Consumers have shown an increasing willingness to pay more for healthier foods raised in sustainable and equitable ways, but they shouldn't have to bear all the costs. Companies like rePlant, Dr. Bronner's, Tablas Creek, and Illycaffè are working to build a new infrastructure that is fairer and more sustainable, bringing us that much closer to our goal of creating a food system that is resilient and regenerative. But as climate change accelerates, we need to move much faster.

While agriculture is where the ideas of regeneration have been gaining the most traction, the idea is more general. At its root, it's about creating or restoring systems in ways that enhance their vitality, resilience, and sustainability. For instance, regenerative systems can also be fostered in social contexts, such as community development and empowerment. Programs that aim to uplift disadvantaged communities, improve education and health-care access, and create sustainable livelihoods contribute to the regeneration of social well-being, help support individuals and families facing economic hardships, reduce poverty, and promote social cohesion. We will discuss these ideas in later chapters

Vincent Stanley, Patagonia's director of philosophy, described to me how understanding the power of regeneration led to an "aha" moment for the company, and that this idea is now the company's North Star.

Since the late 1990s, Patagonia's mission statement was to "build the best products, cause no unnecessary harm, and use business to inspire and implement solutions to the environmental crisis." But as Stanley reflected, the "clause of 'cause no unnecessary harm' acknowledged that almost everything we do to improve our practices is still extractive; they take from nature more than we know how to return and do not actually create positive good."

When the company entered the food business with the founding of Patagonia Provisions in 2012, it began to see the power of regenerative agriculture. In 2017, Patagonia accordingly changed its mission statement to "We're in business to save our home planet." As Stanley told me, regenerative ideas have spread to the company's apparel business, where Patagonia now uses regeneratively grown cotton and other materials and is actively changing its sales, reuse, and repair practices to align with this new mission.

In the next chapter, we turn to manufacturing and production, focusing on ideas of regeneration through a circular economy that minimizes waste and maximizes reusing, repairing, and recycling materials and products. Instead of a linear "take, make, dispose" model, the circular economy aims to create a closed-loop system that regenerates resources and reduces environmental impact.

5

Who Pays for Cheap Goods?

We love convenience, but our consumption habits are increasingly wasteful and resource intensive. Clothing is one example. On average, consumers around the globe buy a new piece of clothing every five days. Prices are so cheap that clothing is seen as essentially disposable. In fact, for every five new garments produced, three are disposed of.[1]

We are overconsuming and doing so at an astounding pace. The volume of clothes we throw away—nearly seventy-five pounds of textile waste per person per year—has increased more than 750 percent since 1960, doubling over the last twenty years.[2] The fashion industry creates ninety-two million tons of textile waste each year, a figure set to increase by about 60 percent from 2015 to 2030.[3]

The clothes may be cheap, but society as a whole pays a steep cost. "You may get a $1 bikini, but it's costing society a lot," said Dana Thomas, author of *Fashionopolis*. "We're paying for all of this in different ways."[4] The environmental impacts of fast fashion

Fast Fashion!

include the depletion of nonrenewable resources, greenhouse gas emissions, and huge expenditures of energy and water—seven hundred gallons to produce one cotton shirt and two thousand gallons to produce a pair of jeans.[5] Textile dyeing is the world's second-largest source of water pollution, because the residual water from the dyeing process is often poured into local ditches, streams, or rivers.[6] The global fashion industry accounts for 10 percent of all greenhouse gas emissions. Textile production alone is estimated to release 1.2 billion tons of greenhouse gases into the atmosphere every year, a number that is expected to increase by at least 60 percent by 2030.[7] For perspective, this is more than the total climate impact of the European Union. Should these trends continue, the annual production of clothing could hit one hundred million tons of greenhouse gases by 2030.[8]

The fast-fashion retailer Zara produces about 840 million pieces of clothing each year for sale in its six thousand stores around the world.[9] The company is a huge business success, but its model socializes its costs and privatizes its profits. Where it can, Zara pays its manufacturing-center workers wages that are significantly below the poverty line, a topic we will consider in more detail in the next chapter.[10] *Fast Fashion*

quote! In China, India, and Bangladesh, where the production of many other fast-fashion companies is centered, rivers are becoming biological dead zones full of carcinogenic chemicals thanks to wastewater discharges. A mountain of cast-off clothing outside the Ghanaian capital city of Accra generated so much methane that it exploded into flames in 2020; months later, it was still smoldering.[11] With fast fashion, every day becomes a new season, yet there is little thought to who is paying for the waste and pollution that result.

Though these detrimental aspects of production are in many ways "out of sight, out of mind" for consumers in the Global North, their effects are being felt worldwide. Plastic microfibers that fall from synthetic clothing during the laundry process are flooding our water supply and food chain and finding their way into our bodies. Researchers warn that they can damage cells and organs as they accumulate. Furthermore, the production of plastic fibers requires large amounts of petroleum and releases volatile particulate matter and acids like hydrogen chloride into the air.

This chapter will explore these problems of waste and, more importantly, what some forward-thinking entrepreneurs are doing about it. While the "take, make, dispose" linear model has pervaded business for centuries, an end-to-end model that emphasizes positive externalities is increasingly important. Some innovators are breaking the overconsumption cycle by reengineering their processes and packaging to be less wasteful and creating circular models where products are refurbished and reused.

For example, Interface, the pioneering global commercial flooring company, takes back old carpet tiles and repurposes them into new ones. Furniture giant IKEA has committed to becoming a circular business by 2030 and has been testing various initiatives, including furniture leasing and buyback programs, and is also increasing its use of renewable and recycled materials. Innovative waste management company TerraCycle specializes in collecting and repurposing hard-to-recycle waste and works with a variety of brands and manufacturers to implement take-back programs and create new products from waste materials. Overall, as we will see, significant savings can be gained by looking backward in supply chains and reducing waste. But also—as with Patagonia, discussed at the end of the last chapter—thinking in this way can unlock creativity to build regenerative systems. In this chapter, we also consider extended responsibility, where producers are held responsible for the end of life for all aspects of their product and its packaging.

Waste as a Design Flaw

"Waste is a design flaw," said Nate Morris of Rubicon, a company that uses technology to solve inefficiencies in the waste streams that are generated by companies during the production process. "If you're producing a lot of waste, there is something not functioning efficiently inside your organization. A very lean and efficient recycling operation is really an indicator of a sophisticated business." He went on, "Waste has not been reimagined really since the ancient Romans, and if you look back, the Romans had very sophisticated sanitation systems. They recycled glass." Why, then, has the contemporary world fallen so far behind? Since we are able to outsource our waste to other countries, arguably it is just our laziness and willingness to accept placing burdens on others.

Morris explained that industry is "built around landfilling waste" and never thinking about it again. "Very few people, if any, ever ask questions about their waste: What's going on with my waste bill? How much is my recycling? How much am I paying each month?" He told me about how, when he met with executives at pizza chain Papa John's, he walked into the meeting and said, "You know, I've started this waste company." And the executive replied, "That's great. You know, I have no idea what we're doing with our waste."

Consider Tyson Foods, the second largest producer of chicken, beef, and pork in the world. The company endured decades of backlash and criticism, not to mention lawsuits, because of its refusal to address the environmental effects of the waste from its production processes. In January 2023, Tyson Foods, among other companies, was found responsible for polluting the Illinois River by spreading manure, which leached into the river's watershed.[12] Companies like Tyson would rather settle lawsuits than invest in large-scale, long-term change.

But change is happening. Many companies are starting to see that it is no longer enough to track and report on the types of waste they produce, be it carbon, plastic, or myriad other forms of waste. For innovative and forward-thinking entrepreneurs, this is creating new business opportunities. For example, Shane Price, the CEO of Toronto-based Green Circle Salons, told me that his company works with hair salons in Canada and the United States to recover and repurpose beauty waste. It's a large and unique opportunity for impact: salons in North America discard about 63,000 pounds of hair, 42,000 pounds of chemicals, and 250,000 pounds of paper and plastics every day.[13]

Price said the idea behind Green Circle Salons came to him while visiting a salon in Toronto and both noticing the amount of waste being produced and recognizing that at the time businesses were paying $3.25 per bag of garbage for curbside pickup. A natural business model emerged where companies can not only save on what they are charged for trash but also contribute to a better planet. As of mid-2023, Green Circle Salons had organized over sixteen thousand "waste warriors" at salons that have since 2009 kept over ten million pounds of beauty waste out of landfills and waterways.

While circularity—turning trash into treasure by reusing it to create new products—is often used as buzzword or seen as an empty panacea, companies and society do, in fact, gain a lot when they think of trash in an end-to-end fashion and consider the waste they create and its disposition.[14]

Going Zero-Waste

Cascade Engineering, a plastic injection molding manufacturer in western Michigan, has been exploring zero-waste options for the past decade. "Nobody had even heard about zero-waste," Sharon Darby, its director of environmental safety and sustainability told me. "But we kept plugging away." At first, the company set up a waste-reduction team to tackle the most obvious and egregious areas. Within the first year, the team cut waste-to-landfill expenses from $268,000 to $181,000. After seven or eight years, they had gotten to the point where everything was recycled. The key to motivating companies to take such efforts, Cascade founder Fred Keller told me, is to help them understand the true cost of their waste, which can lead to unexpected surprises. "There's a prize in there, somewhere. You don't know what it's going to be. In our case, we found that there are financial benefits, adding to our bottom line every year."

Engaging employees in the process is also essential. Kenyatta Brame, executive vice president at Cascade, recalled, "When I first got here, we still had dumpsters. We did something called a 'dumpster dive,' in which we literally climbed inside our dumpsters to see what was in them, to hold ourselves accountable, to make sure that we're not contaminating the streams. If you go into one of our plants, an employee will tell you what you need to do. You just can't dump things in any way." Brame reflected on the fact that it wasn't Fred Keller who dictated the approach but employees on the floor. "I think the bottom-up thing is really kind of an important element, letting the folks own it, as opposed to having it being imposed. The leaders should become cheerleaders, as opposed to enforcers."

Circular Models

Treating the business as an ecosystem clearly resonates with emerging thinking that takes its inspiration from the living world's cyclical model, where there are no landfills to keep trash out of sight and out of mind. One species' waste is another species' food. Yet, as industries grew, we adopted a linear approach. After using something, we throw it in the garbage; we put that garbage in a bin outside our residence; a truck comes and takes it away. When Apple introduces a new phone model, we discard the old one. When we get tired of our old sofa or a household appliance dies, we take it to the curb. We need to turn that on its head and rethink production and consumption in a fundamentally new way.

But overhyping circularity could create another win-win slippery slope, leading to the false inference that, just because one company's trash is another's treasure in some instances, voluntary corporate and market solutions can erase all our environmental externalities. But while it's not a silver bullet, reorienting business systems for circularity can create virtuous cycles, substantially improving their processes, and also help change the mindsets of people, including consumers, employees, and managers.

But first we should acknowledge those limitations. In a 2023 article in the *Stanford Social Innovation Review*, Kenneth Pucker, the former chief operating officer of the environmentally focused footwear brand Timberland, offered a penetrating critique of current ideas of circularity, debunking the idea that it can be achieved solely through market mechanisms and admonishing businesses to acknowledge that many of the proposed solutions "run counter to industry incentives, physical laws, established patterns of consumer behavior, and economics."[15] Emphasizing the need for a fundamental change to business models and the ways companies are held accountable for waste and product degradation, he concludes that significant cross-sector collaborations will be needed to make any of this happen.

While I agree with Pucker about the need to reduce overconsumption and put stronger regulatory supports in place (points I will come back to later), I want to focus first on the importance of circular business models and changing mindsets about production and waste.

We have been conditioned to believe that the linear operating system of today's economy—take, make, waste—is natural, and so it is easy to punch holes in ideas about circularity. Circularity can be defined as "a regenerative system in which resource inputs, waste emissions, and energy leakage are minimized by slowing, closing, and narrowing material and energy loops thanks to long-lasting design, maintenance, repair, reuse, remanufacturing, refurbishing, and recycling."[16]

Interface, the global flooring manufacturer, is often cited as a leading example of the circular economy in action. In the 1990s, Ray Anderson, its founder and CEO, decided that Interface should become "the first sustainable corporation in the world." To that end, the company began reducing fossil fuels in its production of modular carpets and other floor coverings. These carpet tiles and installation processes were redesigned to be easily replaced when they are worn or damaged, so whole carpets won't have to be discarded. But the company's bigger innovation was about more than thriftiness; it introduced a radically new business model.

Instead of selling floor coverings to customers, as carpeting companies typically did, Interface pioneered a service model in which ownership is retained by the producer throughout the product's life cycle, and the customer simply leases the flooring. Installation, maintenance, and removal of Interface flooring and carpets are bundled under one monthly fee. When the consumer no longer needs or wants them, the company takes them back and recycles or resells them. This closed-loop system helps extend the lifespan of resources and minimizes waste.

This kind of model opens new markets in used products and repair services and parts. Those with a traditional mindset may balk at the idea, but consider Richard Henkel, a German manufacturer of steel-tube furniture such as chaise lounge chairs. Eschewing planned obsolescence, the company not only reduces and recycles its production waste, but it takes responsibility for its products through their entire life cycle. Its mission is to create long-term value for investors and customers, not just to grow its sales. So a substantial part of its business is based on repair, refurbishment, and recycling, replacing the traditional linear model with a closed loop.[17] When Richard Henkel refurbishes old lounge chairs, for instance, the rubber cords are recycled. Business models like these encourage investors, partners, employees, and customers to embrace circular thinking. In doing so, they foster innovation and sustainable practices up and down the value chain.

This is in sharp contrast to the approach of a company like Apple. After the launch of the iPhone 14 in 2022, reviewers noted that it shares "the overwhelming majority of features and [has] the same design" as the iPhone 13.[18] So, there was not really a technical or other advantage to the new phone, but Apple needed to meet its schedule for launching a new product, which may in the short term improve profits but only leads to an increase in pollution and waste. When a new phone model is introduced, many people discard the old one or put it in a drawer. Apple deserves credit for its recycling programs, from Apple Trade In to Daisy, its robot that disassembles iPhones so their parts can be reused.[19] But instead of encouraging us to buy and then recycle, how about reducing unnecessary production and consumption?

For instance, Fairphone is an Apple competitor based in the Netherlands that has developed an alternative business model that is making genuine efforts to address the social and environmental challenges of the electronics industry. The company was founded in 2013 as a social enterprise with the goal of making phones with lower environmental footprints than industry leaders. In particular, Fairphone aims to minimize the use of conflict minerals in its devices and maintain fair labor conditions for its workforce. It also encourages its customers to fix their phones when they begin to fail rather than trade them in for new ones.[20]

Fairphone's approach may seem impractical given the demands and expectations that companies face. Of course Apple needs to keep making new products. How else will it grow? But it is important for us to think more about these expectations and question our taken-for-granted assumptions. Our cognitive frameworks have been deeply shaped by the existing models of capitalism and corporate success that have long been formalized and reinforced in institutional systems, such as investors' demands for quarterly earnings growth. However, as many of the examples thus far show, by rethinking production and redesigning products and services, we can move to a more regenerative and circular model.

Promoting Circular Consumption

Beyond cell phones, electronics in general is a very wasteful industry. About 90 percent of the carbon it produces comes from the manufacturing of devices, which are used and discarded as casually as tissues. The World Economic Forum reports that fifty million tons of e-waste is produced every year (approximately fourteen pounds for every person on the planet), and only about 20 percent of it is recycled properly.[21] Not only is e-waste the fastest growing form of waste in the world, but it is also one of the most toxic. The scale of the problem defies comparison. Its weight is the equivalent of 125,000 jumbo jets, more than have ever been produced.

Most of this waste is plowed into landfills in poor communities in the Global South, causing detrimental health consequences as the toxins leach into the ground and water. Overseas, locals work in these dumping grounds—in particular, children—searching for items they can sell. In Guiyu, China, workers sift through over 1.5 million pounds of e-waste annually.[22]

Thibaud Hug de Larauze, the CEO and cofounder of Back Market, aims to make a big dent in this problem by creating a global marketplace for professionally refurbished electronics: everything from iPhones to laptops to appliances. His goal is to make refurbished electronics the first choice for tech purchases. The company is growing steadily, from 1.5 million customers in July 2019 to 5 million in 2021 and 6 million in 2022. As of this writing, Back Market was worth more than $5.7 billion, which makes it France's most valuable start-up.[23]

Despite the impressive growth, consumer awareness is still a hurdle, as ingrained consumption habits focus on new products. But Hug de Larauze told me that five years ago, price was the most important factor for purchasing, and only 3 percent of consumer purchases on Back Market were for ecological reasons, but that number has now jumped to over 25 percent.

Moving Toward Avoidance

As Cascade, Rubicon, Interface, Richard Henkel, and Back Market pioneer new circular models, driving change through their supply chains and helping consumers understand the importance of sustainable production, their ideas and examples will spread. Former Seventh Generation CEO Joey Bergstein told me that his company's goal is "to ensure that 100 percent of [its] products are recyclable and recycled, biodegradable and degraded, compostable and composted." Even Seventh Generation's name is a nod to their long-term perspective on everything from materials and packaging to manufacturing, supply chain, and hiring practices.

While many companies talk about circularity and zero-waste goals, Seventh Generation created a step-by-step approach to the elimination of plastic. A shift in mindset is, when thinking of waste, we should not be considering how to dispose of it properly but how production can be redesigned to avoid it entirely.

There are many ways to encourage companies to design products to be more sustainable. This could involve using less packaging, making products that are more durable or easier to repair, or using materials that are more recyclable. For Seventh Generation, Bergstein told me the process began with a move toward better plastics, then less plastics, and finally no plastics.

Using better plastics means using as much postconsumer recycled (PCR) content as possible. Most Seventh Generation bottles were made with 99.9 percent PCR content. But that wasn't enough, Bergstein said, for one of his team members. "We have an amazing packaging engineer who wasn't satisfied," he recalled. "She had to get the last 0.1 percent, which is the cap. Nobody had actually created a cap from PCR plastic. It's a very difficult thing to do, but she cracked it. So, we now have 100 percent PCR caps as well, which is remarkable."

While recycling is important, Seventh Generation ultimately strives for avoidance—to use less plastic overall, with a goal of zero. Its laundry detergent used to be sold in hundred-ounce bottles that weighed about seven pounds. In 2019, Seventh Generation launched an "easy dose" twenty-three-ounce detergent bottle that washes the same sixty-six laundry loads as the hundred-ounce bottle but is 75 percent lighter because it uses 50 percent less water and 60 percent less plastic.[24] Bergstein hopes that removing liquids from Seventh Generation products will eventually eliminate the need for plastics altogether. They are, Bergstein explained, continually "looking at how to create an effective product for laundry, for dish cleaning, for counter cleaning, and for handwashing" that is a powder or cake.

Recognizing Who Is Ultimately Responsible

A theme of this book, across the many different areas we consider, is that while voluntary action by companies is useful for innovation, creating new models, and raising consumer awareness, it should not be seen as the end goal. As sustainability veteran Kenneth Pucker discusses, seeing circularity as only enabled by market forces and corporate self-interest is yet another win-win trap. We need policies to help drive this change.

For instance, extended producer responsibility (EPR) policies are becoming more common across different industries, from electronics to fashion. Governments can enact laws and regulations that require companies to manage the waste their products create. This could include mandatory recycling programs, bans on certain types of packaging, or requirements for companies to take back and properly dispose of products at the end of their life. When producers are held accountable for the waste generated by their products and materials, they are incentivized to improve their life-cycle performance.

Europe has been a pioneer in requiring companies to take responsibility for end of use, an idea that first took shape around 1990 in Sweden.[25] Though there are a variety of approaches, most require the companies to cover the costs of recycling. In Germany—where the recycling rate is among the highest in the world—waste sorting is serious business, and people can face fines for breaking the rules. As other countries see success with waste management legislation, EPR bills have begun to emerge in legislatures across the United States, with Maine, Oregon, and Colorado as early adopters.

While these new laws appear to be a step forward, some environmentalists advocate that they fall short of what's needed and actually take aim at the wrong issue. Judith Enck, an official in the Environmental Protection Agency during the Obama administration, told me that for as long as the vast majority of plastics are not recycled, most EPR policies simply amount to Band-Aids. When talking with people in Europe, Enck recalls, she realized that while it was good to get the funding for recycling, the problem was that recycling didn't do anything to actually help with plastic reduction.

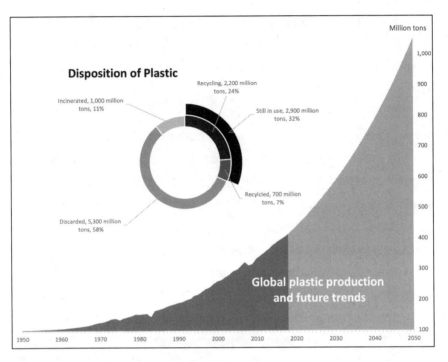

Figure 4: The Past, Present, and Future of Plastic[26]

Her insight was that combating the plastic problem requires a much more radical shift.

The idea that recycling works is so ingrained in people's minds that they don't see the underlying issues with single-use plastic. But a recent report published by the United Nations Environment Programme shows this is not the case. It estimated that less than 10 percent of the over nine billion tons of plastics produced between 1950 and 2017 has been recycled. The report further predicted a sharp increase in plastics production over the next three decades, so even if the recycling rate dramatically rises, we will still need to deal with a huge amount of plastic—as much as double the amount we have today.

Enck's conclusion is that our focus should not be on recycling plastics, as history has shown that to be a failure. Resonating with the idea of avoidance, she told me we need to focus much more on plastic reduction and elimination. The NGO she founded, Beyond Plastics, focuses on EPR policies that set clear goals to replace plastics with reusable options and require producers to redesign, reduce, and reuse. Given that plastic recycling has been shown not to work, "why should we set up a whole system to fund it?" she asks. Although, perhaps unsurprisingly, she has run into some significant opposition.

For example, Enck noticed that, of the bad EPR bills popping up all over the United States, most were designed by petrochemical lobbyists. An organization called the Recycling Partnership sounds promising, but it is 100 percent astroturfed. As Enck told me, it "has a nice name, but the company is actually funded by Dow, Exxon, Coke, and Amazon. They will say they support EPR but then work to make sure the legislation is super weak." For instance, Enck cited to me the Maine and Oregon EPR laws as ones that were co-opted by industry, because their focus is on recovering recycling costs from producers and not on reducing plastic use, which Enck believes should be the focus of any laws.

Such misdirection is common. For example, Maxine Bédat, author of *Unraveled: The Life and Death of a Garment*, discusses how corporate-captured nonprofit organizations are endemic and part of "Sustainability Inc.," akin to the astroturfing by supposed independent climate NGOs. As she illustrates, such organizations hinder progress toward sustainability by setting slow, voluntary targets without real consequences. Bédat cites Tariq Fancy, the former chief investment officer for sustainable investing at BlackRock, as the source of an evocative analogy about the deceptive work of such nonprofits: "It's like a doctor telling a cancer patient to take wheatgrass when chemotherapy is available. Corporate-captured nonprofits are selling the wheatgrass of slow-paced voluntary measures while regulators have the chemotherapy available in the form of legally enforceable sustainability targets."

Judith Enck has been working with New York State legislators on a bill that would establish an EPR program for packaging and a packaging responsibility fund. Introduced on May 5, 2022, the New York EPR bill does not focus on funding plastic recycling. Instead, it includes language outlining packaging design standards and sets benchmarks for reducing packaging by 50 percent, after which 90 percent of the remaining packaging must be recyclable, made of postconsumer recycled content, or compostable within twelve years. While proponents also worked to pass the bill in 2023, at the end of the legislative season in June, it had not yet passed the legislature.

———

As the saying goes, "There is no such thing as a free lunch." As consumers, we take cheap goods for granted without knowing who is paying for the waste and emissions that stem from their production. Those costs are hard to notice given that they are incurred over an extended period and that so many of them are paid by underprivileged workers in the Global South. We will take a closer look at this in the next chapter.

While many companies are working to direct our attention to consumer responsibility as opposed to acknowledging the underlying issues themselves, some companies have been working to reduce waste with noticeable successes. We have seen how companies like Cascade Engineering, Richard Henkel, Rubicon, and Back Market have developed their business models based on the idea of zero-waste and circularity, which again shows that addressing environmental and social problems can go together with business interests.

But such changes cut to the heart of the linear model of today's capitalism, where waste is out of sight and out of mind. A key to this story is to go beyond the buzzword; it takes rigor and creativity to rethink today's entrenched business models and achieve success in this endeavor. It is also essential that policymakers not be fooled by astroturfing and that they support circularity by creating regulations that encourage genuinely sustainable practices. Finally, a crucial element is consumers and consumer behaviors. We will discuss more in Part III how individuals and companies can also support circularity by buying less and better quality clothing, shopping secondhand, and supporting small ethical brands.

6

Who Pays for Cheap Labor and Inequality?

Chocolate, one of the most enjoyed foods in the Global North, comes at deep, deep cost to others. Large chocolate manufacturers are able to keep their prices low because most cacao farmers earn less than $1 a day, which puts them below the extreme poverty line. Unfortunately, children not infrequently join the workforce early on to help their families.

While the previous chapter examined the wastefulness of modern production processes, we now focus on the human costs, in particular, the abuse of labor, not only in the Global South but in the developed world as well. We will also consider the systemic nature of poverty and wealth inequality overall, while highlighting the work that some pioneering organizations are doing to address these issues at their roots.

In West Africa, boys and girls as young as five years old are routinely sold to cacao growers, sometimes by their own relatives.

Fourteen-hour workdays are typical, and the work is dangerous. Children use chain saws to clear forests and machetes to hack bean pods out of cacao trees, and they haul hundred-pound bags through the forest. "Some of the bags were taller than me," Aly Diabate, a former enslaved cacao worker recalled. "It took two people to put the bag on my head. And when you didn't hurry, you were beaten." There are laws in place in most if not all of the countries where this happens that bar child labor and require children to go to school, but they are not enforced.[1] Children will not complain and will not be heard even if they do.

Large chocolate companies have created sustainability programs to address these issues, but they operate only in parts of their supply chains and, as we will discuss more below, primarily address symptoms rather than the underlying factors that contribute to extreme poverty. Child labor mainly occurs in rural economies that are often beyond the reach of labor inspections, workers' organizations, and even producer organizations. No one wants to support sweatshops, but our ignorance of the realities on the ground is facilitated by corporations who don't want to think too hard about the conditions in their supply chains or pay higher costs for their goods, and so they engage in many strategies to deflect attention from the more unsavory aspects of their production. The focus on product rather than people is prevalent among many industries, from manufacturing to mining to tourism.[2]

A 2018 report from the US Department of Labor found that forced labor and child labor are prevalent in the fashion industry in Argentina, Bangladesh, Brazil, China, India, Indonesia, the Philippines, Turkey, Vietnam, and more.[3] As the *Guardian* reported in a 2015 article, fast fashion in particular "has engendered a race to the bottom, pushing companies to find ever-cheaper sources of labour. . . . Child labour is a particular issue . . . because much of the supply chain requires low-skilled labour and some tasks are even better suited to children than adults."[4]

According to data from the International Labour Organization (ILO), there are approximately 170 million child laborers in global supply chains, mostly in the Global South.[5] As many as twenty-five million people, including many of these children, are enslaved. As Sofie Ovaa, global campaign coordinator of Stop Child Labour, put it, "There is no supervision or social control mechanisms, no unions that can help them to bargain for better working conditions. These are very low-skilled workers without a voice, so they are easy targets."[6]

Many companies have strengthened their standards and run frequent audits on their factories and other workplaces to enforce them. But their supply chains are murky and hard to pin down. A big blind spot is the production of raw materials, the environmental impacts of which we discussed in Chapter 3. A 2021 report from the ILO and UNICEF estimates that since 2016 the number of children between 5 and 17 in child labor has risen by 8.4 million, bringing the global total to 160 million, which is about 1 in 10 of all children worldwide. Further, 79 million of these children are working in hazardous conditions.[7] The global risk intelligence company Verisk Maplecroft publishes an annual index that tracks the adoption of child labor laws and international treaties by countries and regions, their ability and willingness to implement and enforce them, and the frequency and severity of violations. As of this writing, the index has not registered any material improvements in Bangladesh, Cambodia, China, India, and Vietnam since 2016.

Privileged consumers in the Global North rally around organic and fair trade certifications and feel good when we buy from companies that earn them. We have been fooled into thinking that buying wild-caught salmon, for example, helps to make the world a better place. But the seafood industry is one of the most complicit when it comes to child labor and modern slavery. Reports from countries like Bangladesh and the Philippines, one of the world's largest fish producers, reveal that their fisheries are rife with sexual abuse, labor violations, and unsafe conditions. Male children are forced to swim and dive for nine hours a day without breaks. Girls are put to work as fishers and in processing plants from a very young age.[8] These children are invisible. They do not receive an education or have any prospects for a real life. European and American seafood companies work diligently to certify their products, to ensure that the fish they sell had lives that were, in many ways, better than the lives of the workers who caught and processed them.

The Rana Plaza incident in Bangladesh in 2013—when a building housing five garment factories collapsed, killing 1,100 workers—is a stark reminder of what can happen when profits are put before safety. Workers had shown their managers the cracks in the building and expressed their concern. But they were compelled to return to work. There are many, many similar cases, such as the fire at an Ali Enterprises factory in Pakistan that killed 289, or the fire at a Tazreen Fashion factory, also in Bangladesh, where more than one hundred people lost their lives.[9] Working under these conditions seems to have become a generally accepted hazard of life in the developing world.[10]

———

Given the shareholder-focused ideology, business leaders have little incentive to find out whether their resources are being well allocated to address issues like poverty and workers' rights. Human-rights-related factors in particular can be difficult to grasp or quantify. True Price, as we have seen, calculates the cost to remedy these harms and includes it in the price of the goods, so that the companies that benefit from exploiting workers can see how much their inputs should really cost. Because of the tendency to consider such practices as "out of sight, out of mind," we need more work to direct our attention to these systemic problems. Sharon Prince—founder and CEO of Grace Farms Foundation, an organization that holds events to promote removing slavery from building and construction supply chains—told me she initially met resistance to her message about these abuses due to cost reasons, as margins in construction are notoriously tight. But she changed tack and now retorts with a much more powerful and evocative description that jars listeners into action: that construction companies "can no longer accept a slavery discount."

In 2013, Tony's Chocolonely, a chocolate company that is tackling issues of human rights in supply chains head-on, partnered with True Price to assess the real price of the cocoa it was buying. Though Tony's did better than most companies in its sector, there was still a worrisome gap between what would provide workers with a humane standard of living and what the company was paying. So it increased wages and kept pushing to eventually eliminate the gap.

Tony's follows five key principles in its production, all of them diametrically opposed to business as usual in the chocolate industry: (1) know the source of the cocoa, (2) pay a higher price for it, (3) strengthen farmer organizations, (4) enter long-term relationships with farmers, and (5) invest in professional production. "We believe that extreme poverty among cocoa farmers is the root cause of illegal child labor, modern slavery, and associated problems like deforestation," Paul Schoenmakers, head of impact at Tony's Chocolonely, told me.

The Tony's Chocolonely origin story clearly illuminates its central philosophy. In 2003, the Dutch journalist Teun van de Keuken read about child slavery on cacao farms. His response was to eat some chocolate bars and turn himself in to the police to be arrested and tried as an accessory to child slavery. The courts didn't bring charges against him because they would have had to prosecute everyone who eats chocolate. He then launched Tony's Chocolonely, which now helps over eight thousand farmers earn a decent wage and is 100 percent slave free. Through cooperatives in the West African nations of Ghana and the Ivory Coast, Tony's Chocolonely is making a real difference, considering that, for most of the industry, barely 5 to 6 percent of the price of a bar of chocolate goes to the farmer.

Tony's has also worked collectively to end child labor and ensure fair pay for farmers in the chocolate supply chain. Since 2013, the company has committed to paying farmers a living income (living income reference price, or LIRP), which includes additional premiums on top of what qualifies as the Fairtrade International premium. Other companies who have followed Tony's lead to pay the LIRP to cacao farmers include ice-cream producer Ben & Jerry's, German supermarket chain ALDI, Dutch supermarket chain Albert Heijn, and Dutch food products companies Jokolade and Vly. These companies and others are also part of Tony's Open Chain, an initiative of chocolate producers to end forced labor and child labor in the chocolate industry. While these are important examples that production can be done in a fair and equitable way, we also need more systemic changes, which will be discussed further in Part III.

Labor Exploitation Is Also Occurring in Developed Economies

Before exploring solutions, it is important to recognize how widespread these issues are and that corporate gaslighting strategies allow labor abuses to occur in the Global North as well. The increasing use of temporary labor and subcontractors, where companies outsource jobs to the lowest bidders, are not as exploitative as slavery, but the practice allows companies to withhold such important employment benefits as health plans and pensions. It certainly lowers their costs and improves their margins, but it puts significant burdens on public systems.

Framing the system as a "gig economy" or "free agent nation," in which people are empowered to control their work life, is a gaslighting tactic. Gig and temp workers receive hourly wages that are $3 less on average than those of full-time workers. Many are among the 138 million Americans who face financial insecurity, and their numbers are growing.[11] The proportion of gig workers in the US labor force increased from 10.1 percent in 2005 to 15.8 percent in 2015.[12] And in 2021, 16 percent of Americans reported that they made money from online gig work alone in the previous year.[13]

A recent NPR *Planet Money* episode investigated the Walt Disney Company's customer service system.[14] The support agent was not a Disney employee and did not answer the phone from Cinderella Castle, as claimed. Turns out, Disney outsources many of its customer service functions to Arise, a company that also works with Airbnb, Comcast, Instacart, Amazon, Apple, and many other major companies. Arise is a pioneer in two trends that have disrupted the American labor market in recent decades: work from home and independent contracting. Arise's independent contractors don't work for the company they are representing or for Arise. As gig workers, they assume all of the costs and risks of employment themselves in return for a very small share of the value they produce.

When Tami Pendergraft decided to contract her services to Arise, she paid about $1,500 for a computer, two headsets, a dedicated phone line, a background check, and Arise's voice-assessment test. She also had to sign Arise's confidentiality form. Pendergraft paid for and passed Arise's introductory training, which took three days. The required AT&T customer service certification course took forty-four days and cost $199. Afterward, she was told she had to do another ten days of training that Arise said she would be paid for, but she ultimately wasn't. Finally, Pendergraft worked for three weeks as a purported AT&T customer service agent, for which she earned a little under $100.

In arbitration, Pendergraft explained that while her contract stipulated she must work at least twenty hours a week, she could rarely find enough available time slots to make the minimum. Typically, it was a half hour here, a half hour there. And here's the rub: Arise only paid her if calls came through during that half hour. Often, Pendergraft sat at the computer with her headset on and no one called.[15]

The gig economy is part of a broader trend in the growth of temporary workers. While in gig work, an employee typically chooses a job and company to work for, for most other temporary employment arrangements there is frequently a middleman staffing agency between the worker and an employer. Many brick-and-mortar and online retailers hire temps during peak seasons, a long-standing way of dealing with spikes in demand. A growing number of warehouses and distribution centers now use temporary workers year-round—more than 15 percent of their workforces, according to the Bureau of Labor Statistics. The number of US freelancers, another form of temporary employment arrangement where individuals work on projects for employers under contract, is estimated to grow from fifty-seven million to eighty-six million by 2027. The temporary workforce in the United Kingdom more than doubled from 2016 to 2019, accounting for 4.7 million people (as of this writing, the data had not been updated).[16]

Gig workers, freelancers, and temp workers are not eligible for the worker protections and benefits that more formal terms of employment bring. The temporary workers suffer more drawbacks than permanent employees, have less influence on work-related decisions such as working hours and wages, and are exempt from many of the rules that ensure occupational health and safety. Costs are lower for companies, but the externalities this situation creates are then passed off to the broader society, which makes up the difference with public pensions, health care, and other assistance programs.

Gabriel Mac, a human rights reporter for *Mother Jones* magazine, became a temporary worker for an investigative piece. The conditions he described were reminiscent of Charlie Chaplin's *Modern Times*. Workers were treated like robots. They didn't know if they'd still have a job or how they'd be paid for it from one day to the next. Sometimes they were paid by the piece, sometimes by the hour. Some days there was no work at all. Anyone who didn't move quickly enough to meet their quotas was quickly replaced; the staffing agencies that provided the temps often had offices in-house, so they could handle the churn more efficiently. As one "workcamper" (a nomad who lives in an RV and travels from one temporary job to another) described it, "We will be fired if we say we just can't or won't get better.... But so long as I resign myself to hearing how inadequate I am on a regular basis, I can keep this job."[17]

But employees are beginning to push back. Uber and Lyft drivers organized themselves into groups like Gig Workers Rising and Rideshare Drivers United and demanded fair and equitable treatment and recognition as actual employees. In 2019, California passed Assembly Bill 5 (AB 5), a law that extended employee status to some gig workers. In August 2020, a California judge ordered that Uber and Lyft classify their drivers as employees with benefits.[18] Ride-sharing companies had argued that their drivers are not really employees because the businesses are not transportation companies but "technology companies." The irony wasn't lost on anyone: a ride-sharing company claiming that the individuals who drive customers from point A to point B aren't necessary for their business? The California ruling explicitly noted the absurdity.[19] Other countries, such as the United Kingdom, have also begun to recognize that gig workers are essentially employees and so should be provided benefits, though at nowhere near the same levels as traditional employees.[20]

Uber and Lyft threatened to leave California; they also spent $200 million on campaigns to sway voters to exempt them from AB 5, arguing that their workers should have independence and freedom of choice. The companies scored a major win with Proposition 22 in November 2020, which essentially exempted ride-sharing apps from AB 5.[21] It did include some concessions on behalf of the workers, who will now be paid 120 percent of the state's minimum wage, but only during active hours—when a passenger is in the car or they are en route to pick one up. Proposition 22 also requires companies to provide gig workers with health-care stipends, not full health-care benefits and plans. It is clear that this was a huge boon for Uber and Lyft, as their combined market value increased by $10 billion after the vote. Not a bad return on their $200 million investment.

Among temporary workers, undocumented immigrants fare the worst. Brookings senior fellow Vanda Felbab-Brown explained that "undocumented workers [in the United States] often work the unpleasant, back-breaking jobs that native-born workers are not willing to do," such as gutting fish or working in farm fields.[22] Dodge City, Kansas, is well-known for relying on undocumented immigrants. This corner of Kansas produces a quarter of the beef eaten in the United States, with more shipped overseas. The employees in its meatpacking factories are nearly all immigrants. A manager of a large packing house in the area explained that "no matter what wages you paid, you are not going to find any reasonable number of 'native-born' Americans who will do those jobs. . . . Your Anglo community is not going to work there, pretty much regardless of the wage. The entire meat-packing industry depends on immigrant labor, and always has."[23] Many analysts have shown that displacement effects are extremely rare. In the United Kingdom, the

Migration Advisory Committee has concluded that immigration has little or no impact on the employment or unemployment rates of UK-born workers.[24]

Even before COVID-19, the situation of low-wage workers in America was steadily worsening. Financial stress contributes to up to 80 percent of workplace accidents, 90 percent of health and welfare issues, and 40 percent of employee turnover.[25] Workers in traditionally underpaid industries, such as fast food and retail sales, often depend on government assistance to survive. And entire groups of our population, such as formerly incarcerated people, can be completely deprived of employment opportunities.

Respecting Workers in an Authentic Way

We need only look back at our own history to see that the "free agent nation" is not at all "natural," that there are other ways of production that respect the contributions of labor. Let's start with retirement benefits. As the economy returned to a peacetime basis in the post–World War II era, companies looked for ways to attract and retain the best talent. Corporate leaders worked with labor unions and governments to deliver comprehensive welfare to communities and employees. Pensions incentivized workers to spend their whole careers at one company. Such systems are not at all revolutionary; the Roman Empire paid soldiers who had served for twenty-five years a pension equivalent to thirteen years of salary.

But then came the neoliberal reaction. In 1978, the nature of pensions was fundamentally changed with the publication of section 2 of the Internal Revenue Code and its subsection 401(k), which stipulates that there will be no tax collected on certain amounts of income that *employees*—not employers—defer to retirement funds. By 1983, surveys showed that almost half of all large companies were offering 401(k) plans or at least considering them. Some offered matching funds to incentivize saving.[26]

The difference between these two systems is significant. Under a traditional pension plan, known as defined benefit, payouts are based on years of service, rank, and salary, and the company pays for all of them. Under defined-contribution plans, such as 401(k)s, the onus is frequently on the employee to sign up for the plan, and it is funded by the employee deferring a portion of their salary. Employers frequently match at least part of the employee contribution.

Today, defined benefit plans are an endangered species. According to data from the Employee Benefit Research Institute, by 2011, 69 percent of employees in work retirement plans participated in defined contribution plans, 24 percent participated in defined contribution and established benefit plans, and only 7 percent participated in a defined benefit plan only.[27]

While certainly people have benefited from 401(k) plans, the discourse around these changes is all too familiar: we should save for ourselves, it is better for employees to be in control of their own investments, and so on. Like so many of the misdirection tactics we have seen, while ostensibly true at one level, this line of thinking is also designed to convince us that practices that save companies money are better for us as well.

Who pays is important. If companies do not provide adequate retirement benefits, taxpayers foot the bill through public assistance programs. The crux of the issue, as ever, is that the companies are passing the buck.

Fair and Timely Pay

The thread running through all this is the issue of fair pay and the reality of how one incident, or one missed paycheck, can spell disaster for so many Americans. A recent Federal Reserve survey found that 40 percent of Americans could not easily pay for a $400 emergency.[28] Many can barely manage their routine expenses. To make ends meet between paychecks, many turn to notoriously predatory payday lenders, a $90 billion industry.[29]

Luckily, some companies are attempting to work against these pernicious trends. When an internal survey revealed that 60 percent of PayPal's hourly workers were struggling to pay their bills, CEO Dan Schulman instituted a substantial set of changes: higher wages that reflect regional costs of living, lower health insurance costs, stock grants, and a new financial education initiative. "If you don't act on values, what you stand for, then you don't really stand for anything," he told *Fast Company*. Schulman calls this "reverse Friedmanism," aligning personal values with work and recognizing the benefits of a more equitable work culture for all involved.

The underlying structural features that led to the rise of the payday loan industry are rarely questioned. According to CNBC, almost 60 percent of Americans now live paycheck to paycheck, and so this industry thrives because unexpected emergencies can lead to a financial bind.[30] But an additional and usually unrecognized reason for this is because, at almost all companies, employees' pay lags behind their work, frequently by two weeks and many times by a month. Employees are essentially giving their companies a zero-interest loan.

Such lagged pay may seem natural, as it is the way it has always been done. But unlike yesteryear, when there were likely technical reasons for this arrangement—such as calculating and distributing payments by hand or with early computer systems that were costly and time-consuming—today it is in fact possible to pay, or at least give access to pay, almost instantaneously. Banks frequently charge interest on loans by the day, but similar calculations to provide more regular access to payment for one's work is of course not in the interests of employers, and many are quite content to accept a zero-interest loan at the employee's expense.

In 2012, Safwan Shah founded PayActiv to pioneer earned wage access (EWA), an "employee financial wellness" program that allows workers to access 60 percent of their wages as soon as they are earned, which are then deducted from the next paycheck. In describing the principle behind the service, he told me, "Everything is streaming now. Why can't wages stream?" PayActiv has designed an app that plugs into employers' time-tracking systems. Shah told me that the name earned wage access perfectly captures its spirit: "It's for wages earned, so it's not early, which connotes impatience; it's wage, not income, because income can be commission or something like that; and it's access, not an advance, which implies that someone did you a favor."

Recognized by the US Consumer Financial Protection Bureau, EWA has the key insight that "the timing of when you are paid is entirely in the control of your employer," said Shah. "It's a technology decision. I said that if technology drives the timing of pay, then we could create technology and a product in which people could access their money as they earn it." PayActiv's clients include Wendy's, Walmart, hospitals, and senior living centers, and Shah claimed EWA has increased some of these companies' staff retention by at least 20 percent and in some cases as much as 40 percent, suggesting it is one of the cases where doing the right thing can benefit companies.

Other companies have addressed the monumental problem of cash-flow misalignment in different ways. Rhino Foods is a Vermont-based company that makes frozen cookie dough and other dessert toppings. More importantly, it was an early adopter of an income advance program for its employees, which provides workers with no-questions-asked loans of up to $1,000 during financial emergencies. Rhino launched the program twelve years ago with a local credit union to help employees weather short-term financial challenges, which in turn helps them build long-term financial strength. Participating employees pay off their loans in small, weekly payroll deductions, building a credit history. Unless they opt out, they continue paying the deductions into a savings account after the loan is paid off. Rhino leaders told me that they are "operating in an environment where a lot of people are coming from generational poverty, and so with income advance people are able to access resources and realize . . . in a nonjudgmental way, there are people in this place who can support me." In 2018, Rhino Foods established a separate foundation to accelerate the adoption of income advance and employee-centered workplace practices by other companies.

Ennie Lim's own financial struggles helped her see the structural and systemic issues that workers face. She founded HoneyBee, a company that partners with employers to provide no-interest, no-fee emergency loans to workers and also on-demand financial education. She told me, "If you look at the payday industry, they're banking on the fact that people can't repay. They're banking on the idea that they will come back continuously." But the goal at HoneyBee is not just to get through the emergency but also, through training and education, to change workers' behavior so they don't borrow more than they can afford. Lim said more employers are acknowledging the need to help workers with their financial health and security, for business if not for humane reasons. "It does trickle into the workplace," she said. "It affects productivity and it affects the company's bottom line. By providing this as a benefit, employers can build stronger trust with workers."

Draining Versus Building Human Capital

When considering the externalities produced by a company's inability or refusal to create a good working environment for its employees, low skill and low education rank high. Skills development not only improves employees' living standards, but it also contributes to the success of companies and society at large. Yet many companies are reluctant to invest in their employees' skills.

Take Amazon, whose founder Jeff Bezos reportedly believes that people are inherently lazy and won't stay committed to their jobs over a long period.[31] This philosophy led the company to build in incentives for low-skilled employees to leave so the company doesn't need to provide further growth opportunities. The constant churn of low-skilled employees is destabilizing and destructive for employees and employers alike.

Back in 1974, Harry Braverman's book *Labor and Monopoly Capital* argued that technological development would create a "deskilled" middle class.[32] We are living in that world today. De-skilling is what happens when machinery and technology are introduced to separate (read: replace) workers from the production process. In Braverman's day, it was automation in factories; today, it is increasingly AI, which is performing jobs that were once deemed highly skilled. Theoretically, de-skilling is supposed to result in cost savings and lower barriers to entry for entrepreneurs. In reality, it leads to underemployment, job loss, and poverty.

Some companies see their employees—even their low-skilled employees—not as cogs in a machine but as human capital that provides a positive benefit, both for companies and for communities, as their knowledge and skills spill over. These companies recognize that the ultimate goal of automation and AI should not simply be the elimination of people. Especially since the launch of ChatGPT by OpenAI, there has been much discussion of how such tools have the potential to automate certain tasks that were previously performed by human workers, such as customer service, data entry, and even computer coding.

But as Daron Acemoglu and Simon Johnson discuss in their recent book *Power and Progress: Our Thousand-Year Struggle Over Technology and Prosperity*, it is the choices we make about technology that drive its effects, which can be harnessed to promote greater prosperity. For example, while factory automation eliminated some jobs, improvements in productivity led to new ones.

To mitigate the negative effects of de-skilling, companies should invest in education and training programs that help workers develop new skills. AI systems can be designed to complement human skills and enable workers to focus on higher-level tasks that require creativity, critical thinking, and problem-solving abilities.

Sama is an AI company based in San Francisco that believes there needn't be a "conflict between human and machine." Instead, its services, which include training and validating machine learning algorithms, are designed around a "human-in-the-loop" work model that requires human involvement, even with advanced technology. "It's really this combination of human and artificial intelligence that will allow us to bring best-in-class technology to solve the world's most pressing challenges," said Heather Gadonniex, Sama's vice president of marketing and strategic partnerships. "Our goal isn't to replace humans with AI but to enable AI through humans, which is why we provide skills training for people who normally don't have access to jobs in the digital economy."

It's all about upskilling or cross-skilling, the antithesis of the de-skilling that we saw earlier. Sama believes that machine learning should simply remove more mundane tasks from day-to-day workloads so that humans can focus on higher-value tasks that require higher cognition. Upskilling begins at Sama's internal education program, known as SamaU, which focuses on basic digital skills. "For most employees," Gadonniex said, "this is their first full-time job that pays a living wage. In and of itself, that has the power to transform economies. Not just lives but full economies."

SamaU then builds on topics like machine learning, artificial intelligence, and soft skills like money management. The soft skill training is just as important as the work focused on introducing or upgrading hard skills. "People who received training and employment at Sama reported 10 percent lower unemployment rates and wages that are, on average, more than 25 percent higher than our control group," Gadonniex noted. "Our upskilling programs, our full-time employment programs, and paying living wages had a particularly significant effect on women."

Wealth and Inequality

As the rich get richer, they increasingly construct institutions and systems that provide them with further advantages. The Biden administration's student debt forgiveness program was widely opposed as unfair to people who didn't have student debt, yet the Small Business Paycheck Protection Program (PPP) loan forgiveness, which mainly went to the wealthy, was enthusiastically accepted. For example, Georgia congresswoman Marjorie Taylor Greene vocally protested that forgiving student debt is "completely unfair," yet she hypocritically had $183,504 in PPP loans forgiven.[33]

Thomas Piketty's *Capital in the Twenty-First Century* has shown that capital tends to grow at a faster rate than the overall economy, and that income from capital is always more unevenly distributed than income from labor. This accumulated advantage can also be seen in the "Matthew effect," well-documented in sociology.[34] The term is inspired by a verse in the New Testament's book of Matthew: "For to every one who has, will more be given, and he will have abundance; but from him who has not, even what he has will be taken away" (Matthew 25:29, RSV). In other words, the rich get richer. Those who have significant influence already get disproportionate credit and value for their work, while those in lower positions are trapped, unable to break through.

Neoliberal orthodoxy, popularized by politicians like Ronald Reagan and Margaret Thatcher in the 1980s, presumes that gains to capital also lead to gains for workers (they will "trickle down") in the form of more jobs that pay higher wages, and that economic dynamism will automatically curb inequality. This is also known as supply-side economics.[35]

But this is gaslighting; history reveals the folly of such assumptions. Before World War I, inequality was at its height. Between 1914 and 1970, legal and fiscal changes were hastened by progressive reaction to the Gilded Age, the two world wars, the Bolshevik revolution in 1917, and the Great Depression. Among these changes was the progressive taxation of both income and inherited wealth. Between 1932 and 1980, the top marginal income tax rate averaged 81 percent in the United States and 89 percent in the United Kingdom. As of 2022, the top marginal tax rate in the United States had come down to 37 percent.

Inequality has skyrocketed, as is clearly seen in the share of the top decile of the income distribution since the 1980s. If perfect equality existed, the top 10 percent of the population would have exactly 10 percent of income. If perfect inequality prevailed, they would control 100 percent. In today's United States, the top 10 percent capture 48 percent of income. China, where the top decile captures 41 percent, is almost as unequal. In Europe, they control 34 percent.[36] As thinkers such as Thomas Piketty and Thomas Scanlon discuss, as inequality grows, the rich have increasingly unacceptable forms of control over the lives of those who have less capital, which the wealthy use to increase their own positions, instead of allowing it to trickle down.

What is particularly striking in the United States is the collapse of the share of the total national income going to the bottom 50 percent, which fell from about 20 percent in 1980 to just 12 percent in 2018.[37] The higher you climb on the income scale, the worse it gets.

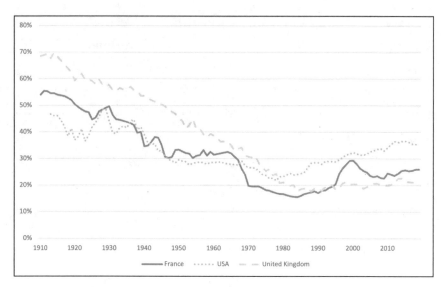

Figure 5: Top 1 Percent Personal Wealth Share in France, United Kingdom, and United States[38]

very sad reality

The top 1 percent of earners have doubled their share of the nation's wealth since the 1980s. The four hundred wealthiest individuals in the United States own more than the poorest 150 million people.[39] The graph in Figure 5 shows the results of the policies of the neo-liberal era. While inequality had been steadily decreasing until the 1980s, since then, following Reagan's tax cuts and other trickle-down policies, it has started an upward trajectory again.[40]

Right now, the wealthiest four hundred households in America pay an average of 8.2 percent in federal taxes, while the average American pays 13.03 percent.[41] Meanwhile, the fortunes of billionaires have soared, especially so during the years of the COVID pandemic. Between 2020 and 2022, the number of billionaires increased by 573, which is a rate of one every thirty hours. And based on World Bank projections, it was estimated in 2022 that about one million people would fall into poverty every thirty-three hours, a shocking parallel.[42] The rising costs of groceries, health care, and energy have been devastating for the poor; while at the same time, for corporate leaders and investors in the energy, food, pharmaceutical, and technology sectors, they have meant record-high profits and salaries.[43]

Executive Compensation and Wealth Accumulation

The gaslighting can get particularly strong in the discourse about how much CEOs deserve their lavish paychecks as their compensation reaches dizzying heights.[44] A 2019 report by the Economic Policy Institute found that from 1978 to 2018, CEO salaries increased by 1,007.5 percent, while the salaries of ordinary workers increased by 11.9 percent. During the pandemic, average CEO compensation rose 16 percent, rocketing S&P 500 CEO pay to nearly three hundred times that of median employees at their firms.[45] Meanwhile, the federal minimum wage has been stuck at $7.25 per hour since 2009.

CEO pay is indicative of deeper problems. To ensure that shareholders' profits are prioritized, executive pay is tied to short-term stock gains rather than long-term investment in employees or even innovation. CEOs enjoy the benefits of rising stock markets even without delivering performance. Boards are typically stocked with C-suite executives, leading to elite back-scratching. In the United States, many directors are appointed by the CEOs themselves, who may also be involved in setting their own pay (such as by appointing the compensation committee). In addition, there is a never-ending upward spiral of executive compensation as companies compare their CEO's salary to peers' salaries.

But some leaders recognize these problems and are working to bring executive compensation under control. As Emmanuel Faber, who was CEO of the global food giant Danone from 2014 to 2021, told me, "Wealth concentration is a time bomb at the planetary level."

Reducing pay gaps is not just about doing good for the world but about attracting the best employees and setting the right priorities.

As Faber explained, "The money I take because 'I can have it, this is legal, and this is a free market' is money that might well be much more useful in the hands of your employees, farmers, consumers, or even shareholders."

During his seven years as CEO, Faber did not take a pay raise, even while also taking on the board chair role in 2017. Faber told me, "My pay didn't change from the day I became a CEO to when I left in March of 2021. I don't want to take any credit for that because I was paid enough for it to just stay like that for a long time. But when it came to not taking a pay raise, it was a fight and a big discussion with the board each time." The board at Danone could not understand why Faber wouldn't take "what was owed to him," while he could not understand why he would ever need that much compensation, particularly when the money could be put to better use.

Faber explained that lavish CEO pay creates inflation to the nth degree, because no company is willing to admit its CEO is below average. "So, if your CEO falls below the benchmark, what do you do? Do you fire the CEO? Or do you say, 'No, my CEO is great, so he couldn't be below average,' and raise his salary? Because of these dynamics, there is a continual inflationary system because boards are often composed of CEOs, who, in a way, depend on each other to get paid more."

In fact, Faber made headlines in 2019 when he waived his severance pay and his "top hat" retirement. "One decision that I made," he said, was "to give away my special pension plan, which was on the books for about $25 to $30 million. I instead put that money in the accounts of the company because I wanted to allow each employee to become a shareholder. In 2019, each of the one hundred thousand employees at Danone became—at no cost for the company, no cost to the shareholders—a shareholder in the company."

As Faber said, "I put my money where my mouth is." When the pandemic struck, Danone introduced a number of programs to support employees, suppliers, and communities, while the board of directors suspended their pay for the second half of 2020 and Faber himself accepted a 30 percent pay cut.[46] Under Faber's leadership, Danone was the first listed French company to become an *entreprise à mission*, a new type of corporate governance, discussed more in Part III, whereby the company's operations were more explicitly aligned with environmental, social, and governance goals.[47]

Faber and the work he did at Danone have been paving the way, and other companies have also set up policies to address these pay inequity issues. Dr. Bronner's limits the salaries of its highest-paid executives to five times the median pay of its full-time employees. At the employee-owned Mondragon Corporation, the highest-paid executive makes at most six times the salary of its lowest-paid employee.[48] And in Chile, there is even collective action to encourage business owners to limit the salary of the highest paid worker to ten times that of the lowest. Known as the "10x Challenge," or "Desafío 10x" in Spanish, over two thousand companies have signed on to this pledge.[49]

Systemic Poverty and Second-Order Effects

As laudable as Faber's and others' efforts are, systemic problems require systemic solutions. For this problem, the solution seems simple: more progressive taxes and, specifically, a wealth tax like liberal US politicians Elizabeth Warren and Bernie Sanders have proposed. In 2022, President Joe Biden unveiled a proposal in which a 20 percent tax would be levied on households worth in excess of $100 million, including all assets and even unrealized capital gains. This tax would help reduce the country's deficit by $360 billion.[50]

Though they poll well, wealth taxes are notoriously difficult to enact, not just because of the resistance of the wealthy (which is considerable), but because they are so inconsistent with what corporate gaslighters have persuaded us to believe. Companies and executives urge us to consider the effects of their philanthropies instead of levying taxes. Part of the issue is the perception in the world today, particularly in developed economies, that wealth is an indicator of success and poverty is a sign of laziness.[51]

Marjorie Kelly of the Democracy Collaborative, a nonprofit working to catalyze the creation of a democratic economy, contradicts this accepted narrative in her recent book, *Wealth Supremacy: How the Extractive Economy and the Biased Rules of Capitalism Drive Today's Crises*. She discusses how a root cause of our systemic problems, from inequality to climate change, is that wealth itself is valorized and so people often don't ask how it was accumulated. She likens this to a cognitive bias—which she calls capital bias—because it's a way of thinking that tells us who matters and what matters, and who doesn't matter and what doesn't matter. In highlighting the potential for systemic change, she draws a powerful analogy to gender bias or racial bias, which are now socially unacceptable but once were accepted. She argues that we need to understand that the level of inequality today, and the capital bias that underpins it, is also unacceptable and that we need to better see its destructive and unethical nature to be able to overcome this bias.

Beyond recognizing that we are biased to valorize wealth, perhaps even more importantly, we need to shift our cognitive frames to better understand that poverty is not simply a result of the actions of poor individuals but that societal structures and institutions hold the poor back in many ways. Unless one has experienced poverty, it is hard to recognize its impact. Most decision-makers at large companies can't relate to the plights and economic realities of their wage workers.

People can become trapped in a cycle of poverty. Poor individuals have limited access to credit and so are forced to seek loans from predatory lenders, who not only charge high interest rates but include hidden fees and unclear terms in their structures. High rates of poverty mean lower economic participation. Companies then shift the externalities of low wages onto the whole society: reduced consumer demand, slower economic growth, increased reliance on public assistance programs, and increased health-care costs due to inadequate access to preventive care. Thus, not only are there dynamics in place to create a race to the top in CEO pay, but, at the same time, there are also mechanisms leading to a race to the bottom in worker pay.

———

Fred Keller, the founder of Cascade Engineering, read Ruby Payne's *A Framework for Understanding Poverty* and was deeply struck by the habits of life poverty engenders. When it comes to food, the focus is on quantity; quality and presentation are secondary. When it comes to money, the focus is on spending it. Any shock can lead to a negative reinforcement spiral: a broken-down car, a child getting sick, or someone in a family becoming addicted to a drug. COVID, of course, was a huge stressor in and of itself, and it exacerbated the factors already in play.

Cascade created a Welfare to Career program to try to break those cycles, helping low-wage workers move from poverty to build careers. The insight was that a well-paying job with good benefits, while important, was not enough. Even with a job in place, it can take six to nine months to transition out of poverty, assuming the proper tools and resources are available. Poverty creates many barriers, including reliable transportation and childcare. These elements need to be addressed, or else the employee could just get caught in a trap of poor attendance as they deal with trying to overcome these lingering issues.

The first step was adding a social worker from the state welfare program to Cascade's staff. "Having a social worker on staff who can call, check in, offer resources, or even just lend an ear is a game-changer for everyone," Keller said. "We live in a society that is care aversive; we need to move back to a care-focused philosophy in (and out of) the workplace." By providing on-site support and connections to workers who had been receiving welfare services, the Grand Rapids, Michigan, company has seen its monthly employee retention rate climb to more than 90 percent—a valuable return on investment, Keller said, that also creates a collaborative workplace atmosphere.

While education and training can provide a way out of poverty, poorer families have limited access to education and high-quality training programs. And as with so much else, education provides disproportionate advantages to the already advantaged. Students whose parents earn more than $200,000 a year score about 250 points higher on their SATs than students whose parents earn between $40,000 and $60,000 a year, and about 390 points higher than those whose parents earn less than $20,000 a year. Higher education is as much of a barrier as a gateway to social mobility, at least when it comes to elite schools.[52]

Wealthy parents don't just put their kids in SAT prep classes; they hire private admissions counselors to refine their applications, put them in dance and music classes, and train them for elite sports such as squash, golf, tennis, crew, and lacrosse that can aid admissions chances. Legacy admissions give privileged applicants an important leg up. At Harvard, the legacy acceptance rate is about 33 percent, while the acceptance rate is only 6 percent for the overall applicant pool.[53] Harvard economist Raj Chetty coauthored a 2023 study of elite US colleges that showed that, among students with the same test scores, those whose parents were from the top 0.1 percent of the income distribution were over two times more likely to be admitted. Chetty said, "The key point is that we don't need to put a thumb on the scale in favor of the poor. We just need to take off the thumb that we—perhaps inadvertently—have on the scale in favor of the rich."

This is all before we come to the issue of tuition fees. Excepting a very few colleges that are wealthy enough to admit students regardless of their ability to pay, those who do not need financial aid are more likely to be admitted than those who do.

The inequality gap does not stop at admissions; it continues to permeate every aspect of life after students are admitted. Elite universities have introduced different recruiting tactics to diversify their student bodies. But in *The Privileged Poor: How Elite Colleges Are Failing Disadvantaged Students*, Anthony Abraham Jack reveals the struggles of poor students who were admitted to elite schools like Harvard and Yale. Not only did these students experience cultural shocks when interacting with their rich peers, but they were unprepared to deal with the social side of campus life and, in many cases, the demands of academic life.[54] As Jack puts it, "Access isn't the same as acceptance."[55] As a result, low-income students are more likely to drop out than high-income students. So much for the meritocracy.[56]

Employees Are the Business

To fully understand how companies can use their positions for the betterment of society, we need to return to the logical but seemingly revolutionary idea that employees are the business. Even the term "stakeholder capitalism" places less emphasis on employees than it should. Judy Samuelson, the executive director and founder of the Aspen Institute's Business and Society Program, said that employees "want the same thing that many executives want: for the business to flourish, while respecting the human and natural ecosystems on which the company depends."[57] When employees become the business, they thrive and their communities also begin to thrive. Societal externalities are reduced with no devastating consequences for the business when companies make employees their priority.

This brings us back to collective action and particularly unions, which, as of this writing, are experiencing a surge in popularity among workers across many industries, including entertainment, retail, distribution, and manufacturing. And unsurprisingly, such action is drawing significant resistance from traditional opponents like automakers, but also from Hollywood studios and newer companies like Amazon, Starbucks, and Apple. For example, when discussing the demands of the United Auto Workers (UAW) in the union's first ever joint strike of the three major US car companies, UAW president Shawn Fain illustrated the inequities in our economic system quite clearly. He said that while automakers' "profits have been through the roof," having made $250 billion in profit in the last decade, and "the price of cars went up 30 percent, workers pay went up [only] 6 percent, and inflation was up 19 percent" at the same time. His assessment, that the position of UAW workers has gone "backwards in the last sixteen years while the CEOs gave themselves 40% pay increases in the last 4 years alone," is a stark illustration of our unequal system.[58] Because of these issues, this strike has gained widespread support, with one survey showing that only 9 percent of the public in the United States supports the large automakers.[59]

This foreshadows the return of the kind of labor-management strife we have not seen since the heyday of economic inequality in the late nineteenth and early twentieth centuries. With the advent of AI, there are increasing challenges to creative and knowledge professionals, and so tensions between workers and companies will likely continue to spread in the future, which the Hollywood strikes of television and film actors and writers in the summer of 2023 likely presages.

While this recent support of workers suggests shifting dynamics in how power in the economy and society should be balanced, significant resistance to unionization remains in corporate suites, even among many companies that are otherwise celebrated for their progressive mindsets. Starbucks is a case in point. Well-known for the benefits it provides employees and its comparatively fair treatment of part-time workers, Starbucks has been accused by the National Labor Relations Board and others of multiple labor-law violations. Its longtime CEO Howard Schultz has defended this with the oxymoronic declaration that "I'm not an anti-union person. I am pro-Starbucks, pro-partner, pro-Starbucks culture. We didn't get here by having a union."[60] This linguistic dance is a prime example of gaslighting.

Schultz's statement also underlines the contrast I have made elsewhere in these pages on the importance of voluntary versus mandatory corporate actions. Many companies and leaders are clearly motivated to develop innovative practices that buck the entrenched systems. For example, part of the reason that Cascade Engineering's work resonates is that they took the time to develop a deep understanding of the larger structural issues that low income, poverty, and inequality create. When I prompted Fred Keller to offer advice to business leaders, his reply was humble and simple. "The first thing I'd suggest is just be present," he said. "Present with the problem, present with people to more deeply understand what they're facing. Let that soak in as part of your problem-solving process." This sounds like common-sense humanity, but the recent labor strife suggests these ideals are not held throughout corporate suites, so ultimately we will need stronger, mandatory measures such as through the state or collective action to address our problems of income and wealth inequality.

While this chapter has focused on how our current system exacerbates issues of poverty and income inequality, in Part III we also examine fairer wealth distribution through employee ownership and other mechanisms. And, in the next chapter, we will turn to racial inequality, a problem even more insidious than income and wealth inequality.

7

Who Pays for Systemic Discrimination?

Shawna Swanson is a Black single mom of five who lives in Yonkers, New York. Throughout her life she has consistently heard "no" when she applied for jobs. "Because I didn't have the experience, or because I wasn't male, or it was different factors—they just looked at me, and it was like, 'No.' So I kept pushing, and pushing, and I kept getting 'No, no, no, no, no.'" At one point her financial situation was so dire she considered putting some of her children up for adoption.

While Swanson's story may seem extreme, it is all too common in the United States in the twenty-first century, where marginalized groups have disproportionately high unemployment rates, financial instability, and food and housing insecurity. Racism and the systemic discrimination that goes along with it are the most significant externalities that have been created by our contemporary business model.

In this chapter, we examine how systemic discrimination pervades corporate practices and daily life for marginalized groups, from people of color to women. This affects their income and wealth in ways that are like weights tied to their ankles, making it hard to advance. But we also examine many companies' policies that are aiming to create a more equitable workforce and society more generally, including new hiring practices and mechanisms to better distribute wealth in society.

To understand the systemic nature of discrimination, it is important to start with companies, as corporate hiring processes that disproportionately screen out candidates based on race, gender, ethnicity, and other factors are pervasive. For example, studies have found that when HR managers screen résumés, Black-sounding first names receive much lower call-back rates, indicating an unconscious bias, which we will discuss in more detail below.[1] Regarding gender, a World Economic Forum study calculated that because of the low rate of change in recent decades in women's participation in the economy, we will need 257 years for gender parity on economic factors like income and workforce participation.[2]

Discrimination not only limits the pool of talent, but it can also lead to social unrest. Negative spirals in equality and wealth lead to disproportionate decay in urban areas that are predominately Black or Latinx, essentially trapping people in places that are underserved by services like public transportation and supermarkets.

Who pays for American capitalism's success? To an unconscionable degree, it is the very people who are excluded from it. Consider that the average Black or Latinx household brings in about half as much in earnings each year as the average white household, and that Black and Latinx households have 15 to 20 percent of the share of net wealth, according to the Federal Reserve.[3] A 2019 study found that median white households had 7.8 times the amount of wealth of median Black households ($188,200 versus $24,100).[4] The numbers are even more stark for women of color, who have far lower incomes and savings.[5]

But recognizing that these issues exist can be a challenge because so many of us—like the proverbial fish who doesn't know what water is—take them for granted, ignoring both the structural dimensions that underlie discrimination and the widespread implicit biases that hold back underrepresented groups.

We have been trained and conditioned to do so. A powerful gaslighting tactic is the manufacture of wedge issues to obscure the underlying problems. For example, there has been a recent focus on "wokeism," in which reformers are criticized for their excessive sensitivity, and attacks on the supposed influence of critical race theory on academic curriculums, falsely described as an "anti-white" ideology.[6]

Despite the propaganda of the Right, critical race theory is neither new nor threatening. It highlights the idea of race as a social construct deeply embedded in institutional systems like criminal justice and housing. It shows how even individuals, companies, and cities can become complicit in racist outcomes, as systems and patterns from periods of more active racism are still present, silently embedded in infrastructure and becoming visible when confronted with a crisis.[7]

This "racism without racists" was exposed in the public services of Buffalo, New York, following a record streak of cold weather and blizzards in 2022, when the streets of predominantly white neighborhoods were cleared more quickly than those in Black neighborhoods. This extreme weather led to the deaths of at least thirty-nine people, more than half of whom were Black in a county where only one out of seven people is Black. It is not as if the plow drivers chose to attend to the white neighborhoods first, but that was how the emergency preparedness system was designed. The only way to combat this is to acknowledge that systemic racism exists and actively work against these systems, which is not at all the same thing as telling white people that they are racist simply because they are white.

Though DEI initiatives are rapidly becoming social, moral, and business imperatives for corporations, too many employers wittingly and unwittingly perpetuate the systemic biases and discrimination that pervade our employment systems.

Systemic Discrimination and Racism

Because of cultural reinforcement over time, systemic discrimination is buried so deeply in people's worldviews that it takes real work to uncover and uproot it; it is the same with institutions and their systems.[8] Although the Fifteenth Amendment gave Black men the vote in 1870, a series of disenfranchisement laws were subsequently enacted. The result has been a lack of investment in education and social welfare in Black communities, a century and a half of housing and employment discrimination, and over-policing and sentencing disparities, which mean that Black people are statistically more likely to be ex-offenders than whites.[9]

Consumers don't become aware of these issues in the companies they engage with until victims take a stand. In 2016, Amazon fired a large group of drivers in Massachusetts, most of them people of color. Two years later, six of them charged Amazon with illegal discrimination. Amazon claims they were fired due to information that turned up during background checks. One complainant, Dexter Andrews, had delivered packages for several months before Amazon fired him. The last time he had been arrested was in 2009; he had worked in construction and mentored at-risk youth in the years since. But when Amazon's background check picked up the nearly decade-old charge, he was summarily terminated. Similarly, Matthew Soler was working sixty to seventy hours a week delivering packages and training new drivers. Then, a background check turned up an old violation: driving on a suspended license. Though his license had been reinstated four years before Amazon hired him, he was dismissed from the company.[10]

Background checks disproportionately affect Black and Latinx workers because their communities are subject to over-policing and over-incarceration. In the 1960s, the federal government established the Equal Employment Opportunity Commission (EEOC) to consider issues of equity and discrimination in the job market. Under its rules, extensive background checks are in fact considered grounds for legal liability. But studies show that the EEOC receives far fewer complaints about discrimination than it should, because the risks of reprisal are so high and the likelihood of actually changing things is low. For instance, the EEOC was unresponsive to several discrimination claims made by UPS employees. Eventually, UPS fired most of the complainants, which discouraged the rest of the employees from making a report.[11] Many companies' employment contracts forbid employees the right to sue, forcing them into private arbitration instead.

In 2018, JPMorgan Chase settled a class action lawsuit, filed by more than two hundred current and former Black financial advisers, that claimed their white colleagues were consistently assigned to wealthier sites and received higher salaries. The bank pledged to invest $4.5 million in a fund to support bias training, branch job reviews, and recruitment.[12] Just two years later, JPMorgan Chase found itself defending yet another racial discrimination lawsuit.[13]

Many job applicants of color have learned to "whiten" their résumés, scrubbing them of anything, including their names, that might identify them as non-white in order to avoid summary rejections. A number of studies have shown that individuals with white-sounding names are more likely to receive job interviews.[14] This is not just the case with lower-level positions; discrimination can be even more intense when it comes to jobs in management. Even when companies institute explicit diversity policies, the people hired are often undermined by being labeled as affirmative action hires or tokens.[15]

In 2020, following the murder of George Floyd and the Black Lives Matter protests that exploded across the country and the world, it appeared that things might start to change. Many companies made shows of their efforts to become a part of the solution via public expressions of support. Amazon, for example, issued a statement in support of the Black Lives Matter movement in June 2020. There was a certain irony in that, of course. Of Amazon's four hundred thousand American employees, 26.5 percent identify as Black or African American; more than three-quarters of them work in the company's lower paying jobs in warehouses and logistics services, with few in management.[16] A public statement is well and good, but if systemic racial issues within the company are not addressed, then it's fair to dismiss it as symbolic gaslighting.[17]

After the killing of George Floyd, McDonald's produced a digital ad to honor Floyd and six other victims of police brutality.[18] "We do not tolerate inequity, injustice, or racism," reads the text that flashes on the screen. "Black Lives Matter." But the reality is that 78 percent of McDonald's majority Black and brown workforce doesn't have access to paid sick leave.[19] That is dangerous under normal circumstances; during a global pandemic, it was deadly, and revealed the company's fine-sounding words as mainly window dressing, or "woke-washing."[20]

If McDonald's, Amazon, or any of the other companies that built their wealth and success on the backs of marginalized people want to show that they are truly engaged in anti-racism, they must begin by scrutinizing their own policies and practices—companies that do not provide universal access to paid sick leave, or that pay employees below the living wage, or any number of other "typical" practices that exacerbate and perpetuate inequality. Without such reflexivity, the cycle will continue.

Understanding Implicit Biases

Recognizing and accepting that everyone harbors biases that are implicit and unconscious is a necessary first step to overcoming them. Unconscious bias doesn't make you a bad person. It's a fact of life; it's part of the way that the human brain works.

However, diversity training that focuses on these issues alone does not have much of an effect on companies, and it may even backfire. Sometimes it is merely window dressing—an easy way for a company to signal that it recognizes the issue. A recent book by the Harvard sociologist Frank Dobbin and Tel Aviv University's Alexandra Kalev, *Getting to Diversity: What Works and What Doesn't*, explores this question thoroughly. Dobbin and Kalev have conducted decades of rigorous research into which corporate diversity initiatives actually work. For a variety of reasons we will discuss, such diversity training programs have achieved approximately nothing.[21]

First, unconscious biases are inscribed over a lifetime. Antibias diversity training might have short-lived effects on discriminatory behavior, but it does not last. Dobbin and Kalev's research shows there is typically a lack of follow-through after the training. Cascade Engineering's Fred Keller reflected to me that frequently challenging problems like diversity are addressed with a quick-fix mentality: "People want to consider the problem and then they want it to go away. They think if I get the right numbers or if I add a department of diversity, I can just push it to the side," he said. But deep-rooted problems are not susceptible to quick fixes, and to adequately address them requires revising the underlying systems and processes.

Furthermore, research has shown that such training can even backfire. While managers may receive diversity training, they may still be required to enforce systemically racist policies and practices, creating cognitive dissonance. Dobbin and Kalev also showed that diversity training can provoke resentment in individuals who believe they are being unfairly scapegoated as racists; the emphasis of this type of intervention on unlearning stereotypes can have the opposite effect of strengthening them. Thus, while diversity training can be one element of a useful intervention, it is mostly ineffective and frequently used as a smoke screen.

Tiffany Jana, founder of TMI Consulting, a firm that does DEI consulting, underscored an important point on such interventions. While a company has no right to tell an employee how and what to think, leaders *can* say that this is what they expect in their inclusive workplace. "That's a very subtle distinction but a really important one," they told me. "People ask us to help 'remove the bias' from employees. Well, you can't do that. But you can identify biased-based behaviors and make it clear that they will not be tolerated."

Focus on Systems and Outcomes

What leads to biased outcomes is not necessarily what is rooted in the minds of managers and members of their team per se, but in the organizational systems, structures, and policies that guide them. So the only way to truly make a difference is to redesign the systems entirely to deliberately and intentionally include and support marginalized individuals. This would affect every aspect of the organization: recruitment, mentoring, project management, job assignments, work-life systems, even layoffs. As Dobbin and Kalev explained, "Each of these systems was designed decades ago to be meritocratic for one slice of the workforce: white men who are not primary caregivers. These systems informally exclude white women and people of colour."[22]

TMI's Jana similarly pointed out that when an organization says, "We are committed to equitable pay across every individual on our team," or, "We are committed to professional development and support," the approach is based on the entire company and organization. That perpetuates the system that inherently will prioritize those who've always been there. Alternatively, Jana recommended companies should reframe these statements and be more specific. Instead, say, "We're going to create equitable pay specifically for our Black employees." For example, following the murder of George Floyd, a number of companies announced plans directed at Black employees. Google committed to improving "Black+ representation at senior levels and committing to a goal to improve leadership representation of underrepresented groups by 30 percent by 2025."[23] Target also announced plans to increase representation of Black team members across the company by 20 percent. Jana emphasized that articulating this more nuanced angle, beyond simple diversity, can help uncover different places where problems and inequities exist. Although for all of these programs, as we will emphasize below, we can't just believe what is announced and follow-up is crucial.

Diversity efforts must extend to the very top of the ladder. Dobbin and Kalev view management diversity as the gold standard in measuring the efficacy of such programs, saying, "Lots of firms have diversity on the front lines. Not nearly as many have retained and promoted people of color."[24]

Data and Tracking

It is hard to identify a problem if you don't know what it is. As Jana told me, "You're never going to move the needle if you haven't decided where the needle is going."

So, an essential step is collecting and making public data on organizational diversity. Unfortunately, many companies are resistant. A prominent example is Nike. Following the murder of Floyd, Nike was celebrated for its marketing campaign about racial justice featuring former NFL quarterback Colin Kaepernick.[25]

As You Sow, an influential California-based organization that has been working for over thirty years on shareholder advocacy around corporate responsibility, was not impressed. As that organization reported, Nike refused to meaningfully disclose its own diversity data—a big red flag.[26] The company is legally required to collect and report on diversity through its EEOC-mandated EEO-1 report. While, after significant scrutiny, many of the largest companies have eventually made these EEO-1 forms publicly available, Nike refused.[27] In fact, Nike actively attempted to block a shareholder resolution that sought release of the company's demographics, as well as hiring, retention, and promotion data (the SEC denied Nike's request). Despite this, in October 2021, 35 percent of shareholders voted to disclose these details.[28] Instead, Nike chose to release an annual impact report with a summary.

Nike did ultimately make certain commitments, financial and structural, that it intends to fulfill in the coming years, and finally agreed to release recruitment and promotion data by race, gender, and ethnicity. But the company is still lagging in releasing other data, such as retention rates by ethnicity. The way Nike has dragged its feet is disturbing and shows how necessary intense public-sector pressure is. Similarly, Amazon has refused to disclose any detailed data and has even refused a civil rights and DEI audit introduced by its shareholders.

What does this data tracking look like, and how does it work? Andrew Behar, As You Sow's CEO, helped me better understand these processes. His organization has developed a research-based set of fifty-seven key performance indicators that measure and grade companies across a number of areas, among them recruitment, retention, and promotion rates by gender, race, and ethnicity. Twenty percent of As You Sow's racial justice scorecard is based on the public declarations of a company and 80 percent on what they actually do. Actions speak louder than words. A big advantage of this data is that it can also be used internally as part of actionable goal setting.

The Unreasonable Group, a venture capital company, is an example of a company that took the approach Jana advocates: everything is specific and action oriented. According to its chief of staff Whitney Heaps, while gender diversity among the leadership team was always an implicit part of the company's ethos, it had never been publicly stated prior to 2019. And while their leadership was diverse, their board wasn't. Articulating the goal spurred action. "So, we actively recruited women. Now 100 percent of independent board members identify as either women or people of color."

Recruitment and Hiring Processes

For nearly forty years, Greyston Bakery, the maker of gourmet brownies, cookies, and those chunky bits in Ben & Jerry's ice cream, has recruited employees through open hiring, a program that is helping to break the cycle of poverty by hiring anyone who wants to work—minorities, dropouts, refugees, the previously incarcerated—without requiring résumés, interviews, or background checks.[29] Greyston gave Shawna Swanson, whom we met in the opening of this chapter, the chance that no one else would. In her words: "They told me 'yes' when everyone else said 'no,' and it means everything,"

"What are we talking about? It's opportunity; it's access," Greyston president and CEO Joe Kenner told me. "We've been bringing folks into the mainstream for decades by investing in their potential, with no judgment." The bakery's demographics reflect its community. Since 2017, approximately 95 percent of its open hire employees are people of color, and a third of them are women. Latinx representation has risen steadily, consistent with the growth of the Latinx population in Yonkers, the company's location.[30] There has also been a significant increase in the number of non-white employees in management positions.

Greyston's open hiring model gives individuals the opportunity to escape the trap of their socioeconomic status, demography, and past criminal behavior. Kenner explained that the company's founder, Bernie Glassman, had been overwhelmed by the myriad of unemployed and homeless people that he saw every day in the Bronx. "The genesis was Bernie's belief that we lose as a society when folks are not realizing their full potential," Kenner said. "Open hiring isn't charity; it's a talent management strategy. . . . We offer jobs to people no questions asked but, at the end of the day, we still need to run a business that needs to make a profit, that needs to supply a product for Ben & Jerry's. There's accountability there."

As Kenner explained to me, Glassman would literally start pulling people off the streets, saying, "Hey, you don't have a job. Do you want to work? Do you want to learn a new skill? The skills are manual, and you can learn them on the job. All you have to do is be willing to work."

Greyston provides resources to help with childcare, mental health, housing, and other issues that perpetuate the cycle of poverty and inequity. "What makes us different is how we invest those dollars from a human resources perspective," Kenner said. "We want to invest in bringing you in and keeping you here, as opposed to expending resources on keeping you out through, for example, interviews and background checks." With about one hundred bakery employees, including seventy or so from open hiring, Greyston operates with an eye on employees' long-term success.

Geographically, the bakery is perfectly situated to enact real change in a community that needs to see it. Yonkers is a poor city: 2017 Census data showed that 15.4 percent of its population lives below the poverty line, including 25 percent of its children. Yonkers's unemployment rate for Black and Latinx people is twice the national average.[31] There are high numbers of formerly incarcerated people as well, and getting a job is practically impossible for them. This is not just bad for them as individuals; it hurts all of us. According to data from the Center for Economic and Policy Research, the social impact of not hiring previously imprisoned citizens results in an annual GDP loss of approximately $87 billion.[32]

Greyston is also providing workforce development and training to Yonkers community members, not just Greyston employees. As Kenner explained: "We want to move people closer to the mid-level skills job, so we are offering additional courses to help people qualify for jobs like medical health professional assistant, customer service, bookkeeping, and a whole host of other things in emerging industries. Maybe you start at the bakery and then move to another employment partner of ours, because we have all the relationships. We do the certificate training, and we do the case management to assess you and see what you want to do, what you're good at, and what you might need to build on. Then we provide the job development services, so we train you, assess you, retrain you, and provide soft skills and essential skills training, such as résumé writing, conflict resolution, and how to interview. The idea is for you to move on to employment, whether it's with us or somebody else. We want you to have a job—that's the goal."

Kenner told me that there are ten million people in America who face some type of barrier to employment, such as homelessness, substance abuse, or a criminal record. At the same time, the Bureau of Labor Statistics claims there are roughly eight million jobs available. So, Kenner said, "Not to say that every one of those ten million folks are work ready, but you can't tell me that there's not an opportunity here."

Greyston recently began scaling the open hiring model internationally. Kenner told me, "If we filled forty thousand jobs through inclusive hiring and open hiring by 2030, that computes to about $3 billion of economic impact—and that's before you consider the savings from corrections, people getting off public assistance, and the tax revenue that they generate from their wages. That is a huge opportunity, and that's only forty thousand jobs." What if, said Kenner, open hiring became so widespread that all of those eight million available jobs were filled by those ten million unemployables? The whole shape of our society would change for the better.

The Greyston Employment Opportunity Center shares its hiring model with many other businesses, large and small, including the Body Shop, Giant Eagle, and Rhino Foods. "We want to educate as many people as we can on the possibility of open hiring," said Kenner. "If a business is skeptical about open hiring, we tell them to open up just one job. It doesn't have to be a whole department. It is low risk. It can be whatever position you think works for your organization."

The Body Shop North America piloted an open hiring program at its distribution center and rolled it out at its retail stores as part of a broader initiative focused on inclusion and equity.[33] Nicholas Debray, the president of the Body Shop Americas, spoke with me about the company's further plans. The next step will be to expand open hiring into a permanent recruitment model for all customer service jobs, as well as entry-level retail and distribution positions.

The Body Shop has developed a comprehensive training program that covers such topics as "leading without bias and building customer service skills through authentic communication," he added. "We want to elevate our employees' soft skills and train everyone to be a leader." Starting in 2021, the programs were also introduced in the United Kingdom and Australia.

Thus far, the results have been overwhelmingly positive, Debray said. "When you give people access to something they have been struggling to find, like employment, they will work hard to keep it. In our case, we saw an overall improvement in both retention *and* productivity"—66 percent and 13 percent, as measured in units per hour, respectively. "In fact, during a time when many employers, especially retailers and warehouses, are scrambling to find employees, we filled all our available positions. Many employees have said that just getting a second chance has given them a reason to be excited to go to work."

Open hiring, Kenner concluded, is "good for business, it's good for the economy, and there are some societal implications. It's good for the hire; it's good for their family; it's good for the community the family lives in." This is why Greyston has changed its mission statement from "To create thriving communities through the practice and promotion of open hiring" to "We want to unlock the power of human potential through inclusive employment, one person at a time."

Social Networks, Within and Between Firms

Open hiring is a specific intervention that strives to eliminate bias in hiring. There are more general practices that companies can adopt as well to address systemic injustices. Dobbin and Kalev's work also highlights the importance of networks, both within and between companies and individuals.

Consciously or unconsciously, employers tend to look for hires from historically white educational institutions, or, even more specifically, from institutions that other members of the management team have attended.[34] If employers truly want to be inclusive of top talent of any marginalized group, they must actively recruit from places where those populations are represented, such as historically Black and brown academic institutions.[35]

Networking has become a priority at SecondMuse, a consulting company focused on building resilient communities. As co-CEO

Carrie Freeman put it, "If you are a primarily white organization with white networks, then the likelihood of getting diverse candidates for your jobs is lower." So, the company consciously broadened its networks to increase that diverse applicant pool. Freeman concluded, "It seems simple, but all these things add up."

To increase the representation of women in technology, Second-Muse runs a program called GET Cities in partnership with a few similarly minded companies. This program focuses on the talent pipeline at the university level and targets "the hiring practices of companies, making sure that young women are getting those internships, for example, and that they are getting the opportunities to be hired," Freeman said.

In Portland, Maine, a staffing agency called MaineWorks is working to dismantle employment barriers by leaning on founder Margo Walsh's experience as a recruiter. MaineWorks connects recently incarcerated people and people recovering from substance abuse with construction companies in need of workers.[36] "That's my superpower—to be able to hustle and meet everybody and put it together in this web," Walsh said.

Overcoming Systemic Wealth Disparities

While these steps focused on reforming organizational systems are an important part of overcoming systemic discrimination, we must also consider the broader wealth disparities in our society that further reinforce racist policies and structures. Take redlining, for example. This practice of steering minorities into segregated neighborhoods has shaped the demography of the entire United States. It is largely illegal now, but its effects linger.[37]

As noted earlier in this chapter, there is a huge disparity between the levels of wealth held by Black and Latinx families and white families. Housing equity has everything to do with it. The Black-white wealth gap is incredibly deep and has been sustained by decades of racist practices. One result is that only about 44 percent of Black Americans own homes in the United States, while 75 percent of white Americans do. Redlining has significantly affected this gap, as have continued racist policies in mortgage lending. According to a recent study by LendingTree, Black homebuyers are denied mortgages 12.64 percent of the time, while the overall mortgage rejection rate is 6.15 percent.[38] Even when existing Black homeowners apply to refinance their homes, they are denied 30 percent of the time (compared to the national average of 17 percent).

Initiatives put into place to "solve" this problem were actually smoke screens that exacerbated it. The Home Owners' Loan Corporation (HOLC) and the Federal Housing Administration (FHA) were initially established during the New Deal to improve the lots of low-income populations. HOLC's mission was to reduce foreclosures, while the FHA was meant to create jobs in construction, and thus increase the affordability of houses across the United States, and also to insure home loans. Instead, both went all-in on redlining. HOLC assigned letter grades to neighborhoods to indicate how "risky" they were in terms of their racial compositions.[39] The FHA created its own maps based on homeowners' compulsory assessments of their neighborhood's risk level. Since the FHA also insured home loans, people in majority Black neighborhoods were effectively unable to obtain them.[40]

In the private sector, the Philadelphia-based company Shift Capital is a neighborhood investment group whose explicit mission is to alleviate cross-generational poverty through its efforts to counter gentrification. Gentrification is the process by which low-income residents of certain neighborhoods are replaced by people with higher incomes, and it has been shown to heavily reduce diversity and inclusion in cities that were already racially inequitable.[41] Other research has shown that public housing is more likely to be demolished in Black neighborhoods as an act of gentrification, contributing to high levels of Black-to-white turnover.[42]

Starting in 2013, Shift Capital began investing in formerly redlined or blighted neighborhoods in Philadelphia. The areas in which the company works all have unemployment rates of over 50 percent and some of the worst public health characteristics in all of Philadelphia. For example, in one project, Shift funded the adaptive reuse of an old mill, which turned it into 116 apartment residences with ground-level cafés and retail.[43] In another project, Shift cleaned out and repaired an almost century-old building, which it aims to transform into a 138-room hotel with ground-level restaurants and a café, a rooftop bar and restaurant, a fitness center, and meeting spaces.

Importantly, Shift Capital's work is not just about creating housing but also about having positive spillovers into the community. For instance, to revitalize Kensington, an area in Philadelphia where 23.3 percent of residents live below the poverty line, Shift formed a cross-sector partnership to specifically attract lower-income entrepreneurs, an important focus area for the company. As of 2021, Shift had supported the creation of fifty-eight enterprises owned and operated by people of color.

Shifting Structural Inequities in Investment Patterns

In 2019, just 2.8 percent of US venture capital went to businesses with all women cofounders. That, sadly, was a record high. In 2022, the number went down to just 2.1 percent.[44] When combined with the capital received by businesses with cofounders of multiple genders, the number only jumps to 9 percent, according to Crunchbase.[45] As venture capital investments hit record heights with each year in the United States—topping $330 billion in 2021—most of it continues to go to companies led by white men. According to a 2020 study by RateMyInvestor and Diversity VC, more than 60 percent of founding teams who received venture capital money are all white. While 21 percent are racially mixed, only 1 percent are all Black, 0.6 percent are all Latinx, and 17 percent are all Asian.[46] Despite growing calls for a more just economy, these numbers make it clear that the system predominantly benefits white men.

As introduced in Chapter 2, Reinventure Capital is looking to change that. Julianne Zimmerman, its managing director, said it invests with the explicit goal of creating opportunities for and advancing the innovations of women and people of color, shifting the venture capital system toward greater equity and inclusion. "What that comes down to is who has authority, who has a say, who has control, who has ownership," she said. "When you look at the distribution of capital, consistently more than 90 percent of venture capital goes to an extremely narrow demographic—in broad strokes, straight, white, US-born men from a dozen universities."

That concentration of capital lands primarily in a half dozen metropolitan areas, she said, further exacerbating inequities. "It also means that we have this perilously unbalanced means of propagating ideas and value propositions and technologies and services," Zimmerman reflected.

"It's also a failure to appropriately price opportunity and risk—the very definition of a market dislocation—in light of findings by BCG, Morgan Stanley, and others that heterogeneous teams led by women and people of color tend to outperform largely homogeneous teams led by white males," she added.[47] Setting the social justice concerns aside, reports from McKinsey and others show that such disparities result in trillions of dollars of lost opportunity for investors and the US economy.[48]

Zimmerman added that the hyperconcentration of venture capital (and other financial resources) is not an obscure or abstract ethical consideration but shapes our social fabric. It's a causal driver, in fact, of some of the most serious issues we're experiencing. So Reinventure works with diverse founder teams to retain ownership as much as possible and also infuse ownership as deeply as possible in the employee base. Zimmerman said: "The funny thing is that you would think that was just sort of sensible. But it's astonishing how often we encounter people, particularly peers in the venture sector, who think that sounds terrifyingly risky and difficult," presumably because investors usually want to retain as much control as possible.

When I talked to Zimmerman in late 2022, she told me Reinventure had six companies in its portfolio, including Canela Media, a New York–based company led by a Latina founder and CEO and a stellar team of primarily Latinx and female employees, focusing its offerings on Latinx markets. When Reinventure first looked at the company, Zimmerman said, experts said the audience is saturated, the media sector is flooded with capital, and there was really no room for anything more than a niche play. But after talking to Canela, she learned that the Hispanic, Latinx, and Spanish-dual-language audience is the most culturally diverse minority group in the United States and the largest population in the Americas, with a real hunger for more authentic, more representative content. In the United States, it is the fastest-growing demographic under twenty-five. Customer-serving enterprises of any kind must pay attention to that rising consumer base. Reinventure led the company's first round of institutional investment in 2020, and in 2022 Canela closed a $32 million series A investment with a number of other investors.

The Unreasonable Group is also working to rebalance the venture investment ecosystem by providing opportunities to organizations and individuals who traditionally don't have access to investment.

Whitney Heaps told me that, from the outset, the company set the objective that at least 50 percent of the members of their collective identify as women, people of color, and/or LGBTQ.

Reparations

Reparations, reclaiming what has been stolen and redistributing it to the heirs of exploited peoples, is one solution that many find radical but that has nonetheless gained traction in recent years. The idea of reparations is not new; it has been around since the end of the Civil War. In 1865, Major General William T. Sherman confiscated land from Confederate landowners to be divided into equal portions and distributed to newly freed Black families—the "forty acres and a mule" order. After the assassination of President Abraham Lincoln, his successor Andrew Johnson rescinded the order.[49] Imagine how different America might be today if the order had stood.

While national policy and action on systemic reparations programs remains stalled, California and a number of US cities are starting to implement programs to right these historical wrongs. California governor Gavin Newsom created a panel to study reparations following the murder of George Floyd, which recommended that the state create a broad program to compensate for the economic harms from racist housing discrimination and mass incarceration.[50] In Evanston, Illinois, where Northwestern University is based, the local compensation restorative housing program passed the city council by an eight-to-one margin, promising Black residents who can prove their ancestors were victims of redlining or racist practices between 1919 and 1969 up to $25,000 per family.[51] These funds are to be used for housing: a down payment, a mortgage, or renovations. Asheville, North Carolina, approved compensation for Black residents and funding for programs that will increase homeownership and career opportunities.

What happened in Providence, Rhode Island, illustrates how controversial these programs can be. The city undertook a study that extensively documented how deeply the city and state were involved in the Atlantic slave trade, and how centuries of racist polices had contributed to the enormous wealth gap between the state's white, Black, and Indigenous residents. In 2022, Mayor Jorge Elorza signed the $10 million Providence municipal reparations program. The controversial element was that, while Black and Native American residents of Providence automatically qualified, because of an income criteria, many white residents could qualify as well.[52]

While state-backed reparations and policy prescriptions may be the only truly fair way to address these issues, it will likely take more time for such ideas to garner public support, so we need to move on multiple fronts. Private actors are working to do just that, for example the growing number of real estate companies that have embraced greenlining—organized efforts to stimulate investment in neighborhoods that were shaped by redlining.[53]

An example of privately financed reparations is Rivendell Bicycle Works, a company in Walnut Creek, California.[54] On October 1, 2020, it announced its Black Reparations Pricing program, which offered a 45 percent discount to any Black customer looking to buy a bike.[55] When Grant Petersen, the company's founder, convened an advisory board of Black cyclists and academics to discuss the idea, they warned him that backlash and lawsuits could ensue. But Petersen stuck to his guns. "Many white people have inherited past interests," he said, "but they don't want to inherit past debts."

While this may seem like an example of an idiosyncratic entrepreneur imposing his values on his company, the history of bicycles reveals just how deeply systemic racism has shaped US culture and commerce. In the 1890s, cycling classes and clubs were a huge fad in American cities, but they were only open to white people. And since bicycles were expensive, they were only available to white elites. As late as 1971, the city of Washington, DC, required expensive bicycling licenses, preventing many Black Americans from being able to use them for commuting.

As predicted, Rivendell has faced a lot of backlash and criticism from predominantly right-wing individuals and groups. Harmeet Dhillon, a former Republican official, wrote: "Rivendell Bicycle Work's [sic] Black Reparations Pricing is illegal. Every customer is entitled to pricing on non-discriminatory terms. We demand you discontinue this policy immediately, or legal action may ensue."

"Those people, the majority of them, had never bought anything from us," said Rivendell general manager Will Keating. "They probably don't even ride bikes. They just saw something that infuriated them on the Internet and had to take the next step." Nevertheless, the program was shut down on the advice of Rivendell's lawyers.[56]

An unfortunate outcome, yes, but it's not remotely the end of the road for Rivendell's efforts to make amends for the history of racism in the bicycle industry. Renamed BRF for Bikes R Fun, the program continues as a charitable fund that supports a variety of causes. In 2021, Rivendell customers donated over $50,000 to it.[57] The original program was enormously risky, Petersen admits, but it gained Rivendell a dedicated, loyal following of customers.

———

Much is still needed to combat systematic discrimination. While we need innovations and understanding to be more embraced in the corporate world, scrutiny of NGOs and policy interventions are also crucial. Sadly, as I pointed out in this chapter, some companies only see the wave of anti-racism movements as a PR opportunity, rather than as a chance to make changes. They have gaslighted the public into supporting their businesses for supposedly championing racial

aspect

important

very

justice while maintaining embedded discriminatory policies and practices.

While all of us should speak out against discrimination wherever we see it, it is important to recognize that fine words are not enough. The systemic nature of these issues must be recognized, and policies and procedures to overcome them must be implemented. The efforts of companies like Greyston Bakery, Rivendell Bicycle Works, SecondMuse, Shift Capital, and Reinventure Capital are showing the way. These companies and others are not just meeting the baseline of creating an enabling environment with a diverse management team and supportive policies but also engaging in changing the underlying racist and sexist systems themselves.

In the next section of the book, we will move beyond these interventions on specific issues that we have discussed and focus more on how companies, investors, governments, and individuals can work alone and together to engage in systemic change more generally.

PART III

BUILDING A REGENERATIVE ECONOMY FOR THE TWENTY-FIRST CENTURY

8

Governing with the Commons in Mind

Emmanuel Faber embedded purpose into every part of Danone's structure during his time as CEO, transforming the French food giant into an *entreprise à mission*, a new type of corporate form with governance and accountability innovations that align a company's social and environmental missions with its overall financial goals.[1] Faber seemed like an unstoppable force. And yet, forces representing the status quo ultimately sidelined him.

When Danone's share price took a significant hit during COVID, the investment group Artisan Partners, which held a significant stake in Danone, blamed Faber, arguing that he was too focused on ESG to deliver shareholder returns.

Many see Faber's downfall as a rebuke to his ideas, but I have a different conclusion. Change always inspires resistance from those who are threatened by it; with every fight for two steps forward, the status quo pushes back one step. The moral of Faber's story is that more, not less, reform is needed.

As more government and business leaders attempt to address our social and environmental challenges, corporate governance and accountability standards will need to be redefined. While Milton Friedman's influential 1970 *New York Times Magazine* article was a clarion call for shareholder primacy, it took decades for his ideas to become embedded in our institutions.[2] The effort to change the capitalist system to be redefined from a linear take, make, waste model to one that fosters regeneration will also be a generational project and include many of the types of work that resulted in the dominance of neoliberalism, including legal and policy changes, shifts in investment priorities, and new types of corporate practices.

One important issue we will need to address is alignment. How can a company respond to the needs of the public commons if its legal foundation and the duties of its directors are primarily focused on shareholders? A second issue is accountability. If companies want to be thought of as greener and more socially responsible, then they should have to prove that they really are. This chapter profiles a number of important voluntary and legal actions that are redefining corporate purpose, and shows how companies are held accountable for their impacts on society and the environment. All of this can create a system where addressing negative externalities is the baseline and fostering the creation of positive externalities can be achieved.

As far back as 1919, in *Dodge v. Ford*, Michigan's Supreme Court stated that "a business corporation is organized and carried on primarily for the profit of the stockholders."[3] But the real watershed for shareholder primacy came in 1986, when the Delaware Supreme Court decided *Revlon, Inc. v. MacAndrews & Forbes Holdings*. The court articulated that when a publicly traded company is being sold, its directors' fiduciary responsibility is to ensure that its shareholders receive the best price. In *eBay v. Craigslist* in 2010, the Delaware Court of Chancery further held that a corporate mission that "seeks not to maximize the economic value of a for-profit Delaware corporation for the benefit of its stockholders" is invalid.[4] The bottom line of these decisions is that executives and directors have a legal duty to put shareholders first.

But the pendulum is swinging back, and the legal duties of companies and directors are being shifted away from these Friedman ideals. Following Maryland in 2010, almost forty US states plus Washington, DC, and Puerto Rico have passed "benefit corporation" legislation, which defines a new type of company like the *entreprise à mission* that is legally focused on a long-term mission beyond delivering short-term profits and is committed to creating value for stakeholders beyond shareholders. Delaware, the most business-friendly state in the country, where most large corporations are legally domiciled, passed benefit corporation legislation in 2013.

According to these laws, the directors of a benefit corporation have a fiduciary duty to support the articulated social and environmental mission of the company. To ensure accountability and transparency, they are required to provide annual "benefit reports" for shareholders and the public. As former Delaware chief justice Leo Strine told me, the language defining the benefit corporation was carefully crafted. It doesn't say that companies "may" consider their obligations to stakeholders; it says they "shall" do so. This adds an additional layer of accountability because it allows shareholders and others to take action if they believe that stakeholder interests are not adequately represented.

Benefit corporation status signals a commitment to sustainability and community, so these businesses attract investors and customers with similar values. More than ten thousand such companies exist worldwide, although they still only account for a small fraction of corporations.[5] States as diverse as California, Kansas, Texas, and Vermont have adopted benefit corporation bills, and governors across party lines—from Deval Patrick (Democrat of Massachusetts) to Mike Pence (Republican of Indiana) and Nikki Haley (Republican of South Carolina)—have signed them.

While a good start, these changes are clearly not enough. We need to go deeper into the governance of firms—including the duties of directors and corporate accountability systems—and have these types of changes move from voluntary to mandatory and diffuse around the world more fully.

Ripples of Change

Robert F. Kennedy's famous "Ripple of Hope" speech, which he delivered in June 1966 at the University of Cape Town, South Africa, when apartheid was its height, contains an evocative metaphor that can be applied to systems change of all kinds. He said, "Each time a man stands up for an ideal or acts to improve the lot of others or strikes out against injustice, he sends forth a tiny ripple of hope, and crossing each other from a million different centers of energy and daring, those ripples build a current that can sweep down the mightiest wall of oppression and resistance."[6]

The ripples unleashed by the move toward benefit corporations have grown into deeper currents. One reached Italy in 2015. Paolo Di Cesare and Eric Ezechieli founded a company called Nativa to provide consulting services on issues of corporate sustainability.

In drafting the company's founding documents, Ezechieli said, "we took a stand about Nativa's purpose. In the bylaws, we put 'happiness' as the purpose for the entire Nativa team, and 'stakeholder inclusion and paradigm shift toward regeneration' as its social objects." But when the cofounders went to the chamber of commerce to get the license, "they had completely crossed out everything that wasn't about profits." After resubmitting the papers four more times, the Nativa team wore the bureaucrats down. "Eventually they said, 'OK, we will take it as you want it. But please be aware, this is not recognized by the law because the civil code that defines all businesses says that the only purpose of a corporation is to distribute dividends to shareholders—there cannot be any other purpose. We'll give you the license, but please be aware, this is not legal. It's your own problem if someone raises questions.'"

So they sat down and thought about how they could change the law. Di Cesare reflected on some of the options they considered: "We could establish a political party—no, that would take too long. Maybe an online petition, talk with some parliamentary reps? What if Italy could become the first sovereign state to introduce benefit corporations?" They approached an Italian senator, Mauro Del Barba, who was interested in the idea, and formed a working group to craft the legislation. It was formally proposed in April 2015 and approved on January 1, 2016. One thing Di Cesare and Ezechieli learned over the course of their journey was that they were not alone; other Italian business leaders shared both their desire to advance sustainability and regeneration and their sense of urgency. Within a few short years, more than one thousand companies, including multibillion-dollar corporations such as Chiesi Farmaceutici and, as noted earlier, Illycaffè had become benefit corporations.[7]

Benefit corporation legislation was adopted in Colombia and Puerto Rico in 2018, in British Columbia, Ecuador, and France (as the *entreprise à mission*) in 2019, Peru in 2020, and Rwanda in 2021. As of this writing, it is under formal consideration in more than ten other countries.

Catching on in Public Markets

There has been a substantial shift in both public opinion and the markets. When I originally started teaching this topic at Harvard

Business School, soon after the first benefit corporation law was passed in 2010, many of my students balked at the idea. Such structures may work for small companies that are tightly controlled, they said, or even a handful of larger ones that have strong missions. But the overwhelming consensus was that larger investors would never go for such structures.

Those assumptions have now been overturned, and the ripples of change have started to penetrate the public markets, as witnessed by the strong opening-day performance of the online insurer Lemonade, a company focused on bringing transparency and affordability to a notoriously shady industry, which went public in July 2020.[8] Up until then, the only benefit corporation on major US exchanges was Laureate Education, which had its initial public offering (IPO) on NASDAQ in 2017. Following Lemonade, Vital Farms, which produces ethically raised egg and dairy products, went public on NASDAQ, and its stock climbed 60 percent on its first day.[9] Many other companies have followed, including AppHarvest, a company focused on sustainable indoor farming, with Martha Stewart on its board; Coursera, the well-known online education platform, listed with a market cap approaching $6 billion; and the shoe company Allbirds, mentioned previously for its innovations in carbon emissions accountability.[10]

One of most telling examples of this trend took place in late 2021, when the eyewear retailer Warby Parker listed its shares on the New York Stock Exchange (NYSE). Right before going public, Warby Parker reorganized as a benefit corporation and also certified as a B Corporation, a type of company whose social and environmental performance is verified by the independent nonprofit B Lab. This was notable because, while Warby Parker had been one of the earliest B Corps, under pressure from investors and directors it had let its certification lapse in 2018.[11] But this model is now well tested in the public markets, as shown by analysts' positive or neutral reaction to the ten-plus benefit corporations that went public in 2020 and 2021, and so the company rejoined the B Corp community before going public.[12]

When Zymergen, a bio-manufacturing company, had its IPO as a benefit corporation in 2021, Pam Marcogliese and Sarah Solum, its lawyers, explained to me that the company did so to provide a "favorable fiduciary duty framework for directors." Marcogliese and Solum, who also coauthored a book about public benefit corporations, emphasized that the model has been shown to help in recruitment, retention, morale, and brand building, while also attracting impact investors.

While activist investors successfully pressed for Faber's ouster at Danone, it is worth noting that 99 percent of shareholders supported the company's conversion to an *entreprise à mission*. Faber told me that the long-term benefits it brought to Danone were significant. Danone was able to renegotiate the terms of a €2 billion syndicated banking loan so that the interest rate fell over time, so long as the company continued to meet its ESG goals and got a certain percentage of its sales from B Corp–certified divisions.

Recruitment numbers jumped considerably as Danone climbed the ranks of French students' fifty favorite companies. Employees supported the company, even when COVID forced it to cut two thousand jobs. Four out of its five major labor unions approved its reorganization plan, which is unheard of in France.

As Faber told me, "The benefit model allows directors to say, 'We're going to make some trade-offs.'" Even shareholders recognize that some of those trade-offs are necessary, as the externalities will inevitably hit their pocketbooks in time, a topic we will discuss in more detail in the next chapter.

A number of public companies in the United States have followed Danone's cue. Veeva Systems, an NYSE-traded cloud-computing company focused on life sciences, passed a shareholder resolution to transition into a benefit corporation in February 2021.[13] Founder and CEO Peter Gassner told me that the change not only reflected his ideals but also made good business sense. "We've always believed that doing the right thing for customers and employees is ultimately good for shareholders," he said. "Aligning our purpose and charter will give customers continued confidence to partner with Veeva over the long term and help attract world-class talent to the company for decades to come." Amalgamated Bank and United Therapeutics recently converted as well.

Unlike undergoing an IPO, where a company discloses its corporate form in a prospectus and investors then choose to buy or not, a conversion to a public benefit corporation needs the approval of the board and a majority of shareholders. So it is notable that these companies are convincing their existing shareholders to change the corporate structure from one that prioritizes shareholders above all to one that emphasizes all social and environmental missions. Overall, as of this writing, there are over fifteen benefit corporations in US public markets and about twenty-five others with similar structures in geographies as diverse as Brazil, Chile, Taiwan, the United Kingdom, and more.

Taking Legal Accountability to the Next Level

Faber told me that a crucial lesson from his case is that it is not enough to simply shift corporate form. New governance mechanisms are needed to ensure that the board and majority investors are aligned with the change. The board that ousted him was inherited from the past; the company's decision to replace nearly all its board members, announced in 2021, means that it will soon have a board that is entirely in sync with its *entreprise à mission* structure.

Enter the Better Business Act (BBA) in the United Kingdom, another ripple outward, which proposes to redefine all corporations by revising section 172 of the UK Companies Act. As of this writing, it has garnered support from more than two thousand companies and 76 percent of the UK population.[14] Chris Turner, who chairs the campaign for the BBA, explained to me the act includes governance changes to better align directors. "We describe this as the 'job description' for the director, outlining their responsibilities to company mission and stakeholders in law. In current legislation this is incredibly ambiguous."

The European Union is also in the process of implementing a Corporate Sustainability Due Diligence Directive, which proposes that directors of large businesses should be required to take the interests of those affected by the company's decisions into account as part of a broader, integrated commitment to long- and short-term sustainability strategies.[15] The implications of this law, if it makes it through the complex EU processes, could be significant, as it does not just apply to EU-headquartered companies but to companies that do business in the EU, which include many of the largest and most important companies in the United States and China. Thus, the EU policy may result in a shift in global corporate governance standards.

While the history of these efforts to shift corporate governance has not been linear, the direction of travel is clear and illustrative of how systems change works. What started as new and voluntary practices in the United States became more rigorous over time as they spread to other regions and countries so that now, in the UK and EU, the work to make governance that holds companies accountable for broader sustainability mandatory is in process.

Trust but Verify

Transparency and accountability are crucial to reform and should be much more widely embedded in these new business models. There have been many innovations regarding how to measure and track the social and environmental impacts of companies, yet they remain, for the most part, up to the individual company to undertake.

For many of the early actors in this space, the implicit theory of change reflected Supreme Court justice Louis Brandeis's famous dictum that "sunlight is the best disinfectant." But it is not clear that theory holds up in today's information environment. As awash as we already are in information and misinformation, voluntary reporting and related initiatives provide the illusion of accountability but are unlikely to result in systemic change. Thus, while the innovations made are a good first step and essential for creating new models and understanding what is possible, as I detail below, the ultimate goal should be changes in policy.

Over the past two decades, a veritable alphabet soup of voluntary systems have been created that provide transparency and accountability, like the Global Reporting Initiative (GRI), the Sustainability Accounting Standards Board (SASB), and the Carbon Disclosure Project (CDP). The Task Force on Climate-Related Financial Disclosures (TCFD), created in 2015 by the Group of Twenty and Financial Stability Board, has developed a widely recognized system that evaluates companies' compliance with climate-related disclosure regulations.[16] Its framework was incorporated into the United Kingdom's legal systems in 2021 and may be adopted by other countries including Canada and Australia.[17]

B Lab's B Impact Assessment (BIA) tool is another nonprofit-based voluntary system that uses objective metrics to assess company performance on governance, workers, customers, community, and environment, taking the company's size, sector, and geographical region into account. As of late 2023, there were about 7,500 B Corps worldwide—a relatively small number in the grand scheme of things, due, in part, to the rigor of the BIA assessment.[18] But more than 250,000 non–B Corps companies also use the BIA to assess the management of their operations. Cutting-edge private equity and venture capital investors like Bridges Fund Management also used it to assess investment prospects.

We should not discount the importance of these voluntary systems. For the last two-plus decades, entrepreneurs across sectors have significantly developed and refined them. Without their innovation and rigorous approach, our understanding of how to hold companies socially and environmentally accountable would be much less advanced, and the idea of ESG accountability would not have diffused so widely. But as helpful as these assessments are, if the goal is systemic change, such disclosures must become mandatory through governmental policy.

To that end, on March 21, 2022, the SEC proposed that Scope 1 and 2 greenhouse gas emissions should be included in annual filings to the government, such as 10-Ks.[19] Indirect emissions from upstream and downstream activities (Scope 3) would also need to be included if material, or if the company had set an emissions target. This sounds like a hugely positive development, except for the words "if material." Unfortunately, the reigning standard for deciding what companies have to disclose is financial materiality: whether such disclosures would affect the companies' financial position or, as the US Supreme Court defined it in the 1970s, whether there is "a substantial likelihood that the . . . fact would have been viewed by the reasonable investor as having significantly altered the 'total mix' of information made available."[20] As SEC chair Gary Gensler put it when testifying before the Senate Banking Committee, "It's the investor community that gets to decide what's material."[21]

But in ceding "materiality" to investors, policymakers are propping up the doctrine of shareholder supremacy. From the perspective of governments, what's material, and what should be their core concern, is what's important to the society and the planet. Scope

3 emissions, which can account for between 70 and 90 percent of corporate greenhouse gas emissions, are also clearly essential to consider. But corporate and industry groups such as the Business Roundtable vehemently oppose the SEC's efforts. In formal comments filed with the SEC, twenty-one Republican state legal officers, led by West Virginia attorney general Patrick Morrisey, argued that the SEC is trying to transform itself from the federal overseer of securities "into the regulator of broader social ills."[22] As Morrisey put it, "The woke left is going full throttle in their mission to change every facet of American life . . . and erode our democratic institutions to suit their liberal agenda."

While the opposition is fierce, it is only in recent years that Republicans have ginned up controversy over these kinds of disclosures to rally supporters. Most are just piling on a hot trend, encouraged by lobbyists and others with highly pragmatic agendas. While BlackRock's Larry Fink's pronouncements have garnered a lot of press coverage in recent years, ESG investing has actually been routine on Wall Street for years.[23] As far back as 2010, I wrote a Harvard case study about how and why Bloomberg introduced ESG indicators onto its platform.[24] The "why" was because investors were clamoring for them. And more recently, a 2022 investment industry survey showed that environmental, social, and governance issues have become a priority for 85 percent of asset managers.[25]

Given widespread agreement that many of these metrics, especially climate-related disclosures, have potential future financial impacts on firms, to argue against them makes it clear which set of actors are putting their ideology above economic reality.

For instance, a recent report published by the public policy consultancy Pleiades Strategy looked closely at 165 pieces of anti-ESG legislation that Republican lawmakers introduced in thirty-seven states.[26] After examining the news articles, fiscal notes, and statehouse testimony related to each of them, the researchers found that the majority of these laws bore a striking resemblance to model bills crafted and circulated by four influential right-wing think tanks: the American Legislative Exchange Council, the Heritage Foundation, the Heartland Institute, and the Foundation for Government Accountability, all of which are very cozy with the fossil fuel industry. For all their complaints about ESG's relevance to company finances and the fiduciary malfeasance of putting a liberal political agenda before profits, most of these organizations are just a smoke screen for advancing the interests of fossil fuel companies.

Unfortunately for those ideological holdouts, the writing is on the wall. The European Sustainability Reporting Standards (ESRS), which were created by the European Commission in 2023 to modernize and strengthen the rules concerning mandatory disclosures, are likely to be a game changer.[27] Crucially, the ESRS differ from other regulations and systems in three important aspects: the definition of materiality, the topic coverage, and the application to companies beyond those headquartered in the European Union (including US companies) if they want to compete there. This last aspect will have the effect of making the ideological thrashing over the SEC regulations meaningless.

Importantly, the ESRS regard financial materiality and social and environmental impact as parts of the broader concept of "double materiality," which differs substantially from the US SEC's prioritization of investors. Further, the ESRS provide more detailed guidance on the environmental, social, and governance information required. This significantly broadens the scope of what companies are required to report and does not rely on investors as the primary judge, as is the focus of the SEC and commentators like Larry Fink.

The ESRS will also go beyond the environmental bias in US standards. Because it overweights financial materiality, the SEC hones in on environmental factors, where it is easier to make this link. As Dan Romanoff, an equity research analyst who covers Amazon for Morningstar, told CNBC, of the three ESG categories, social factors are "not something that investors are really focusing on all that much."[28] These new EU standards will require companies to report on their policies and their impacts on their own workforce, workers in their value chain, their consumers, and affected communities.

EU companies will have to submit their first reports in 2025, and non-EU companies—including US ones—in 2027 or 2028. So while US states, regulatory bodies, firms, and investors are getting tied in knots about the wokeness of ESG, such debates will be moot in the future, if these companies want to compete in the European Union.

———

Shareholder primacy did not get established as a powerful paradigm overnight and neither will a shift in the other direction. While voluntary alignment and accountability standards are important first moves to test ideas and refine models over time, there needs to be much stronger legal alignment not just to shareholders but to a broader set of stakeholders. Directors need a new job description that recognizes this change too.

A further point is that relying solely on companies to voluntarily adopt ESG standards will not be sufficient to drive social change. While the many systems that have been created are important for their innovations in understanding social and environmental impact and diffusing the idea of sustainability and corporate responsibility more widely, there are significant flaws with a lot of ESG thinking nowadays.

At the core of ESG metrics as they are mostly conceived today is investor materiality, which from a public standpoint is flawed, as it is a fluid concept open to various interpretations and by definition determined by the financial position of a company. What is needed is a more encompassing idea of materiality that prioritizes societal concerns, such as is emerging in the European Union, and mandatory accountability.

This chapter has also illustrated that systems change is complex and multifaceted and requires action on many fronts: governments, investors, and corporations. When these different currents come together, larger waves are created on the horizon. In the next chapter, we will see some more of these important ripples. While shareholder activism can be a tool for short-term, shareholder-focused action, it is a double-edged sword, and we will explore next how it can also be used to force companies and investors to adopt system-first thinking.

9

Commons First Finance
and Ownership

Spend enough time exposed to society's ills, and eventually you'll feel the need to do something about them—at least, that was the case with Rick Alexander. For close to three decades, this modern revolutionary worked as a corporate lawyer, helping companies fulfill their shareholder-primacy mandates. During that time, he was recognized as one of the top ten corporate governance lawyers worldwide and made the list of five hundred leading lawyers in the United States. Shareholder primacy "isn't an amoral model," Alexander told me. "It just posits that externalities are the concern of government and not of industry." Even so, he found it harder and harder to live with the consequences.

In 2015, he shifted his career from being part of a group of Delaware lawyers who were the de facto trustees of American corporate law and became head of legal policy at B Lab, the global nonprofit that certifies B Corporations based on their ESG performance. During his four years in that role, he spearheaded the creation of public benefit corporation law, which, as we have seen in the last chapter, allows companies to align their operations with their beliefs by pursuing both profits and ESG principles.

But making this shift did not initially come naturally to him. He recalled that when the B Lab cofounders approached Delaware about changing its corporate law, "we thought they were kind of silly and naive and not something we wanted to mess with." But when he read the late Cornell law professor Lynn Stout's book *The Shareholder Value Myth*, things clicked into place and he realized that what "I've just assumed for twenty-five years are just bad assumptions." He told me he was particularly affected by the argument that if a person acted the way that corporations are allowed to act, if they "did everything possible to maximize their own value, as long as they follow the law, without caring how much they hurt other people or the environment, we would call that person a sociopath." And yet, as he has come to understand, this is what traditional investors expect boards of directors to do. Instead of considering a company successful as long as it provides a return on capital, Alexander now believes we should consider a company successful if it provides a return on our capital *without* depleting other capitals, be they human, natural, or social.

But while Alexander's work on benefit corporation law was crucial in getting change off the ground, he was impatient to do more. In 2019, he founded the Shareholder Commons, a nonprofit focused on the power of advocacy—specifically, how to effectively use shareholder proposals to hold companies accountable for their externalities. As investors increasingly recognize the effect of externalities on their portfolios, they can become a potent lever for change. We'll dig into his work in this chapter and also detail many other ways that individuals, companies, and industries are using their ownership stakes to shift the paradigm away from the short-term shareholder focus of Friedman and his followers.

We'll also look at the Long-Term Stock Exchange (LTSE), an SEC approved and regulated market like the NYSE and NASDAQ. The key difference is that companies listed on the exchange have agreed to measure their impacts over years and decades rather than quarters, while developing structures to facilitate long-term planning and value creation. Finally, we will consider new ownership models that aim to democratize the distribution of capital. Overall, these different constituencies and their actions are aiming not only to develop new methods to address negative externalities but also to shift attention to the positive side of the externality ledger and address systemic issues in ways that create virtuous-cycle spillovers to employees, communities, and the environment.

The Costs of Externalities Are Unavoidable in Large Investment Portfolios

Most investors are trained to think about the returns of individual companies. Alexander and a growing number of investors look at the economy in a systems-first way—that is, they take a more macro view and consider investments from the perspective of their effect on overall portfolios, as opposed to in a one-off fashion, as has been the traditional approach. They see large institutional investors like pension funds, mutual funds, and insurance companies as powerful levers for change.

These investors are what is known as "universal owners," a term that refers to an entity that holds a portfolio that is highly diversified across various asset classes, such as stocks, bonds, real estate, and other financial instruments, and, therefore, their overall returns effectively represent the whole economy. These actors are quite substantial. For instance, as of 2021, the pension assets of countries in the OECD group were worth $60 trillion, which is 105 percent of overall OECD GDP.[1] That is, these investment portfolios are essentially the size of the overall economies.

Instead of simply attempting to pick winners and avoid losers, universal owners in theory should acknowledge that the health of their portfolios depends on the health and stability of the market. They cannot ignore externalities because they are inevitably affected by them. If one company in their portfolio takes a shortcut on pollution abatement or employee benefits to boost its returns, the consequences will likely spill over to other companies in the portfolio, and thus negatively affect returns. For example, perhaps there would be higher insurance costs from pollution crises or natural disasters, so insurance companies in the portfolio would have lower returns.

But as Alexander explained, the effects of externalities are really not yet being considered by most investors. Therefore, there is a significant flaw in how they think about their investment portfolios. Here, Alexander described the "big, entrenched financial system that is still based on individual company financial return as the measure of success." He emphasized that, ironically, this objective is not in the best interest of the overall investor in diversified portfolios, because diversified investors cannot easily escape the systemic risks and challenges faced by the global economy. Environmental and social consequences and costs inevitably affect their returns in one way or another.

Antimicrobial resistance is a telling example. As we discussed in the opening chapters, AMR is a systemic risk, a problem that affects multiple interconnected systems simultaneously and can lead to the failure of an entire system or a significant segment of it. Companies in the food industry use antibiotics to fight the bacterial infections that livestock are susceptible to in factory farm conditions and also to help them grow faster. So, in short, such practices can lower costs for food companies and lead to higher profit margins. About 70 percent of all medically important antibiotics in the United States are sold for use in animals. The problem is that when antibiotics are used extensively, bacteria exposed to the drugs can develop resistance. These antibiotic-resistant bacteria, often referred to as "superbugs," can spread from animals to humans through various pathways, such as contaminated food, water, and direct contact with animals.

Because of this, the World Health Organization considers AMR one of the biggest threats to global health, food security, and development today.[2] In 2019, 1.27 million people died as a direct result of drug-resistant infections.[3] If we don't take action to decrease the use of antibiotics, it is projected that AMR will kill as many as ten million people a year by 2050, matching cancer's annual death toll.[4] At some point, even a simple cut or toothache could be fatal.

As a result, the potential financial costs to economies and investors are gigantic. By 2050, low-income countries are likely to lose more than 5 percent of their GDP because of AMR infections, costing the global economy as much as $100 trillion.[5] Clearly this is an externality of factory farming that is of real urgency, and one that governments must address so the world does not keep underwriting agribusiness profits. But systemic risks like this impact the portfolios of large investors because many of their investments are also exposed to this risk, so, as I discuss below, they can also provide a lever for change.

Using Shareholder Proposals to Reshape Corporate Action

Proxy voting, shareholder resolutions, and active ownership practices can have potent effects to reorient companies' priorities. This is where investors can play an important role. In the United States, shareholders who own at least 1 percent of a company can put forth a shareholder proposal. Once submitted, it must be added to the agenda of the next annual shareholders' meeting unless the company has formally challenged it and the SEC has allowed it to be excluded.

The philosophy of the Shareholder Commons is premised on the simple idea that asset managers must prioritize the returns of their whole portfolios over the performance of their parts. To that end, it helps shareholders use their power to demand sustainable practices, improve corporate governance, and address social and environmental challenges. "Part of what we want investors to do is be more aggressive in insisting that companies stop externalizing costs," Alexander told me.

One company the Shareholder Commons has engaged with directly is Yum! Brands, which owns Pizza Hut, KFC, and Taco Bell. AMR issues are particularly salient for the fast-food industry, and Yum! Brands has said it cares about the problem. So, in 2020, the Shareholder Commons filed a shareholder proposal demanding that "the board commission and disclose a study on the external environmental and public health costs created by the use of antibiotics in the supply chain of our company (the 'Company') and the manner in which such costs affect the vast majority of its shareholders who rely on a healthy stock market."[6] The company agreed to study the issue and eventually published a report that acknowledged the problem and stated that "one of the most significant barriers to meeting the challenge . . . is the balance between the rewards of proactive AMR mitigation and the cost of changing established husbandry practices." Follow-up and an action plan is clearly needed, but the company's recognition of the issue and commitment is a start.

As I write, Legal & General Investment Management (LGIM), Britain's biggest asset manager, is leading a shareholder revolt at McDonald's over its continued overuse of antibiotics in mass meat production. At the 2023 annual meeting, LGIM urged McDonald's to adopt World Health Organization rules on the use of antibiotics across its supply chain.[7] Although LGIM owns a significant amount of McDonald's shares, enough to make it a top-twenty shareholder, its concerns over system-wide AMR issues outweighs its interest in McDonald's short-term performance.

Another example of shareholder activism focused on systemic risks is a proposal, put forward by the Shareholder Commons, to the Tractor Supply Company, whose starting wages are 32 percent below the 2019 living wage as calculated by MIT's Living Wage Calculator. It read, in part, "Our proposal asks Tractor Supply to report on 1) whether it participates in compensation and workforce practices that prioritize its own financial performance over the economic and social costs created by inequality and racial and gender disparities and 2) how any such costs threaten returns of diversified shareholders who rely on a stable and productive economy." Both points are important because, as we have seen, greater inequality in a society has a significant negative effect on GDP, which should be a concern of universal owners as it affects overall portfolio return.

Andrew Behar, the CEO of the pioneering NGO As You Sow, which also works with shareholder activists, told me that sometimes the group doesn't even have to take action after threatening to put shareholder proposals to a vote. "Once we file a resolution," he said, "nearly half of companies agreed to get on the path to change and the resolution was withdrawn based on a written agreement with specific metrics and milestones."

In November 2022, for instance, As You Sow published a call for a resolution questioning AT&T's stand on racial justice.[8] While AT&T claimed equality as a core value, between June 1, 2020, and March 25, 2021, it contributed at least $228,000 to state lawmakers who introduced or sponsored legislation restricting public protests. The resolution had an effect. Five months later, in April 2023, AT&T reached an agreement with As You Sow, in which it promised to provide shareholders with increased transparency about its political spending.[9]

Behar told me that As You Sow is most effective when members sit down with company executives and highlight how they are hurting their own businesses. "Let's say the company scored a five out of one hundred on our Racial Justice Scorecard, and their competitor scored a twenty-seven. We show them six key performance indicators and break down the cost and return on investment of adopting them," he said. "We also show them the risk. A brand associated with racial injustice is not a competitive brand and may alienate their customers and miss out on investment opportunities. Inevitably the company will agree that our analysis and plan make good business sense."

Searching for Stronger Measures

In many ways, traditional shareholder advocacy is a long-term game. An active proponent of stakeholder capitalism, the investment adviser Trillium Asset Management helps companies improve their ESG policies. "Take, for example, a shareholder proposal filed at ExxonMobil asking it to amend its written equal employment opportunity policy to explicitly prohibit discrimination based on sexual orientation," Susan Baker, Trillium's director of shareholder advocacy, said. "The proposal was first filed in 2001 and was voted on for the next fifteen years, yet the company did not act on it until 2015, when they adopted a nondiscrimination policy that included protections for the LGBTQ community. In recent years, workforce diversity proposals have been receiving 40, 50 percent and several majority votes showing that investors want to see progress on this issue."

She continued, "Companies that are best able to attract, develop, and retain employees are likely better performers. The expansion of parental leave, sick time policies, and diversity and inclusion programs is an important area of focus. We press companies to demonstrate environmental responsibility . . . that goes beyond regulatory compliance."

A quicker way to incite change through shareholder activism is to target the board, though of course this is easier said than done. With regard to fossil fuel companies, activists are coalescing around the position that these companies need to be told "no new oil fields, or shareholders will vote against current directors."

The idea of bringing the case to those on the board is in some ways the most powerful and direct way to force corporate action. Shareholder votes against directors can have reputational consequences for both the directors and the company, generate negative publicity, and erode investor confidence, potentially impacting the company's stock price and market perception. To protect their reputations and maintain shareholder support, directors are especially compelled to respond to concerns that target them directly.

A conference of leading asset owners held at the University of Cambridge developed principles for asset owners who advocate voting against directors and taking other actions because "current academic evidence suggests that investors have the greatest impacts on company behaviour when they threaten to vote against the (re-)election of directors, decline to provide new capital, and encourage regulators."[10]

As You Sow uses all of these tactics. Starting in 2013, the NGO pushed ExxonMobil, Chevron, and others to share their plans for energy transition. Exxon shared a carbon asset risk report with them the following year, but, as Behar reflected, "it failed to address the key issues in a meaningful and accurate way."[11] As You Sow kept pushing, but "Exxon would not reveal any serious plans and a campaign was organized for a no-confidence vote. When that did nothing to change corporate behavior, shareholders concluded that they would have to run a dissident board slate."[12]

Exxon clearly believed it was in a strong position, perhaps because of how dispersed its ownership was, but As You Sow put together a slate and negotiated for three board seats in 2021. Engine No. 1, an activist hedge fund that was also pushing Exxon to take climate change seriously, ran a slate as well and won three seats. As You Sow subsequently lost one of those seats, but with five out of twelve board seats in the hands of the activist shareholders, the balance of power was beginning to shift. As of 2023, the substantive effect of these changes is not yet clear, but the activists continue to work on the board because, to truly force change, they need to hold a majority of the seats.[13]

As You Sow extends its activism into the courtroom as well. Behar told me the group is a plaintiff in a case at FirstEnergy and seven midsize oil and gas companies. "As shareholders and owners of companies," Behar said, "boards report to us. The board's job is to set strategy and incentivize the executives to carry it out. If boards will not consider and address the risks we are identifying, then exercising our responsibility as a shareholder is the last resort."

Shareholder Commons filed a class action lawsuit against Meta for using algorithms that spread disinformation, fuel violent arguments, contribute to mental health problems in adolescents, and encourage vaccine hesitancy.[14] Meta did not respond to the legal charges of ignoring harmful externalities. Instead, the company merely restated the core tenet of shareholder supremacy: that Meta's sole aim is to maximize share value and that it is not a public benefit corporation (which we discussed in the last chapter), which exempted it from the mandatory duty to promote public welfare. While Meta can find plenty of wiggle room under the current legal system, the lawsuit reminds shareholders in social media companies that this type of behavior causes adverse impacts in society and so has negative effects on other parts of their portfolios, and as ideas of universal ownership become more widespread, it is likely these companies will come under more scrutiny.[15]

Long-Term Stock Exchange

Some activists want to phase out the current system of stock market exchanges altogether and replace it with a new model that eliminates the short-termism baked into financial markets, which leads to underinvestment in innovation, workers, and anything else that creates value in the long run.[16] Enter Eric Ries and the Long-Term Stock Exchange. First proposed in his book *The Lean Startup* in 2011, the LTSE rewards companies that prioritize stakeholder approaches.[17] In 2015, Ries and Michelle Greene, the LTSE's honorary president and a member of its board of directors, raised $19 million from venture capitalists to get it off the ground. The SEC approved it and, on September 9, 2020, the Long-Term Stock Exchange began operations—the first new stock market exchange in California since the Pacific Exchange collapsed after the Internet bubble burst in 1999.[18]

The LTSE's requirements for listing and information disclosure are basically the same as the NYSE and NASDAQ. What's different are its corporate governance requirements and its demand that companies adhere to its five long-term development principles, overturning the shareholder-first institutions that have come to define the mainstream markets. In brief, these principles are:

- that companies consider a broader group of stakeholders and the critical role they play in one another's success;
- that they measure success in years and decades and prioritize long-term decision-making;
- that they align executive compensation and board compensation with long-term performance;

- that their boards have explicit oversight of their long-term strategy; and
- that they engage with their long-term shareholders.[19]

For each principle, the company must adopt and publish a specific operating policy that the LTSE will regularly audit to ensure that it complies. Companies that are found to not be in compliance will be delisted.[20]

LTSE's listing criteria is designed to match long-term investors with companies. The longer investors hold stocks, the greater the voting rights they are granted.[21] And the LTSE provides remedies when short-termism creeps in.

Etsy's NASDAQ IPO provides a cautionary tale in this regard. Etsy raised $267 million when it went public in 2015, but when a hedge fund holding 2 percent of the company started recruiting other major shareholders to promote "strategic options" (including the sale of the company), Etsy's board was forced to fire 8 percent of employees (eighty people). Had Etsy's IPO been on the LTSE, its founding management team would have been able to use "super voting" power to defend its mission against the hedge fund's attack.[22]

After decades of shareholder supremacy, the tide is turning. Initiatives like the LTSE that rethink the economy and capital may be small—there are only a handful of companies listed on it thus far—but they are generational plays and have the potential to drive the change that is needed system wide.

Democratizing Private Investment and Ownership

While this chapter has focused thus far on institutional investors, universal owners, and changing market structure, other investment and ownership mechanisms—including crowdfunding and employee and foundation ownership—promote fairer distribution of wealth in society as well.

Crowdfunding platforms are reshaping relationships between companies and investors while allowing consumers and less wealthy individuals to play roles in start-ups. Until 2016, direct financial investment in businesses was largely restricted to accredited investors in the United States, typically high-net-worth individuals or institutional investors. Crowdfunding platforms allow anyone to invest in a start-up they believe in and share in its potential return, regardless of their wealth or income level.

One pioneer in this space is Wefunder, whose founders advocated for new funding regulations that would remove private investment restrictions. They joined President Barack Obama in the White House Rose Garden when he signed the JOBS Act in 2012, which included the initial regulation crowdfunding provisions (Reg CF) that opened up this market. Initially, it allowed companies to raise up to approximately $1.07 million from non-registered investors in a twelve-month period. The limit was raised to $5 million as of March 2021.

Wefunder's platform hosts small and start-up companies and allows investors to contribute a minimum of $100 to their funding campaigns. Its goal is to make the economy more just, equitable, and community oriented through democratized, pre-IPO investing. As Jonny Price, Wefunder's director of fundraising, told me, "If you have a more democratic approach to who can be an investor, maybe we can level the playing field a little bit." He pointed out that crowdfunding also helps democratize investment recipients, as it makes it possible to get more capital to "entrepreneurs of color and women in Tennessee or Ohio as well as San Francisco, New York City, and Boston." As of late 2023, Wefunder has helped fund over three thousand start-ups and small businesses with over $641 million raised.

While Wefunder hosts a diverse range of companies—from tech start-ups to restaurants, breweries, and even indie film productions—a wide variety of crowdfunding platforms focus on specific areas such as causes (GoFundMe) or artists (Patreon). Indiegogo prides itself on being one of the only crowdfunding platforms that fosters investment in tech, hardware, and innovation products. Andy Yang, Indiegogo's CEO, said his company's mission is "to create a world-wide network of communities that connect trustworthy, professional entrepreneurs and the enthusiasts who power their innovation." Green tech is a particular strength for Indiegogo. Between 2020 and 2021, green tech funding raised on the site grew 145 percent and support grew 900 percent.[23]

The broad scope of investors these platforms serve accelerates the speed of change in investment markets while providing entre-preneurs with like-minded communities who will support both their brand and their mission as they grow. "There's this crazy gap between bank loans and venture capital," Wefunder's Price said. "Bank loans are usually only for established businesses. And then with venture capital, it's like, 'Unless you can show me the $1 billion total addressable market [the overall revenue opportunity from an investment], then you're not a good fit.' There is a striking homoge-neity of investment structures, and so there are a lot of businesses in the middle that fall between these two stools."

Although there are always risks for investors, both Wefunder and Indiegogo have a variety of fail-safes in place. Wefunder, for exam-ple, runs fraud and background checks and follows SEC and Finan-cial Industry Regulatory Authority guidelines, reminding would-be investors that "potential earnings are projections rather than guar-antees." Both companies were established as benefit corporations and have achieved B Corp certification, so their business models and procedures have been stress tested by a third party. Price shared a story with me about the time Wefunder noticed a company's investor notes were overly focused on the opportunity to "make a ton of money." When the Wefunder team investigated, they saw that the company was partaking in fraudulent activity, and its crowdfunding campaign was immediately halted.

Employee ownership is another powerful tool for democratizing investment. As noted, traditionally, investment in businesses has been the domain of a select few, typically wealthy individuals or institutional investors. One lesson I have learned is that no matter how sustainable and socially responsible a business aspires to be, if it is organized with traditional ownership structures—publicly traded, venture capital or private equity owned, family owned, LLC—by definition a disproportionate amount of its earnings will be funneled to its owners at the expense of its workers.

Companies may enjoy a good image because their products may be environmentally friendly and produced in ethical ways. But because greater gains in the business will flow to owners as opposed to employees, they will also be driving economic inequality. One way to close the gap between capital and wages is to distribute the ownership in a business to its workers. Sustainable business pioneer Jeffrey Hollender, cofounder of green consumer products giant Seventh Generation, told me: "I don't think you can be a responsible business without being committed to employee ownership, because otherwise your business acts as a way to concentrate wealth."

Corey Rosen and John Case, authors of *Ownership: Reinventing Companies, Capitalism, and Who Owns What*, argue that employee ownership enables people to become owners, not through their savings (with wages stagnant in real dollars since the 1970s, they are rarely enough to accumulate substantial ownership) but through their work. When companies share ownership with employees, both sides gain. Rosen and Case assert that the data is unambiguous: employee-owned companies grow faster and create vastly more wealth. When a company is owned (wholly or in part) by its employees, it allows a broader group of individuals to have a stake in the business. This not only provides employees with a direct financial interest in the company's success but also promotes a more equitable distribution of wealth. It gives employees a voice in the company's direction and decisions, fostering a sense of collective responsibility and commitment.

But as is all too common with people whose mindsets are deeply baked in free market ideology, many leading economists reflexively oppose employee ownership. As former US Treasury secretary Larry Summers put it at a 2019 conference, "When you put workers in charge of firms and you give them substantial control, the one thing you do not get is expansion. You get more for the people who are already there."[24]

But the real story is quite different. Researchers have shown that incentives are better aligned in employee owned and controlled firms: workers understand that they succeed when their organization succeeds and so are more productive. Cooperatively owned firms typically have higher profitability than their publicly or privately owned peers.[25] Ironically, this is the exact same logic that elite venture capital investors give for the stock options and control rights that are lavished on the employees of tech start-ups.

An in-depth piece in the *New Yorker* about Mondragon Corporation, a voluntary association of ninety-five employee-owned companies, provides many examples of the advantages employee ownership confers, especially employee retention.[26] "If I worked outside of Mondragon, I would earn more money," Ion Beltza, an engineer and industrial director at Fagor Automation, said. "But I prefer to live here with a lot of people and friends than alone like a king."

I have seen scores of companies implement this model. For all the talk about the freedom of the gig economy, Kimberly Jones, the

CEO of the media and communications agency Butler/Till, said that employee ownership "strengthens communities, fosters a financially savvy workforce, increases resiliency during recessions, and offers big benefits during economic booms." Consider the marketing agency Global Prairie, founded by Anne St. Peter and Douglas Bell in 2008. Employee ownership was one of Global Prairie's goals from the very beginning, and St. Peter connected the dots for me between employee ownership and "building a better business." She said that the company's strong year-over-year growth (it now has offices in nine cities around the world) is a direct result of the decision to focus on being 100 percent employee owned.

Paul Burns founded Fireclay Tile, an eco-friendly handmade tile company, in 1986. Recently, Fireclay's leadership team agreed to buy his shares in the company, which amounted to a little under a third of the company's ownership. CEO Eric Edelson had thought about selling the company and even began the process. When a sale didn't materialize, he decided to buy out the owner. "Convincing our board and investors to redistribute almost all of the ownership to our employees took about eight or nine months of negotiation," he said. "Usually when you buy out an owner, you simply retire their shares and all the other owners collectively increase their ownership. That's the natural approach. The unnatural thing in this case was taking almost all of it and creating a new stock-option plan to redistribute that ownership among our employees." Employees are eligible for the ownership program from their first day on the job. Edelson wasn't simply driven by feel-good sentiments; Fireclay has seen increased employee engagement, reduced turnover, and bottom-line benefits. The company's revenues have increased 800 percent since it created its first stock-option plan in 2013. "Anyone who's come to visit Fireclay feels something different about it," he said. "They walk through our factory and they see engaged team members. They meet our team, and our team just speaks positively about each other and about the culture."

In Europe, a common form of ownership is through enterprise foundations: independent, self-governing entities with philanthropic as well as business objectives. They are most common in Denmark, accounting for almost half of domestic stock market capitalization, including three of the four largest Danish companies: A. P. Moller-Maersk (A. P. Moller Foundation), Novo Nordisk (Novo Nordisk Foundation), and Carlsberg (Carlsberg Foundation).[27] Other well-known European companies—including Bosch, Rolex, and IKEA—are all owned by enterprise foundations.

As such, ownership by foundations helps democratize wealth by ensuring that the benefits of a company's success are shared more broadly and used to create societal value. For instance, the Beneficial State Foundation is a nonprofit charitable organization that owns the majority of Beneficial State Bank. To its cofounders—Kat Taylor and 2020 presidential candidate and billionaire investor Tom Steyer—it seemed a natural way to maximize the bank's positive social and environmental impacts. As Taylor told me, "Banking is really a utility that should be governed in the public interest. We had a hunch that this powerful positive public system was going terribly awry. Somebody had to set an example for the banking industry that said, 'You can be financially sustainable without trashing people or the planet.'" With about $1.5 billion in assets, Beneficial has offices in California, Oregon, and Washington.

Such ownership structures became even more well-known when, in 2022, the ownership of Patagonia was transferred from the Chouinard family to two foundations that will ensure that the company's values are upheld and that Patagonia's profits are used to combat climate change. Patagonia's Vincent Stanley told me how this step was a natural evolution to ensure the full realization of the company's purpose, independence, and values, which include not only climate action but also worker well-being. Patagonia thus added two important principles to the company's legal structure: purpose orientation, which turns profit generation from an end to a means, and self-governance, which requires voting rights to be distributed to "stewards" whose values align with the company.

———

Profit maximization is driven by the short-term financial concerns of companies. It is not the natural state of the world per se but how financial systems have been constructed over the past fifty-plus years that focused investors on individual returns instead of considering the risks of externalities to their overall portfolios. It follows that these ideas can be reversed, and so, in the right hands, ownership can lay the groundwork for systemic change in our markets and economy. Organizations like the Shareholder Commons and As You Sow are using the standard mechanisms available to investors as a lever to push big companies to better understand how systemic risks affect their returns and so change for the better. They are focused on effective use of shareholder activism and advocacy to hold companies accountable for their externalities.

Beyond this, there are many ways that other individuals, companies, and industries are working to shift that paradigm via new approaches to finance that use ownership stakes to put systems first—that is, prioritizing the commons. For example, the LTSE and crowdfunding platforms are changing the rules of investment with their commitment to stakeholder benefit. Other forms of ownership that broaden considerations beyond traditional shareholders, such as employee ownership and purpose trusts, aim to change how capital is distributed throughout society more generally.

In the next chapter, we will see how businesses are generating change within themselves and working together to create broader movements as well.

10

Corporate Activism
for the Commons

As the daughter of a leader of one of Canada's first environmental protection groups, Char Love has always had climate advocacy as a big part of her life. From an early age, she saw how individuals can work collectively for change. As an adult, she has exemplified what real corporate activism—not the gaslighting kind—can and should look like. In 2023, she was global director of advocacy for Natura &Co, where she coordinated a worldwide network of partners for the Brazilian-headquartered company, which includes Avon Products.

"Those of us who work in business actually have a special kind of power," Love said. "It is vital that we find ways to help channel that power in a direction that can drive system-level changes." She emphasized that, perhaps more than anyone else, business leaders are the best positioned to change destructive policies and systems and make decisions that affect real, lasting change.

She quotes Harvard political scientist Erica Chenoweth's research, which found that when 3.5 percent of any population, but especially mass movements that include people with some form of power, engage in nonviolent civil disobedience, they can shift systems and worlds.[1] Examples include the People Power movement that toppled the Marcos family in the Philippines in 1986, the Singing Revolution in Estonia in the late 1980s that led to the state's independence, the Rose Revolution in Georgia that ousted President Eduard Shevardnadze in early 2003, and many others.

Collaborating with leaders of companies of varied sizes and industries, Love saw the potential they had to get people involved in social and environmental advocacy, especially those from what is referred to as the "moderate flank"—people who care about issues and want to help create change but won't be chaining themselves to buildings. "Right now, I feel like the world needs some very strong and solid examples of big businesses willing to set ambitious, radical climate strategies rooted in what we know is needed rather than limited by what feels possible," she said.

Love told me about a definition of activism she saw that really inspired her: "Seeing your edge and being able to step beyond it." "I love that so much," she said, "because it means activism is actually a relative term. For example, someone who has never been to a protest could step beyond that edge by simply joining a protest. Speaking up in a meeting where you would have normally stayed quiet is another way to step beyond that edge. Activism is a relative concept, and it's important that we all understand our individual edges so that we can figure out how to push beyond them."

This chapter, following Love's lead, will spend some time outlining how businesses can work, alone and together with others, to engage in corporate activism. Changing the system, as discussed earlier, requires us to create a tipping point whereby the economy better recognizes the costs of business on society. Business activists can help us advance that idea by drawing attention to new models and building partnerships with other organizations to amplify efforts and bring more resources and expertise to bear on the issue. Finally, another important way to effect change is to advocate for policies or laws that directly address the issue at hand.

Taking a Stand with Products and Services

The first things that likely come to mind when we think about corporate activism are media campaigns that use social justice issues as marketing hooks. Many are so transparently disingenuous that we simply ignore them or roll our eyes. But while we need to stay vigilant for greenwashing and gaslighting, we shouldn't throw the baby out with the bathwater either. Sometimes, companies really do set an example for change. Love pointed to Patagonia, which took a stance against misinformation by suspending all of its advertising on Facebook and encouraging others to do the same.

A conceit of neoliberalism—one that has done incalculable damage to our communities and to the planet itself—is that the economic sphere is separable from the social sphere. As Love described, corporate activism can help to change that. As polls have shown, a majority of consumers want companies to take a stand on social issues. A June 2020 survey, for example, found that 57 percent of respondents expect companies they buy from to support racial equity, social justice, and antidiscrimination and engage their employees in that work; 46 percent expect corporations to vet new products for their impacts on the environment.[2] The Internet fosters more conversation between consumers and companies—and allows customers to organize when they are unhappy with a company's positions.

When I asked Vincent Stanley from Patagonia about corporate activism, he said, "We've made a shift to take a stronger public stance on issues that might be more controversial, but they are issues that we've been involved with for thirty years. We know what we're talking about, and we're connected to the people who know more than we do." The most important thing, he said, is that Patagonia's activism is genuine: "If it's used as a marketing ploy, it's just going to turn people away. But we have seen a change in generational values. Millennials and Gen Z are much more responsive than boomers and Gen X to doing business with companies whose practices they value."

Authenticity and knowing one's customers are essential for developing an effective corporate activism platform. But while these efforts may resonate with certain consumer segments, they can also spark backlash in our polarized social and political climate. Efforts might be attacked as "woke" activism if the causes a company supports include such "controversial" topics as diversity, inclusion, and environmental sustainability. Taking a public stance on sensitive matters can potentially alienate a portion of a company's customer base, which can lead to negative publicity, boycotts, and potentially lasting damage to a brand.

In April 2023, beer brand Bud Light found itself engulfed in controversy when it hired Dylan Mulvaney, a transgender social media influencer with millions of Instagram and TikTok followers, to participate in a product promotion during the US collegiate basketball championships. Following Mulvaney's post promoting the beer, there were calls for boycotts, which significantly affected Bud Light's sales and Anheuser-Busch's share valuation, leading the brewer to announce that two of its marketing executives would take a leave of absence.[3]

But corporations today are in a tough place, as it's impossible to avoid politics altogether. "In a politically polarized world that is saturated in social media, you're not going to escape politics," said Jerry

Davis, a professor of management and sociology at the University of Michigan. "This is a sea change—in the past, companies kept their heads down and did their best to never be seen."[4]

When Warner Bros. released the movie *Barbie* in 2023, Fox News repeatedly attacked the film over everything from its feminist themes and "wokeness" to its inclusion of a transgender performer and even its support of Chinese propaganda (a map is briefly seen on screen that was said to include China's "nine-dash line," marking its disputed claim to the South China Sea). Fox broadcasters vowed that *Barbie* would get "the Bud Light treatment," but the movie's blockbuster performance made them look foolish.[5]

Companies need to walk a fine line between pretending it's all business as usual and dealing with potential backlash from customers with opinions that run counter to those the brand is supporting. The best way for companies to build positive and lasting relationships with the communities they serve is to genuinely align their actions with their values. While taking a stand on certain issues may alienate some consumer segments, it can strengthen brand loyalty among others, as many of the activist companies I've profiled in these pages have shown. We can specifically learn some important lessons from companies who have been effectively pushing social change for decades.

Learning from the Activist Old Guard

As Love noted, corporate activism is not a new phenomenon. Well-known and incredibly successful companies like Ben & Jerry's, Patagonia, and the Body Shop have successfully engaged in this type of work since their inceptions, and taking a stand is deeply tied to their identity and mission.

Since its founding in 1978 as a scoop shop in Burlington, Vermont, Ben & Jerry's has become the top-ranked US ice-cream brand and sells its products in thirty-eight countries.[6] But the strength of its brand is inseparable from its founders' three-part mission: economic, social, and product. Ben & Jerry's work on progressive issues—including racial justice, the environment, and refugees—has led to greater customer loyalty and stronger bonds with its employees and business partners.[7] In addition to supporting its own employees' engagement in movements like Black Lives Matter, the company has urged the US Congress to pass H.R. 40, the Commission to Study and Develop Reparation Proposals for African Americans Act.[8]

Reflecting on how Ben & Jerry's contrasts with traditional corporate responsibility initiatives, Rob Michalak, Ben & Jerry's long-time director of social mission special projects, told me, "We quickly understood that philanthropy is a wonderful thing, but that philanthropy is quite ephemeral in terms of, you sign a check and you provide a grant, and once it's spent, it's gone. That's when we started to examine how we could take those attributes of philanthropy and incorporate them right into the business structure."

In 2019, Ben & Jerry's launched Justice ReMix'd, a new flavor featuring cinnamon and chocolate ice creams, and directed its revenue into a variety of causes supporting criminal justice reform. As part of the company's "Silence is not an option" campaign following the murder of George Floyd, it issued four policy-oriented calls to action.

"Well before same-sex benefits were being discussed," Michalak said, "there were some LGBTQ couples who realized that married heterosexual couples were getting benefits that LGBTQ couples weren't getting. So, we were one of the first companies to offer LGBTQ couples the same benefits as married heterosexual couples. We thought, 'Wait a minute. We're living those values and we need to be brave enough to support them.' So, we had campaigns, and continue to advocate for LGBTQ rights."

In 1989, when Ben & Jerry's first codified its mission statement, it was clear that the company was determined to speak out on social, economic, and environmental issues. "It's kind of spiritual, almost biblical, like the golden rule," Michalak continued. "As you give you receive. The more you stick to good ideals and values that treat others as you want them to treat you, then you will also be treated well. While we have many people who disagree with us, others deeply agree and are very loyal and we've seen great success over the years by holding true to our values and publicly advocating for them."

By sharing its values transparently, Ben & Jerry's has grown a large and loyal following, but the company acknowledges it has also likely alienated some. "We respect that some people will have a set of values that are meaningful and important to them, and we may lose some customers," Michalak said. "But what we've also learned is that those who share our values are more deeply loyal." He told me the company did some internal research that suggested that the supporters are actually two-and-a-half times more loyal than regular customers, and they appreciate that the company stands for something and is authentic about it. But ultimately, profits and consumerism is not why Ben & Jerry's takes on these issues.

I heard similar sentiments from Patagonia's Stanley, who described to me that, following the 2016 election of Donald Trump, the company decided to take a stronger stance on issues it had long supported. Stanley pointed out that "history and consistency is critical, particularly for larger companies," emphasizing that companies today appeal to customers on the basis of values as well as products. "We're all so afraid of talking about values because it supposedly puts people at odds with each other, but if you make the values deep enough, you connect to people—even with people you might disagree with."

Another pioneering activist brand, the Body Shop, began in Brighton, England, in 1976 as a small, green-painted shop that sold products made from ethically sourced, naturally based ingredients.[9] Its founder, Anita Roddick, believed that social and environmental issues were woven into the fabric of the company, and so having a voice on these matters was a natural strategy, in addition to how the company produced its products. The Body Shop has achieved incredible success, with more than three thousand stores in over seventy countries. It has campaigned actively for fair trade and women's rights and against racism. It has a full-time activism team on staff at its headquarters and local teams around the world.

Roddick founded the Body Shop to make a living for herself and her two daughters while her husband was traveling.[10] In an interview, she said that "the original Body Shop was a series of brilliant accidents," and her focus "wasn't a sophisticated plan, it just happened like that."[11] In addition to the importance of authenticity and ethical production practices as the first line of activism, being a newcomer to business systems was helpful to maintain focus on what mattered to her. Roddick did not have formal business training nor did she receive any outside investment, and so, not being socialized into how business is traditionally run, she was able to focus the business on the values she held as a person.

Spurring Collective Action for Good

Beyond individual companies' actions, generational shifts, and the importance of product ingredients, Natura &Co's Love pointed out that a key "way to engage in activism as a business is by joining forces with other businesses, recognizing that no *one* business will ever be able to solve all the problems our planet is facing. We must actively find ways to work together." To this end, for instance, Avon, one of Natura &Co's brands, is working with local organizations to fund vital frontline services for victims of gender-based violence.

Collective action is an essential element of corporate activism for many reasons. For example, some companies might be intimidated by potential backlash, worried about possible escalation of commitment, or unsure about how to get started. Being part of a collective not only gives companies a cover against attacks like that against Bud Light but also creates an "ambition loop" in which companies will push one another and aim for higher goals than they would as individuals. Through such collaborations, learning and benchmarking can also occur.

As we have seen, food production is a huge contributor to the climate crisis. At the same time, as much as a third of that food is wasted.[12] Toast Ale, a UK-based brewing company, is working to tackle the food-waste problem head on. Using surplus bread to brew beer, the brewer is creating a circular and sustainable economy that is regenerative by design, as it also uses less land, water, and energy and produces less carbon emissions.

In order to spread this circular economy, Toast Ale recently partnered with twenty-four breweries, including Guinness and brands owned by Heineken and Asahi, to launch a series of twenty-six brand-new beers that are all brewed with surplus bread and other sustainably sourced ingredients.[13] More notably, all twenty-four partners signed an open letter calling on world leaders to make concrete commitments to tackle the climate crisis at the UN's COP26 in Glasgow, Scotland, in 2021. The partnership shows that even rivals can work together to support big issues.

Toast Ale then went on to form partnerships with the Rainforest Trust UK and Soil Heroes to protect 3.25 million trees in tropical rainforests and support farmers in their efforts to replenish the health of the soil by sequestering CO_2.[14] The brewery also devised a funding model that requires investors to reinvest their net capital gains in other businesses with environmental missions whenever they sell their Toast Ale shares. Beyond beer making, Toast Ale's biggest mission is to create system-wide change, Louisa Ziane, Toast Ale's cofounder and chief operating officer, told me.

For systemic issues like climate change, where no one government is responsible, collective action is paramount. At the UN's COP25 in December 2019, for instance, more than one hundred companies joined an initiative to be carbon-neutral by 2030. In the fall of 2021 in Glasgow, the decision-making body of the UN Framework Convention on Climate Change announced the Glasgow Climate Pact, which was much weaker than many hoped. But Nigel Topping, the UK's high-level climate change champion, and Gonzalo Muñoz, a Chilean business entrepreneur and environmental activist, used the occasion to promote the Race to Zero campaign to businesses. With more than one thousand cities, five thousand businesses, and one thousand universities from 120 countries, it is the largest-ever alliance committed to the achievement of net-zero carbon emissions.[15]

Two hundred and fifty companies and civil society groups gathered at COP27 in Egypt in 2022 to reaffirm their commitment to help national governments limit global temperature rise to 1.5 degrees Celsius above preindustrial levels.[16] The Alliance of CEO Climate Leaders, under the World Economic Forum, has pledged to reduce one gigaton of emissions annually by 2030 and lower Scope 1 and 2 emissions by 22 percent from 2019–2020 levels.[17] But while such mobilization is essential to make positive change in the world, our discussion of astroturfing and other corporate gaslighting tactics above should alert us to the point that those who are opposing change are also mobilizing. For instance, while there has been notable progress from the COP process, in recent years, there have also been significant concerns that these meetings have been co-opted by fossil fuel interests. At COP27, for instance, there were more oil and gas industry lobbyists than the combined number of delegates from the ten countries most affected by climate change. Sultan Ahmed Al Jaber, chief executive of the Abu Dhabi National Oil Company

(ADNOC), led COP28 in Dubai, and COP29 will be in Azerbaijian, another oil-rich locale.

While international cooperation is important to create action on systemic global issues, collective action can be even more powerful when done to pressure individual governments. Founder and CEO Gregg Renfrew launched the personal care company Beautycounter in 2011 with a promise to advocate for safer products, and the company has been influential in revising cosmetics regulations in the United States for the first time in over eighty years.

The first step was Beautycounter researching industry ingredients and establishing a "Never List," which now includes 1,800 questionable or harmful ingredients that are not used in its products.[18] In addition to voluntarily regulating its own products, Beautycounter partners with unlikely allies—such as car and plane manufacturers—to develop cross-industry and stakeholder engagement to change ingredients and sourcing up and down the supply chain. This includes advocacy at the federal and state level in the United States, investments in research, and a focus on issues surrounding ingredients such as mica, a key component of cosmetics and other consumer products. When the company found out that child labor was widely used in mica mining, it set out to create a fully traceable supply chain—a goal that no other company has achieved as yet. To that end, Beautycounter created "The Mica Toolkit" and shared it as a guide for other companies to responsibly source mica. Building on the OECD's "Due Diligence Guidance for Minerals" and the ILO's labor standards, the tool kit lays out eight steps companies can take to better understand where and how they are sourcing mica.[19]

Beautycounter also developed two critical partnerships in its effort to do something about the mica issue. The blockchain technology group Sourcemap is helping Beautycounter trace the mica's origins, while the Kailash Satyarthi Children's Foundation is giving the company a fuller understanding of mica mining's effects on communities. "A lot of international brands dive into local communities and make decisions about what they think is best for them without actually listening to them," Beautycounter's chief impact officer Lindsay Dahl told me. "We did not want to take that approach." Instead, the company works with the foundation to explore solutions.

In 2020, Dahl told me that, as the culmination of all of this work, the company began working to update the Federal Food, Drug, and Cosmetic Act, a law that hadn't been substantially revised since 1938 when it comes to cosmetic safety.[20] Beautycounter's efforts bore fruit. When Congress passed its fiscal year 2023 spending bill, the Modernization of Cosmetics Regulation Act was included.

A further type of collective action for good that businesses can engage in is using their brand and product as a platform for activism. Certainly, some of the pioneers discussed above provide examples here. Patagonia created a platform so people can look up their area of interest on the website, pair it with their location, and get the names of environmental organizations to support. Vincent Stanley told me this is a natural extension of the company's activism, to help make a connection between interested customers and grantees.

In 2004, Jeff Skoll founded Participant, a media and filmmaking company whose mission is to advance social change via civic engagement.[21] Many of its films have received awards and critical acclaim, notably Al Gore's 2006 Academy Award–winning climate wake-up call *An Inconvenient Truth* and 2011's pandemic precursor *Contagion*. As of 2023, Participant's films have received eighty-six Academy Award nominations and twenty-one wins, including Best Picture awards for *Spotlight* and *Green Book*.

During the 2020 US election, many companies, Participant among them, focused on voter turnout and voter education. "It might look like magic that we happened to have several films that really speak to the importance of civic participation in, arguably, the most important election of our lives," said Holly Gordon, Participant's chief impact officer. But "when you think about artists and activists," Gordon continued, "the thing they have in common is that they're generally on the front lines of change. They often sense early on what is not right in the world . . . and are able to inspire people to get involved." Participant doesn't just connect organizations with audiences via its movies; it also launches activist campaigns under its own corporate brand.

In the fall of 2020, in conjunction with the release of *John Lewis: Good Trouble*, which focuses on the civil rights leader's fight against voter suppression, Participant launched its own voter turnout campaign. Donations made through the Make Good Trouble campaign website helped send more than fifty-three thousand registration forms to eligible voters throughout the country, and Participant's voter hub website made it easier for potential voters to request mail-in ballots.[22] "It's about raising awareness about disenfranchisement, getting more people to care, and then to protect the vote. So one by one, we built these campaigns that were really rooted in the narrative of the film," Gordon explained. Another influential move targeted at the 2020 election cycle was Participant's *Slay the Dragon*, a documentary about gerrymandering efforts in Michigan. The film resulted in the state's independent redistricting commission receiving 120 applications for its thirteen open positions, as citizens rallied to challenge problems with the way redistricting resulted in people being disenfranchised.[23]

When asked about the importance of brand activism, Gordon referenced John Lewis: "I think brands should be making good trouble. Brands help us imagine what's possible. They help us imagine the culture that we want. Brands are but an expression of companies, and corporations are communities of people. They are institutions themselves."

"We can't let governments off the hook," Gordon said. "We can't let individuals off the hook. We all have agency. We have the ability to make change. It's a huge opportunity for the kind of transformation that we need in the world. When a CEO decides to change a policy in a business or stands up for something the way Ben and Jerry's recently did on white supremacy, it has this ripple effect through the thousands of employees at the company and through the millions of people that consume the product. So, they're just leverage points for change."

Pushing Toward a Tipping Point

While systems change is a long-term game, corporate activism and especially corporate collaboration on global challenges can bring us to a tipping point faster.

The need to play a long game in this regard came home to me when I was talking to Jeff Clements, a lawyer who previously has served as assistant attorney general and chief of the Public Protection and Advocacy Bureau in the Office of the Attorney General in Massachusetts. During his career, Clements watched what he calls "the change in what the Constitution means," the effect of that change on people across the political spectrum, and the loss of the public commons to private enterprise.

He reflected on his role with the Office of the Attorney General and involvement with tobacco litigation. He told me that he and his colleagues were trying to enforce basic laws regarding a buffer for tobacco marketing around schools. As is now well documented, big tobacco targeted children with advertising outside of schools to get kids addicted. Industry scientists had said that if you can get kids hooked on tobacco at fifteen, you have them for life, but if you wait until twenty-one, they're not going to be as susceptible to being a lifetime customer.

The tobacco companies sued, saying the rule against marketing cigarettes around schools and playgrounds violated their First Amendment free speech rights. Clements emphasized that the companies didn't debate the public policy; they just said Americans weren't allowed to touch them because their First Amendment rights would be violated if they were unable to use cartoon cigarette ads in places where children go to school. Massachusetts appealed all the way up to the Supreme Court, but then lost five-to-four in *Lorillard Tobacco Co. v. Reilly*. Clements told me, "That is a dangerous change in what free speech is supposed to be about in America."

He eventually came to the conclusion he couldn't sit on the sidelines anymore. In 2016, he founded a nonpartisan organization called American Promise to support a grassroots movement focused on reducing the influence of money in politics.

Clements and American Promise are looking to pass a constitutional amendment that will overturn the campaign finance model put in place by *Citizens United*.[24] They are also part of a larger movement on taming corporate political spending that includes the University of Michigan's Erb Institute, which has launched an initiative for companies to commit to a set of "Principles for Corporate Political Responsibility." These standards assess if corporate political activities are aligned with a company's values, purpose, and commitments to all stakeholders, and if it is transparent on that. Companies as diverse as IBM, Pirelli Tire North America, Danone North America, Aspen Skiing Company, and DSM North America have signed onto these principles to ensure their political activities are responsibly aligned with their business.

At first glance, Clements's approach for a constitutional amendment may seem quixotic. Only one constitutional amendment has been passed in the United States in the last fifty years, and our politics could not be more polarized than it is now. But our discussion gave me hope that there may be historical precedent. The Supreme Court's *Dobbs v. Jackson Women's Health Organization* decision overturning *Roe v. Wade*, *Citizens United*, and other recent decisions have convinced a large swath of the public that the court has overstepped its bounds.[25]

Moreover, constitutional amendments have typically come in waves, as reactions to turbulent times in US history. Three amendments were ratified between 1865 and 1870, in the wake of the Civil War. Four more became law between 1913 and 1920, the tail end of the Progressive Era, which was itself a reaction to the excesses of the Gilded Age. Two more were passed in 1933, at the outset of the New Deal. And four amendments were added between 1961 and 1971, during the civil rights movement. Reform eras account for thirteen of the seventeen amendments that have been ratified since the Bill of Rights.[26]

In our modern Gilded Age, more and more people are frustrated by our public officials' seeming inability to address the climate crisis and other challenges of our time. Clements believes that the wind is at his back, as a majority of Americans from across the political spectrum—including business leaders and legislatures in twenty-two states—have signaled their support for the amendment.

Is it too much to hope that the extreme polarization of our politics can lead to a new era of collaboration? Char Love told me that if she was asked to give just one piece of advice to activists, it would be this: "Find friends and fellow travelers and other businesses or organizations you can learn from. Engage with them and build trust with them." And then, she said, "you need to find people who will make you feel uncomfortable, since that is how you become radical. Challenge your own comfort first, then fight for the comfort of others."

Love also identified the importance of getting to root causes. "You should be asking whether your activism is linked to the idea of changing the rules of the game," she explained. "It shouldn't be seen as an incremental step forward. Now is the time for a system change."

Radical action and radical collaboration aren't words you expect to hear from someone in the corporate world, but as Love explained, the word is derived from the Latin *radix*, meaning "root." "When we talk about radical action or radical collaboration, it doesn't mean the action is necessarily extreme, but rather deeply rooted in its urgency," she concluded.

In the next chapter, we will delve into the challenges and opportunities of radical culture change.

Consumption and the Commons

Beliefs to Action

"Don't buy this jacket!" Patagonia said. KLM advised its customers to "fly more responsibly," urging them to choose more energy-efficient forms of travel or to use digital technology to connect with loved ones instead, and they did this in 2019, before COVID really did ground millions of frequent fliers. IKEA has furniture repurchase programs. All of these are great ways to raise attention about overconsumption, but they put the onus for reducing it solely on individuals. Could that ever be enough?

As discussed earlier, an important element of systems change is the need to shift ingrained cultural assumptions. For the majority of people, this has proven to be an incredible challenge. While many signal their support for sustainable consumption in surveys, they don't act on that belief when faced with higher prices. This chapter focuses on what companies can do to lead culture change and what we as consumers should support when it comes to sustainable production.

As is well known, Patagonia is a model and go-to resource for companies seeking to be sustainable and mission driven. For years, its vests were a favorite accessory of Wall Street and Silicon Valley capitalists when they trekked to ideas conferences in Davos, Switzerland, and Aspen, Colorado. When the fictional Logan family attended a conference inspired by the annual Allen & Company Sun Valley conference, informally known as "summer camp for billionaires," on HBO's *Succession*, they were all dressed in puffy vests. It seemed a cultural triumph, but it made the company uncomfortable. In 2019, Patagonia announced that it would stop offering jackets and vests with corporate logos, as these corporate giveaways drive excess and unneeded consumption. Patagonia's principles were the foundation for taking this step, even though it cut off a revenue source.

Patagonia launched its controversial "Don't buy this jacket" ad campaign on Black Friday in 2011 to take a stand against overconsumption.[1] The move required a board vote, as there were concerns about the potential hit to profits. But the response was overwhelmingly positive, Patagonia's Vincent Stanley said, so they kept going. "In 2016, for Black Friday, we were all set to close the stores and encourage customers to spend their day helping environmental organizations," he told me. "Then the Monday of that week, a mid-level employee came in and said, 'We should keep the stores open and give 100 percent of sales to grassroots environmental groups.' By that afternoon, approval had been secured all the way up the line."

For the last half century and more, we have been led to believe that if we care about ills like pollution, climate change, and child slavery, we should exercise the power of the purse in our purchases, recycle conscientiously, and read labels carefully to make sure that the goods we are buying are organic, sustainably produced, green, and a host of other buzzwords.

And it does seem there has been some traction. During the COVID pandemic, the mission-driven marketing company Futerra partnered with market researchers OnePulse to carry out a survey, which suggested that up to 80 percent of US and UK respondents would be willing to change their lifestyles to stop climate change, in much the same ways as they had to curb the spread of the virus.[2] Young people in particular have been transitioning toward ways of living that leave smaller footprints on the world. Movements like minimalism, simplicity, and mindfulness are taking Gen Z by storm and seem to be here to stay. As young people become core consumers, companies will increasingly adapt to their demands, offering them more and better information, such as reliable third-party certifications, that allow them to align their principles with their consumption choices.

But that won't be enough. Yes, it's us that's doing the overconsuming, but, as I have argued all along, companies need to address their own culpability. Consumption habits are quite difficult to affect directly, especially when companies are spending at least $600 billion a year to convince us to buy more. The kinds of campaigns that activists can afford don't stand much of a chance against the fast-fashion industry. Overconsumption is the massive problem that it is because markets encourage consumers to behave irresponsibly. The global population will likely reach 8.5 billion by 2030 and 9.7 billion by 2050. We would need three planet Earths to provide the resources for that many people to maintain their current lifestyles.[3] If we continue at this rate, we will experience widespread societal, environmental, and political chaos. Systems are needed that decouple quality of life from resource consumption while establishing regenerative solutions.

In this chapter, we focus on how rethinking production includes focusing more on quality over quantity and how companies like Patagonia promote consumer-facing circular solutions. I also suggest principles we can all follow in our own consumption to help make this shift.

Promoting Reduced Consumption

Patagonia's founder Yvon Chouinard's well-known maxim that we should "consume less but consume better" is hard to argue with, and the company has put its money where its mouth is, prioritizing sustainability over consumption even in its marketing.[4] While this may seem counter to business as usual under the short-term paradigm of shareholder primacy, as we have discussed before, thinking in this broader and more long-term way allows companies to have deeper and more impactful relationships with their diverse stakeholders, including consumers. But such ideas are still on the vanguard, so companies need to do more to help consumers make the shift.

For instance, the aviation industry accounts for approximately 2 to 3 percent of the world's anthropogenic CO_2 emissions, but if more airlines follow KLM's lead and urge their customers to fly less, we might see this number decrease.[5] KLM knows that individual flight reduction is not the only thing needed and has invested in opening a sustainable fuel plant in the Netherlands. Its Fly Responsibly website also states that the company is working to improve the sustainability of onboard catering and to reduce the emissions from its ground operations.[6]

But it is also clear that we need to be on guard for gaslighting. For instance, in June 2023, the European consumer rights organization lodged a complaint at the European Commission against seventeen airlines for the use of terms such as "sustainable," "responsible," and "green." Commercialization of technologies for low-emission flights are far off, so activists assess that such claims by the airlines can be nothing more than greenwashing. More recently, KLM's Fly Responsibly website acknowledged flying was not sustainable and listed its environmental initiatives.

Although I think these greenwashing accusations are not without merit, we also should entertain the alternative possibility that the company is simply preparing for a future where there are significantly more environmental constraints on its work, and given current trends, more airlines would be prudent to consider such long-term strategies. As we have discussed a number of times, expectations on companies are changing, and it is the forward-looking ones that will thrive in the new era.

Promoting Circularity

More effective than appeals to the better nature of consumers are programs that incorporate recycling into their operations or business models, significantly reducing waste. While in an earlier chapter we examined process innovations in how companies are converting trash into treasure, here we consider the consumer-facing aspect of this work: how companies can market and message to help consumers understand the value of engaging in circular consumption. These innovations are critical in taming waste.

IKEA has committed to becoming a circular business by 2030. An initial step is a buyback program. Customers returning an IKEA product they no longer want can then receive credits worth between 30 and 50 percent of the original price, depending on its condition. The returned items would then be made available for repurchase.[7] Hege Sæbjørnsen, IKEA's sustainability manager for the UK and Ireland, said that the plan would help to promote IKEA's progress toward achieving its "fully circular" and "climate positive" 2030 goals.[8] "Encouraging circulation," she said, "is both the right thing to do and a good business opportunity."

The company has also announced plans to extend its buyback program to US stores.[9] IKEA has further considered rental services, aimed at extending the lifespan of furniture and reducing greenhouse gas emissions and waste. The Swedish retailer already recycles about 71 percent of its waste in stores and refurbishes and resells some forty-seven million products worldwide. These initiatives stand in stark contrast to its aggressive campaign from the early 2000s, which encouraged consumers to replace their furniture more often, inspiring the derisive characterization of its products as "disposable furniture."[10] Peter Jelkeby, national retail manager at IKEA UK and Ireland, called sustainability "the defining issue of our time" and said the company "is committed to being part of the solution."[11] Sæbjørnsen sees "circularity" as both a huge business opportunity and a social imperative.[12]

REI's used gear division has become an important and growing part of the outdoor equipment co-op's business. Members can trade in used items for gift-card credits of up to 50 percent of their original prices. "Buying a piece of used gear is one of the best ways you or I can reduce our carbon footprint," said Ken Voeller, REI's manager of new business development and re-commercialization.[13]

Patagonia, also a leader in circularity, launched an initiative alongside its "Don't buy this jacket" campaign in 2011 to encourage customers to reduce, repair, reuse, and recycle their clothing and equipment. "We realized that what was really needed was a mutual responsibility between company and customer for the full lifecycle of stuff," said Rick Ridgeway, Patagonia's vice president of environment.[14] The company has a used clothing program wherein consumers can either get their clothing repaired or trade it in for store credit.

Patagonia will also help customers sell their clothing through eBay and Patagonia.com. If the clothes are too worn out to repair, Patagonia offers to recycle them. When I talked to Vincent Stanley, he told me that he sees this business continuing to significantly grow in future years, and that since Patagonia makes "high-quality, durable products that last a long time, it makes sense to offer a platform for people to buy what's used and still perfectly good but at a lower price. It's a huge environmental advantage to keep things in circulation longer." Finally, Patagonia works with farmers who grow cotton regeneratively, meaning they have replaced chemical pesticides and fertilizers with "knowledge and labor."[15]

The apparel company Eileen Fisher is also adding circularity to its branding proposition. "We actually think maybe we don't have to sell so many clothes," its eponymous founder said. The company, which designs clothing to last as long as possible, buys back its used garments for $5 each and either repairs and resells them or incorporates the fabric into new clothes at factories in Irvington, New York, and Seattle, Washington, which are sold under its Renew brand. It also sells a line of bags and pillows made from clothes that were too worn to reuse. The company bought back its millionth item in 2019.[16] It also opened a concept store in Brooklyn, where it runs workshops that teach consumers how to live more sustainably.

The Swedish company Nudie Jeans offers free denim repairs in its twenty stores and provides customers with mail-order repair kits so they can fix their own jeans at home; online videos show them how. "We've been repairing, reusing, and recycling denim since long before circularity even had a hashtag," the Nudie Jeans sustainability report states.[17] If customers don't want to repair their jeans, they can return them and the company will resell them.

It's a fantastic start. But to create the kind of cognitive shift that can tip the system in the way we need, many more companies across many more industries must have programs promoting reduce, reuse, and recycle so that it will seem shocking to encounter one that doesn't.

Overcoming Challenges in Shifting Consumer Perception

None of these circularity efforts can have a lasting impact unless more people know about them. One company that's trying to change that is the Fors Marsh group, a research and strategy firm. "If it's a product or a service or communication—whatever it is," said CEO Ben Garthwaite, "you can't design and build something better for people without bringing them to the table."[18]

"People care about ethical business practices. People care about workers' rights, about voting rights, about racial equity and anti-racism," said Fors Marsh research director Michael Karim. "It can feel awkward or uncomfortable at first to put your values front and center and to take a risk, because 70 percent of people is not 100 percent. But it is still the vast majority of Americans who care about these issues and are passionate about them."

Fors Marsh has found that the biggest barrier people face when they are looking to buy from a company with a mission is that they don't know where to start. They wonder if they can find the products in stores, or if they have to shop online. They don't know what to make of the various certifications they've seen on products. The more barriers that emerge during their shopping experience, the less likely they are to push through.

What fuels this is something called the attitude-behavior gap, which has been extensively studied by psychologists. The fact that consumers value a particular behavior does not necessarily mean they will engage in it. So, while studies by McKinsey and NielsenIQ and others show that consumers in general value sustainable products, that doesn't guarantee that they will buy more of those products. The biggest barrier to their doing so is simply access to information.

Many people and organizations are actively working to reduce or remove these informational and perceptual barriers. Carbon labeling, as we've seen, is an important emerging practice, because it requires companies to be rigorous in their measurement but also because it increases consumers' awareness of the impacts of their purchases. But other ways of engaging and informing consumers are needed.

Cullen Schwarz started his career as a political communications professional, and he has worked in the Michigan statehouse, the US Capitol, and the Department of Agriculture. When he was still in college, he began working to end abuses in the garment industry. The work made him realize that consumer spending was an underutilized tool that could create significant social change. "Even back then," he said, "I thought if you could galvanize a large number of individual consumers to use their purchasing power to get businesses to pay better wages or produce more sustainably, we could collectively have a really huge impact."[19] In 2015, he launched an online e-commerce platform called DoneGood that offers products from companies that are good for the environment, for workers, and for communities. It has been called "the Amazon of Social Good."

It began as a Yelp-style app that rated brick-and-mortar stores in the Boston area. "Even though we had 1,200 businesses in the greater Boston area on the app," he said, "once you put just a few search filters in, the universe of businesses gets really small. The behavior change we were asking of people was to travel extra miles, and that can be a big ask, especially if they don't have extra time. So, we decided that online shopping is the direction we need to go. Instead of asking people to walk more miles, we're asking them to move their mouse a few inches."[20]

The shift to online shopping was the right approach on a number of levels. Research shows that, due to shipping efficiencies, online shopping actually can lead to less carbon emissions than stores.[21] And it allows DoneGood to work with several hundred businesses across the country that it can be certain share its values. "We aggregate data from independent third-party certifying organizations and then we do our own research," Schwarz said. "We actually have interviews with people at the company. We ask them to follow up to demonstrate that their claims are accurate, and we have them sign an affidavit that everything they're saying is true." DoneGood no longer requires third-party certifications, as they've realized that there are great businesses that haven't been certified for a variety of reasons, and they didn't want to exclude them.

"Our mantra now is 'stories not data,'" Schwarz said, which makes sense because stories resonate with individuals more than dry facts. To illustrate this point, he provided a contrast between a bigger clothing company that powers its production facility with 100 percent clean energy and uses organic cotton and nontoxic dyes, and a little company that's a few people in a garage making dog collars out of upcycled cowboy boots. He asked, "Who gets a better environmental score?" He went on, "On the one hand, the bigger company is helping to show other companies that it's possible to produce at a larger scale in really innovative, highly sustainable ways. On the other, the folks making dog collars are removing waste from the waste stream and probably have a lower carbon footprint overall." So now DoneGood just tells consumers that the clothing company is running purely on renewable energy and describes their other sustainable practices, and that the other company is making dog collars out of upcycled cowboy boots. Then consumers can make their choice about which companies they want to buy from.

Direct consumer engagement is also essential. The clothing retailer Reformation has set an ambitious goal of becoming climate-positive by 2025.[22] One of its strategies is raising carbon footprint awareness in the general public by promoting easy-to-adopt and accessible climate actions. In 2019, Reformation introduced "Carbon is canceled," a program that offers shoppers simple ways to reduce or offset their carbon footprint. Chief sustainability officer and vice president of operations Kathleen Talbot explained that "we basically took solutions we use as a brand and made them available for our customers."[23] Customers can use the Reformation website to opt for wind energy from their power utility and receive a $125 Reformation credit for doing so. They can purchase climate credits that are applied to verified carbon-offset projects, such as renewable energy and reforestation efforts. By raising climate awareness among individuals, Reformation fortifies them against greenwashing and gaslighting tactics. By sharing its climate-positive strategies with other businesses, Reformation encourages other leaders to rethink their company's positioning in the circle of responsibility.

How do initiatives like these change perceptions and redefine expectations of what's possible? By engaging people directly in opportunities to act on their values, these programs create a collaboration between the individual and the company. But there are deeper barriers that must be overcome as well. One of them is the opportunity cost of buying sustainable products. To produce these products, companies need to make trade-offs. In food products, it may be taste and price; in clothing it might be appeal. A recent survey showed that while many Europeans say they are willing to change their consumption habits to fight climate change, they balk when it would threaten their quality of life.[24]

This idea of a trade-off has deeper cognitive effects as well. Fors Marsh's Karim noted the "fundamental psychological belief that something that is two things is worse at any one of those things." That is the way human cognition works. It is natural that, when we see a product that is good for the environment, we assume it doesn't work as well as one that simply does what it's supposed to. When we see a company that treats its workers well and cares about its impact on the world, we assume it will probably make things that are too expensive and that work poorly.[25] The only way to overcome this psychological process is by example and reinforcement over time, by making quality products that are affordable and don't produce negative externalities.

Roberta Graham, associate director at Space Doctors, a cultural and creative consultancy, told me there are lessons in how systems and cultural change can happen effectively from the fast-food industry. Those lessons can be used in fast fashion as well, as both rely on our need for convenience, affordability, and consistency. Graham further pointed out that both industries have relied on a discourse that was gaslighting consumers: placing the blame on them for not making the "right choices" with where they put their money.

With fast food, consumer consciousness and increased demand for healthy options and ethical supply chains have led to real change in the industry, although, as we saw in Chapter 4, extensive systemic barriers remain in place. Healthy eating and large movements toward organic and plant-based options have driven more people to seek these alternatives out, Graham pointed out. Food companies, in turn, have begun adapting, providing caloric and nutritional information on their menus and expanding and improving their vegetarian and plant-based options. Stricter government regulation and legislation around ingredients and supply chains play a critical role in this as well.

Part of making this shift is about helping consumers better understand the implications of their actions. As Basil Demeroutis— managing partner of FORE Partnership, a real estate development firm funding sustainable projects in the United Kingdom and western Europe—put it to me in relation to his industry, "We need our plastic straw moment. People said, 'Oh plastic straws are bad, and I know they're bad because there's a picture of a plastic straw in a turtle's mouth or a dolphin's snout.' Suddenly, plastic straws were being replaced with sustainable alternatives. In real estate, the measurements of environmental impacts are too abstract. Energy intensity is measured in kilowatt hours per meter squared, which is confusing to people. We need to distill it down into something that is, first of all, easily relatable and, second of all, blatantly, egregiously wrong, so there's no possibility other than to act."[26]

Some Principles of Sustainable Consumption

Goal Twelve of the UN's seventeen Sustainable Development Goals is "ensuring sustainable consumption and production models."[27] As a share of GDP, consumption hovers around 70 to 80 percent in developed economies.[28] So although we need to first and foremost hold companies accountable, we also need to recognize that our personal decisions, from the food we eat, to the clothes we wear, to the car we drive, to the home we live in, have global consequences.

We as individuals must refuse to be gaslighted and demand systems-level change. But we must do our part as well. For example, when a utility asks its customers to reduce their power consumption to avoid a brownout or blackout, most people turn off their lights and raise the thermostats on their air conditioners, because they recognized that they're all in it together.[29]

We can change what we eat, what we wear, and how much we drive. First, we need to raise our awareness about sustainability in general and what companies are doing about it. As discussed in an earlier chapter, accountability matters, and so certifications and labels like B Corp and Fair Trade Certified can tell us a lot. So can online databases, like the Ecolabel Index and the International Trade Centre's Standards Map.[30]

Then, we need to transform that awareness into action by voting with our wallets for companies that have smaller environmental footprints and that respect the rights of their workers. Consuming mindfully leads to lower consumption, as we are less likely to succumb to trends and more likely to look for quality and durability. Consuming locally is not just good for local merchants; it reduces packaging and lowers greenhouse emissions.[31]

Throwing away better—that is, being thoughtful about products' end of use—requires us to take the "hows" and "whats" of recycling into account. Know your local government's rules and respect them. Moreover, think creatively about what you're getting rid of. There are apps to help you donate leftover food and old clothes and furniture to those in need. You and your actions matter. You can reuse and repair, and support the many brands we have discussed in these pages that focus on circularity.

Think collaboratively. There is much power in collective action, and you can influence others to act more responsibly. Research has shown that solar supporters who had solar panels on their houses were able to recruit nearly 63 percent more residents to buy and install solar panels than community organizers who did not.[32] Positive influences reinforce each other, and the sustainable efforts will snowball over time. You and your community matter.

Finally, as discussed earlier, you can engage in political activities. Macro-level policies must be supported by grassroots initiatives. To get to the tipping point needed to change the system to a more sustainable and equitable state, we need to all work on many different fronts.

After decades of gaslighting and greenwashing, many of us have finally—if belatedly—recognized the implications of the climate crisis and want to make a difference. In Chapter 2, we saw how big companies create narratives to shift the blame to individual consumers. This chapter offers an alternative to the individual-responsibility narrative and shows how some companies are pushing back. From Patagonia, IKEA, and KLM to Fors Marsh and DoneGood, many businesses are using insights to help consumers make better choices. All of these show that businesses and consumers can work together toward a common goal.

Thanks to decades of education and public discussions, nowadays many of us have recognized the social and environmental injustices present in our society and are willing to work to address these problems. By following the principles outlined, you will be on your way to a more sustainable lifestyle.

Whether as voters or consumers, we have more power than we realize. We are all in this together.

Conclusion

We Are Up to the Challenge of Systems Change

When new ideas—good or bad—push up against established beliefs, they inevitably come under fire. Why is that? In part, because we take our culture and norms for granted. New ideas that don't fit into our cultural frames seem out of place and even dangerous. Sometimes they are.

In discussing the resistance to evolutionary theory, the English polymath William Whewell, the former master of Trinity College at Cambridge who coined the word "scientist," is reported to have said that every important new idea passes through three stages: "First people said, 'It is absurd!' Then, 'It is contrary to the Bible!' And finally they said, 'We always knew it was so!'"

From Copernicus and Galileo to Nelson Mandela and Martin Luther King Jr., there are countless examples of this in the scientific world and even more in the social world. Interracial marriage was outlawed for centuries in many countries. Through legal challenges, activism, and shifting cultural attitudes, those restrictions have been largely dismantled, and it is now overwhelmingly accepted.

Similarly, in the areas of gender equality and LGBTQ and disability rights, decades of activism have moved the needle forward in much of the Global North.

We need to also remember that ideas like markets, profits, and capital are historical constructions that depend on choices we make. Those choices shape—and are shaped by in turn—our political, legal, social, and educational systems.

Important factors underlying the first two phases in Whewell's model are the powerful and vested interests who see the new ideas as a challenge to their privileged positions. For example, the presentation of misleading evidence that there is no connection between carbon emissions and global warming from interested actors like fossil fuel companies—and the hold this idea has on actors like former president Trump and other right-wing politicians—clearly reflects the stage when resistors claim, "It is absurd!"

Companies have worked for decades to place the blame for the externalities they create on their customers. We should not be "litterbugs," we should work to reduce our own carbon footprints, and of course we should recycle. All are actions that direct our attention away from the idea that this book aims to expose: we need to shift the blame to be much more squarely on the companies themselves and label them for what they are—profiteers, making excessive profits by exploiting the inequitable situations and market imperfections that form the foundational logic of our current economic system.

Throughout history, businesses have defined the assumptions that guide the lived reality in our economy and society to obscure the inequalities that are fundamentally immoral in order to concentrate power and profits for the few. Part of the work that I've undertaken throughout this book is to expose the systemic and fundamental injustices that underlie our economic system and the dishonest practices that perpetuate them.

Instead of working to address the structural problems, we've been convinced that it's up to us, that we can take responsibility in our own homes and with our lifestyle choices. The theory is, if we all do the same, we will make a change. Or, we hear, if we pull ourselves up by our bootstraps, we can climb out of poverty. The people in power will show us a story about a kid from a low-income neighborhood, with a marginalized background, graduating top of his class and going to Harvard because he was a "hard worker," but they don't show the dozens of other hard workers who are left behind, who worked just as hard but couldn't climb out.

At the same time, billionaires like the Koch brothers and other allies in the fossil fuel industry have funded endeavors to lobby against businesses' ethical, social, and governance programs, which has prompted some Republican-controlled states such as Texas and West Virginia to pass anti-ESG legislation. Presidential hopefuls like Ron DeSantis, Vivek Ramaswamy, and others argue that ESG factors place intolerable restrictions on companies and so defy the principles of free market capitalism that America is built on, of course not recognizing or perhaps not being aware of the fact that these ideas have mainly come to the fore in the last fifty years. "Anti-wokeism" is itself reflecting an ideology, another way of saying that such ideas are "contrary to the Bible."

But, as I hope I have shown, there are better ideas out there, and we can work together to embrace them to build a system where virtuous cycles are the norm and not the exception. We begin by knowing the full story—and then switching the narrative. As Joy Anderson, an impact investor with a PhD in history, once said, "We made this shit up. We can make up better shit."[1] That is, the world is constructed based on human actions and assumptions. This should be recognized, and our efforts should be put toward creating a new economic and societal system.

Changing the System

Throughout history, seasons of change have set in gradually. But, like Ernest Hemingway said of bankruptcy—it starts slowly, and then happens all at once—those changes eventually reach critical mass and the unthinkable happens: war, famine, economic collapse.

So it is with climate change, perhaps the biggest existential threat humanity faces today. Most of us have traditionally assumed that the relationship between climate change and its consequences is linear, that a small increase in deforestation would have a correspondingly small effect on human civilization. But recent evidence is showing powerfully that these relationships are nonlinear and thus can suddenly manifest surprisingly intense effects that are hard to predict. Whether it's environmental degradation, the effects of COVID-19, or the growing societal inequities in our global system of surveillance capitalism, all of these press on each other and threaten to cascade, leading to abrupt and dramatic systemic failure, like the St. Matthew Island reindeer discussed in Chapter 1.

This is how societal change frequently occurs: things build up slowly and suddenly tip over into another steady state—"We always knew it was so!" in Whewell's typology. While we can see this in retrospect, it is hard to predict or even understand when such dramatic shifts will occur as we are living through the changes.

It's how our brains are wired. We have a cognitive bias to expect things to grow or change at a steady, constant rate. Exponential growth, which involves accelerating rates of change, is harder to see, but this is how most social change occurs. One illustration is the wheat and chessboard parable, in which a subject asks a king to reward him by placing one grain of wheat on the first square of a chessboard and then doubling the amount on each subsequent square. The king agrees without hesitation. But by the time he reaches the sixty-fourth square, the amount of wheat is more than the entire kingdom produced in a season. While things move slowly at first, a tipping point can occur when a critical mass is achieved, leading to a rapid acceleration or transformation of the system, as any number of thought experiments illustrate.

History shows this as well. In *1177 B.C.: The Year Civilization Collapsed*, the American archaeologist Eric Cline examines why eight major Mediterranean civilizations simultaneously imploded.[2] For decades, it was hypothesized that war and local conflicts caused the catastrophe. But its true cause, according to Cline, was climate change. Sea surface temperatures were cooling, leading to less rainfall. As the climate became more arid, famine and drought became the norm. Frequent earthquakes and devastating fires made things worse. It was a perfect storm, and it was enough to decimate the Bronze Age civilizations and the global networks they had built. The story seems eerily familiar.

But what's important to recognize is that positive change can be exponential as well. We are not destined to be victims of nonlinearity. Our system tipped to neoliberalism in the 1970s and 1980s, following the ideas of Milton Friedman and many others who worked to create legal and corporate systems that oriented corporations to short-term shareholder primacy. The diverse tactics that enabled this revolution in societal systems provide clues to how to reverse course. Like the shareholder-primacy activists in the 1970s and 1980s, we need to chart a change path focused on many forces across many fronts, including governmental levers, new financial models, and corporate practices that align business with society. A tall order no doubt, but there are many indications the time is right to intentionally tip the system back in a better direction.

There has been much talk about the calls for sustainability issuing from Davos, the Aspen Ideas Festival, and other elite forums. But most of their proposed solutions are "fixes that fail," as at best they deal with the symptoms of the problem and not its root causes. Many of these proposals are totally ineffective, purposeful distractions by the culpable. By focusing on doing well by doing good, we are only reinforcing the idea that profit or economic gain should be the ultimate objective of action. As Berkeley cognitive scientist George Lakoff said, "When we invoke the frame, we reinforce the frame."[3] This is natural and what frequently happens at the beginning of periods of dramatic upheaval. In addition to misdirecting our attention, the elites themselves start to make calls for change. Witness the Business Roundtable, World Economic Forum, and BlackRock CEO Larry Fink. But today's focus on stakeholder capitalism and the promotion of ESG deny the fundamental conflict between caring for society and the environment on one hand and optimizing shareholder value on the other. As I have argued, relying on win-win solutions that will allow us to continue to put profits first is a potent but dangerous fantasy that creates cognitive dissonance and misdirects attention away from fundamental solutions.

I don't deny that at times profit motive can be used to incentivize better corporate behavior, but we can't fall into the trap that business self-interest will solve our problems. As discussed in these pages, innovative companies have advanced a host of solutions that provide proof of concept and insight into how business can be reorganized in regenerative ways, but they cannot do it on their own. Ultimately, it is the neoliberal system itself—and the existing assumptions, practices, and policies—that needs to be fundamentally dismantled and replaced with a new understanding of how society and the economy should be governed.

———

When I was a student at the University of Michigan, I studied social movements theory with Mayer Zald, one of the foundational thinkers on the topic. What I learned is that successful change projects throughout history—from abolition in the Civil War era to the anti-abortion movement's success in overturning *Roe v. Wade* in our own day—all have three key elements: They mobilize diverse constituents. They have an effective messaging or framing strategy. And they capitalize on an "opportunity structure" that reflects the political and societal openness for change at the time.[4]

In that light, our own moment seems quite propitious. Throughout this book, we've seen many stories and instances of mobilization, of innovative, socially minded politicians, companies, and individuals who are eager to collaborate and shape a better future. This makes sense because, as Nobel laureate Elinor Ostrom articulated, collective action is a way to overcome the tragedy of the commons. Corporations are opting into third-party reviews and outside accountability processes for assessing their ESG behavior, as well as embracing new corporate governance structures. Some governments have also started to instate policies to require everyone to take a longer view.

In Part II, I introduced a number of practices innovative companies are using to overcome problems with specific types of externalities, the underlying idea being that "the future is already here—it's just not very evenly distributed." Innovators have found a surprising number of solutions. Hopeful models of circular, regenerative, and equitable business are here and are proven concepts. What we need is wider mobilization.

For instance, Allbirds partnered with its competitor Adidas to create the lowest carbon footprint sneaker ever. rePlant Capital is funding regenerative solutions for farmers, organizing large companies to change their supply chains and directing billions of dollars toward the transition of farmland from agrochemical practices to organic agriculture or "soil to shelf." Ecosia is working with scores of partners in reforesting major swaths of the Global South. Dr. Bronner's, Patagonia, and others are working to popularize a "regenerative organic standard."

Other pioneers include Rubicon, a technology company helping businesses effectively deal with their waste. PayActiv developed a technology to allow employees early access to pay they have already earned to avert emergencies, and Greyston Bakery is working to get gainful employment for those systematically excluded from the workforce.

All of these companies are addressing a number of key externalities, from carbon emissions to degradation of land, from industrial waste to inequalities in labor practices. But while these leading companies show change is possible, it is not preordained.

They have all created a variety of important new models, but we also need to think more systemically, through partnerships with other organizations, groups, and individuals to bring more resources and expertise to bear on the issues and through governments to write and enforce new commons-first policies. Of course, while businesses can't solve every problem we face, for better or for worse they have a crucial role to play in society. They can continue to be profiteers and tip the scales toward the benefit of the few, with toxic side effects for all. Or, as we have seen, they can provide innovation to highlight better, more equitable long-term solutions.

Beyond Silver Bullets

When I talk to social entrepreneurs and change agents, I am always inspired by the passion and commitment that has driven them to come up with innovative solutions to vexing challenges. However, sometimes I am also surprised by how overly focused they are on the power of their specific ideas. They believe if everyone went all in on the solution they advocate, the world would transition to a more sustainable state. As such, they are frequently dismissive of other potentially viable and even complementary solutions. Perhaps seeing deeply into one area is like having blinders on, making it harder to see the broader picture.

I am reminded again of the Eisenhower quote: when he ran into a problem he could not solve, his strategy was to make it bigger, as seeing more context and other, connected pieces of the issue allowed him to begin to see the outlines of a solution. To get to the tipping point, to a new economic model that creates virtuous cycles, we need to see one-off solutions as elements of a bigger system of changes, but they alone are not enough.

With framing and messaging—the second component of Zald's social change model—we need to clearly articulate the idea about working on many fronts, across many sectors, not simply developing silver bullets. There is not one idea that will reshape the whole system in one fell swoop. Like what followed Friedman's call for focusing on profits first, we need multifaceted actions, each seemingly small, but their diversity and interconnectedness create a self-reinforcing dynamic that has the potential to help the system tip to the more sustainable, equitable, and ultimately regenerative reality that is better for all.

Part III outlined a number of such systemic solutions across different domains, including policy changes to align corporate governance with stakeholders and accountability processes to ensure such structures are authentically followed. New investment models play an essential role as well, not only because externalities are affecting returns but because we need to bring investment opportunities to Main Street. Corporations and individuals can also advocate and support such models to hasten the adoption curve.

Again, we need to acknowledge that what is needed is systemic change; for each of these individual ripples to eventually come together into a wave and create a new paradigm for responsible business, multi-sector, coordinated action is necessary. There will need to be scores of actions across many of these different domains: policy, markets, corporations, and individuals.

———

I have found that while people can easily grasp the importance of mobilizing and framing as general concepts that can enable social movement success, Zald's third element, "opportunity structures," is a bit harder to grasp. Basically, it means taking advantage of timing.

Is the world ready? There are many indications that the time is clearly ripe for a paradigm shift of the kind Thomas Kuhn identified and defined in the sciences. The tipping point that occurs when the dominant paradigm no longer works leads to a fundamental shift in the basic concepts and practices. That is, "there is nothing more powerful than an idea whose time has come."

In our modern Gilded Age, more and more people are frustrated by our public officials' seeming inability to address the climate crisis and other challenges of our time. But overwhelmingly, the solutions thus far only focus on symptoms that are embedded within the discredited logic of the neoliberal, shareholder-first model we need to move past, such as the Business Roundtable's exhortations about the win-win nature of stakeholder capitalism.

We have had nine consecutive "hottest years ever," with hundred-year floods happening monthly in some parts of the world, and sea levels rising. Wildfires, too, have become a more frequent and severe consequence of climate change, from Canada to the US West Coast to countries like Greece, Italy, Lebanon, and Turkey. Russia lost a record forty-six million acres to fires in 2021. By September, Canada had lost over forty-five million acres in 2023, an area so great that it is larger than the total land area of half of the world's countries. Extreme weather prompted intense flooding across China, western Europe, the north Indian Ocean region, and Australia. China's Sichuan province had to evacuate eighty thousand people due to reservoir and river overflows. Species are going extinct, and the degradation of ecosystems has far-reaching consequences for ecological balance, food production, and the provision of ecosystem services.

COVID-19 highlighted the vulnerability to pandemics of weak health-care systems and the need for global cooperation in addressing such crises. The gap between the rich and poor continues to widen in many countries, leading to social unrest, political instability, and reduced opportunities for economic mobility. Addressing economic inequality is crucial for achieving sustainable development and social cohesion. Rapid advancements in emerging technologies, such as artificial intelligence and genetic engineering, bring both promising benefits and potential risks.

As we have seen from history, world-shattering crises tend to erupt quickly, and by many estimates our pace to a tipping point is accelerating. With the world's population projected to reach nearly ten billion by 2050, it is not a question of if the increasing strain on resources such as water, energy, food, and land will lead to dramatic crises, but when.

With these cascading climate disasters, we may now have that missing element to galvanize action. Will our future be any different? It is up to us, and our time is running short. Let's hope we seize the opportunity while we can.

ACKNOWLEDGMENTS

O ver the past two decades, I have had the privilege of teaching many of tomorrow's business and societal leaders at world-leading institutions, including Harvard and Cornell in the United States and Cambridge in the United Kingdom. Being on those campuses on a daily basis, I have been continually confronted with questions about today's most important challenges and have dedicated my teaching and research to understanding how businesses can contribute to a more sustainable world. Students in classes on social impact and innovation, sustainable business, and climate change leadership at all levels—doctoral, executive, masters, and undergraduate—have inspired me and pushed my thinking forward on the topics and ideas contained in these pages.

I am also grateful to have had the opportunity to connect with and learn from hundreds of business, governmental, and nongovernmental leaders for my series of *Forbes* columns on sustainable business. Many of their specific stories of innovation to make the world better animate this book, and I thank all of them for their generosity in sharing their time, ideas, and details about work. Entrepreneurialism across sectors is a potent engine of change, and these leaders are individually and collectively building to a sea change in how market systems are constructed and business is conducted around the world.

For most of my academic career, I have been employed by business schools, which some may find an unusual perch for a critic of our current economic model. While over the past two decades I have heard many of my colleagues voice some of the free market assumptions critiqued in these pages, I have found this to be positive, as while I may not agree with them, being in such an environment pushes me to better question and defend my own ideas. We are all increasingly in closed bubbles with others of common thoughts, and I am grateful for having been in academic environments where different ideas are discussed and celebrated, as that is what fosters the kind of friction needed to deepen and advance new thinking.

But also, business schools are vibrant centers of discussion on economic reform, and I have found wonderful and supportive communities focused on sustainable and responsible business at all of these institutions. From my earliest days as a faculty member at Harvard, I was fortunate to find many faculty and students focused on social enterprise and corporate social responsibility. I have particularly benefited from the recent two years at Cambridge, which has been some of the most professionally inspiring time of my career, as relocating across the Atlantic has provided a new context, allowing me to see these issues from a new angle. I am very grateful to Christoph Loch, the dean at Cambridge Judge Business School who recruited me and Yasemin Kor, for being such an enthusiastic recruiter. Teaching with other leading sustainability scholars such as Jennifer Howard-Grenville and Matthew Grimes has also pushed my thinking forward on these topics in new ways. Executive education has been a particularly generative activity for me at Cambridge. I lead the university program on climate and sustainability with Boston Consulting Group, and I am especially grateful to BCG leadership for their commitment to this topic, and to the hundreds of BCGers who have come to Cambridge to learn about tomorrow's key climate and sustainability issues. Many of the faculty involved in the program have also been quite influential to my thinking and work, especially Emily Shuckburgh, who runs Cambridge Zero, the university-wide center on climate topics and achieving net-zero.

Another key aspect of my time at Cambridge has been being elected as a fellow at Jesus College. For this, I very much thank Peter Williamson and Julian Huppert for their support and also Master Sonita Alleyne for leading such an engaging interdisciplinary community.

Many others have helped shape these ideas and their expression over the years of research. A very special appreciation to the Bark Media team, especially Jennifer Kongs, Susie Fagan, James Duft, and Jessica Kellner, who have always pointed me in interesting and important directions and shaped my thinking on these topics. Many have read different iterations and sections of the book and provided feedback, and I especially appreciate discussions with Lionel Paolella, Steve Piersanti, Kunyuan Qiao, Ellen Quigley, and Mia Sannapureddy. Fuyuan Luo and Kuangheng Li provided essential research assistance. I have benefited from the editorial help of Effie Sapuridis and also especially appreciate Arthur Goldwag's insightful commentary, editorial guidance, and streamlining on later stages of the manuscript. These pages are much more persuasive as a result of all of this feedback and guidance.

I also greatly appreciate the insight and support of Jane von Mehren from Aevitas Creative, who helped me sharpen these ideas and better consider how to communicate them to a wider audience, and

I thank Mauro Guillén for introducing me to Jane. John Mahaney and PublicAffairs have also been great partners in helping me more clearly and powerfully communicate the messages in this book.

I also have many personal debts of gratitude. My amazing children, Alex and Ava, are both inspirations for me in different ways and also reminders that we need to act now to protect our planet and world for future generations. And finally, my biggest source of inspiration has been Ying (Claudine) Li, who has been by my side from the start of the work, accompanied me on research trips, discussed the ideas herein, and also been patient and kind as I have been very occupied during these recent years in writing this book.

Notes

Introduction

1. GE, "Jack Welch, the 'Ultimate Manager' Who Oversaw GE's Rise to the Most Valuable Company, Dies at 84," news release, March 2, 2020, www.ge.com/news/reports/jack-welch-the-ultimate-manager-who-oversaw-ges-rise-to-the-most-valuable-company-dies-at-84.

2. Films for the Humanities and Sciences, "The CEO EXCHANGE," YouTube video, posted by Dr. Peter Lewa, April 4, 2015, www.youtube.com/watch?v=oSiEcLbcyNE; Ted Borden, "'CEO Exchange' Visits 'U' Campus," *Michigan Daily*, October 17, 2001, www.michigandaily.com/uncategorized/ceo-exchange-visits-u-campus.

3. Kirk Johnson, "Experts Look to Old Mill for Answers to Pollution of Hudson," *New York Times*, January 16, 2001, www.nytimes.com/2001/01/16/nyregion/experts-look-to-old-mill-for-answers-to-pollution-of-hudson.html.

4. Charlie Cray, "Toxics on the Hudson: The Saga of GE, PCBs and the Hudson River," *Multinational Monitor*, August 2001, www.multinationalmonitor.org/mm2001/01july-august/julyaug01corp1.html.

5. Brendan J. Lyons, "Dredging Up the Truth," *Times Union*, March 9, 2014, www.timesunion.com/local/article/Dredging-up-the-truth-5294643.php.

6. Tom Perkins, "Revealed: Top US Corporations Raising Prices on Americans Even as Profits Surge," *Guardian*, April 2022, www.theguardian.com/business/2022/apr/27/inflation-corporate-america-increased-prices-profits.

7. Damian Carrington, "Global Fossil Fuel Subsidies Almost Doubled in 2021, Analysis Finds," *Guardian*, August 31, 2022, www.theguardian.com/environment/2022/aug/31/fossil-fuel-subsidies-almost-doubled-in-2021-analysis-finds.

8. Dave Anderson, "Sports of the Times; Hootie Is Handling the Heat on the Eve of the Masters," *New York Times*, April 10, 2003, www.nytimes.com/2003/04/10/sports/sports-of-the-times-hootie-is-handling-the-heat-on-the-eve-of-the-masters.html; Michael Pearson, "Augusta National Golf Club Admits First Female Members," CNN, August 21, 2012, www.cnn.com/2012/08/20/us/augusta-female-members/index.html.

9. Thomas Piketty, *Capital and Ideology* (Cambridge, MA: Harvard University Press, 2022); Michael Sandel, *The Tyranny of Merit: What's Become of the Common Good?*

(London: Penguin Books, 2020); Robert Reich, "The Myth of Meritocracy," *Salon*, April 15, 2019, www.salon.com/2019/04/15/robert-reich-the-myth-of-meritocracy_partner/.

10. Michael Young, *The Rise of the Meritocracy* (1958; New York: Routledge, 2017).

11. Michael Young, "Down with Meritocracy," *Guardian*, June 29, 2001, www.the guardian.com/politics/2001/jun/29/comment.

12. Simon Leadbetter, "We Are Stealing the Future, Selling It in the Present, and Calling It GDP," *Blue & Green Tomorrow*, October 10, 2013, https://blueandgreentomorrow .com/energy/we-are-stealing-the-future-selling-it-in-the-present-and-calling-it-gdp/.

13. The Fair Housing Act, 42 U.S.C. 3601, US Department of Justice, last modified June 22, 2023, www.justice.gov/crt/fair-housing-act-1.

14. Rebecca Henderson, *Reimagining Capitalism in a World on Fire* (London: Penguin Books, 2021); Rebecca Henderson, "To Save the Climate, We Have to Reimagine Capitalism," TED, video, October 2020, www.ted.com/talks/rebecca_henderson_to_save_the _climate_we_have_to_reimagine_capitalism?language=en.

15. Karen Bennett and Matthew Goldberg, "Survey: ATM Fees Hit Record High While Overdraft and NSF Fees Fell Sharply," Bankrate, August 30, 2023, www.bankrate .com/banking/checking/checking-account-survey/#interest-checking.

16. Kieran Bol et al., "The Value of Personal Advice: Wealth Management Through the Pandemic," McKinsey, May 25, 2021, www.mckinsey.com/industries/financial -services/our-insights/the-value-of-personal-advice-wealth-management-through-the -pandemic.

17. Sylvia Allegretto et al., "The Public Cost of Low-Wage Jobs in the Banking Industry," UC Berkeley Labor Center, October 27, 2014, https://laborcenter.berkeley.edu /the-public-cost-of-low-wage-jobs-in-the-banking-industry/.

18. Gary Gerstle, "The Rise and Fall(?) of America's Neoliberal Order," *Transactions of the Royal Historical Society* 28 (December 2018): 241–264, https://doi.org/10.1017 /S0080440118000129.

19. David Gelles, *The Man Who Broke Capitalism: How Jack Welch Gutted the Heartland and Crushed the Soul of Corporate America and How to Undo His Legacy* (New York: Simon & Schuster, 2022).

20. Jori Kandra and Lawrence Mishel, "Wages for the Top 1% Skyrocketed 160% Since 1979 While the Share of Wages for the Bottom 90% Shrunk," Economic Policy Institute, December 1, 2020, www.epi.org/blog/wages-for-the-top-1-skyrocketed-160 -since-1979-while-the-share-of-wages-for-the-bottom-90-shrunk-time-to-remake-wage -pattern-with-economic-policies-that-generate-robust-wage-growth-for-vast-majority/.

21. Facundo Alvaredo et al., *World Inequality Report 2018* (Paris: World Inequality Lab, 2018), https://wir2018.wid.world/.

22. Robert B. Reich, "When Bosses Shared Their Profits," *New York Times*, June 25, 2020, www.nytimes.com/2020/06/25/opinion/sunday/corporate-profit-sharing-inequality.html.

23. Chris Isidore, "What's Killing Sears? Its Own Retirees, the CEO Says," CNN, September 14, 2018, https://money.cnn.com/2018/09/14/news/companies/sears-pension-retirees /index.html.

24. Gelles, *Man Who Broke Capitalism*.

25. David Leonhardt, "The Jack Welch Effect," *New York Times*, June 5, 2022, www .nytimes.com/2022/06/05/briefing/jack-welch-david-gelles.html.

26. Milton Friedman, "A Friedman Doctrine—The Social Responsibility of Business Is to Increase Its Profits," *New York Times*, September 13, 1970, www.nytimes.com /1970/09/13/archives/a-friedman-doctrine-the-social-responsibility-of-business-is-to.html.

27. Kyle Westaway, "How Jack Welch Broke Capitalism," interview with David Gelles, YouTube video, May 31, 2022, www.youtube.com/watch?v=RUHTZawNCSY&t=905s.

28. Data source: Bivens, Josh, and Jori Kandra, "CEO Pay Slightly Declined in 2022: But It Has Soared 1,209.2% Since 1978 Compared with a 15.3% Rise in Typical Workers' Pay," September 21, 2023, https://www.epi.org/publication/ceo-pay-in-2022/#full-report.

29. Michael C. Jensen, *A Theory of the Firm: Governance, Residual Claims, and Organizational Forms* (Cambridge, MA: Harvard University Press, 2000).

30. Samantha Prince, "EBay Domestic Holdings, Inc. v. Newmark, 16 A.3d 1 (Del. Ch. 2010)," in *Entrepreneurship Law: Company Creation* (self-pub., Pressbooks), accessed January 13, 2023, https://psu.pb.unizin.org/expsk909/chapter/ebay-domestic-holdings-inc-v-newmark -16a-3d-1 del-ch-2010/.

31. *Fishing with Dynamite*, directed by Paul Wagner (Charlottesville, VA: American Focus, Inc., for the Olsson Center for Applied Ethics, University of Virginia Darden School of Business, 2020).

32. Roger L. Martin, "The Age of Customer Capitalism," *Harvard Business Review*, January 1, 2010, https://hbr.org/2010/01/the-age-of-customer-capitalism; Francesco Guerrera, "Welch Condemns Share Price Focus," *Financial Times*, March 12, 2009, www.ft.com /content/294ff1f2-0f27-11de-ba10-0000779fd2ac.

33. Juliana Menasce Horowitz, Ruth Igielnik, and Rakesh Kochhar, "1. Trends in Income and Wealth Inequality," Pew Research Center, January 9, 2020, www.pewresearch .org/social-trends/2020/01/09/trends-in-income-and-wealth-inequality/.

34. António Guterres (@antonioguterres), "We are all floating on the same sea, but some are in superyachts & others clinging to drifting debris," X (Twitter), July 18, 2020, https://twitter.com/antonioguterres/status/1284494828034760706.

35. Data source: Lucas Chancel et al., *World Inequality Report 2022* (Paris: World Inequality Lab, 2022), open access datasets 2, https://wir2022.wid.world/www-site /uploads/2022/03/WIR2022TablesFigures-Chapter.zip.

36. Orsetta Causa, Alain de Serres, and Nicolas Ruiz, "Growth and Inequality: A Close Relationship?," OECD, 2014, www.oecd.org/economy/growth-and-inequality-close -relationship.htm.

37. Fiona Harvey, "World's Richest 1% Cause Double CO_2 Emissions of Poorest 50%, Says Oxfam," *Guardian*, September 20, 2020, www.theguardian.com/environment/2020 /sep/21/worlds-richest-1-cause-double-co2-emissions-of-poorest-50-says-oxfam.

38. Harvey, "World's Richest 1%."

39. Bjoern Soergel et al., "Combining Ambitious Climate Policies with Efforts to Eradicate Poverty," *Nature Communications* 12, no. 1 (April 27, 2021): 2342, https://doi .org/10.1038/s41467-021-22315-9.

40. Jean-Marc Ollagnier, Peter Lacy, and Mauricio Bermudez Neubauer, "Accelerating Global Companies Toward Net Zero by 2050," Accenture, November 2, 2022,

www.accenture.com/us-en/insights/sustainability/reaching-net-zero-by-2050?c=acn_glb
_netzeroby2050mediarelations_13237252&n=mrl_1022.

41. Hannah Ritchie and Max Roser, "CO$_2$ and GHG Emissions," *Our World in Data*, accessed June 28, 2023, https://ourworldindata.org/co2-emissions.

42. *Poverty and Shared Prosperity 2020: Reversals of Fortune* (Washington, DC: World Bank, 2020), https://openknowledge.worldbank.org/bitstream/handle/10986/34496 /9781464816024.pdf.

43. Su-Lin Tan, "Pakistan Is Bearing the Brunt of the Climate Crisis Despite 'Small Carbon Footprint,' Minister Says," CNBC, September 6, 2022, www.cnbc.com/2022/09/06 /pakistan-finmin-on-floods-country-is-bearing-brunt-of-climate-change.html.

44. Jocelyn Timperley, "The Broken $100-Billion Promise of Climate Finance—and How to Fix It," *Nature* 598, no. 7881 (October 20, 2021): 400–402, https://doi.org/10.1038 /d41586-021-02846-3.

45. Piketty, *Capital and Ideology*.

46. Nir Kaissar and Timothy L. O'Brien, "Who Helps Pay Amazon's Low-Wage Workers? You Do," *Bloomberg*, March 18, 2021, www.bloomberg.com/opinion/articles /2021-03-18/who-helps-pay-amazon-walmart-and-mcdonald-s-workers-you-do.

47. "Statement on the Purpose of a Corporation," Business Roundtable, August 19, 2019, https://opportunity.businessroundtable.org/ourcommitment/.

48. Audre Lorde, "The Master's Tools Will Never Dismantle the Master's House," in *Sister Outsider: Essays and Speeches* (Berkeley, CA: Crossing Press, 2007), 112.

49. Alan Murray with Catherine Whitney, *Tomorrow's Capitalist: My Search for the Soul of Business* (New York: PublicAffairs, 2022), 175.

50. Renae Merle, "Jamie Dimon Defends JPMorgan Chase's $16.50-an-Hour Minimum Wage, Saying It's Not an 'Arms Race,'" *Washington Post*, April 12, 2009, www .washingtonpost.com/business/2019/04/12/jamie-dimon-defends-jpmorgan-chases-an-hour -minimum-wage-says-its-not-an-arms-race/; Robert Reich (@RBReich), "JP Morgan CEO Jamie Dimon made more than $31 million last year, but many of his employees can barely make ends meet," X (Twitter), April 12, 2019, https://twitter.com/RBReich /status/1116795068403163136.

51. Andrew A. King and Kenneth P. Pucker, "The Dangerous Allure of Win-Win Strategies," *Stanford Social Innovation Review* 19, no. 1 (2021): 34–39; Andrew A. King and Luca Berchicci, "Material Sustainability and Stock Return: Faith Is not Enough," *Journal of Financial Reporting* 7, no. 2 (2022): 41–42, https://doi.org/10.2308/JFR-2022-011.

52. Andrew A. King and Kenneth P. Pucker. "ESG and Alpha: Sales or Substance?," *Institutional Investor*, February 25, 2022, www.institutionalinvestor.com/article /b1wxqznltqnyzj/ESG-and-Alpha-Sales-or-Substance.

53. Michael E. Porter, George Serafeim, and Mark Kramer, "Where ESG Fails," *Institutional Investor*, October 16, 2019, www.institutionalinvestor.com/article/b1hm5ghqtxj9s7 /Where-ESG-Fails.

54. Cam Simpson, Akshat Rathi, and Saijel Kishan, "The ESG Mirage," *Bloomberg*, December 10, 2021, www.bloomberg.com/graphics/2021-what-is-esg-investing-msci-ratings -focus-on-corporate-bottom-line/.

55. Steve Johnson, "ESG Outperformance Narrative 'Is Flawed,' New Research Shows," *FinancialTimes*,May3,2021,www.ft.com/content/be140b1b-2249-4dd9-859c-3f8f12ce6036.

56. Aneesh Raghunandan and Shivaram Rajgopal, "Do Socially Responsible Firms Walk the Talk?," SSRN, April 1, 2021, https://ssrn.com/abstract=3609056.

57. Jerry Useem, "Beware of Corporate Promises," *Atlantic*, August 6, 2020, www.theatlantic.com/ideas/archive/2020/08/companies-stand-solidarity-are-licensing -themselves-discriminate/614947/.

58. Peter S. Goodman, "Big Business Pledged Gentler Capitalism. It's Not Happening in a Pandemic," *New York Times*, April 13, 2020, www.nytimes.com/2020/04/13/business /business-roundtable-coronavirus.html.

59. Peter S. Goodman and Patricia Cohen, "It Started as a Tax Cut. Now It Could Change American Life," *New York Times*, November 29, 2017, www.nytimes .com/2017/11/29/business/republican-tax-cut.html.

60. Geoff Colvin, "America's Top CEOs Didn't Live Up to Their Promises in Business Roundtable Letter, Researchers Find," *Fortune*, August 5, 2021. https://fortune .com/2021/08/05/business-roundtable-letter-statement-on-the-purpose-of-a-corporation -stakeholder-capitalism-american-ceos/.

61. Adam Lowenstein, "How a Top US Business Lobby Promised Climate Action—but Worked to Block Efforts," *Guardian*, August 19, 2020, www.theguardian.com/environment /2022/aug/19/top-us-business-lobby-group-climate-action-business-roundtable.

62. Andrew Ross Sorkin, "Business Reaches a Turning Point," *New York Times*, November 6, 2018, www.nytimes.com/2018/11/06/business/dealbook/business-reaches-a -turning-point.html.

63. Larry Fink, "Larry Fink's 2022 Letter to CEOs: The Power of Capitalism," BlackRock, accessed June 28, 2023, www.blackrock.com/corporate/investor-relations /larry-fink-ceo-letter.

64. Irina Ivanova, "BlackRock Touts Investment in Fossil Fuels After Threat from Texas Official," CBS News, February 18, 2022, www.cbsnews.com/news/blackrock -texas-fossil-fuels-boycott/.

65. Silvia Amaro, "Blackrock's Former Sustainable Investing Chief Now Thinks ESG Is a 'Dangerous Placebo,'" CNBC, August 24, 2021, www.cnbc.com/2021/08/24/blackrocks -former-sustainable-investing-chief-says-esg-is-a-dangerous-placebo.html.

66. Kate Aronoff, "The Right Has It In for Woke Investors. The Only Problem? They Don't Exist," *New Republic*, February 15, 2023, https://newrepublic.com/article/170229 /right-woke-investors-problem-dont-exist.

67. Adam Tooze, "Has Covid Ended the Neoliberal Era?," *Guardian*, September 2, 2021, www.theguardian.com/news/2021/sep/02/covid-and-the-crisis-of-neoliberalism.

68. Arundhati Roy, "Arundhati Roy: 'The Pandemic Is a Portal,'" *Financial Times*, April 3, 2020, www.ft.com/content/10d8f5e8-74eb-11ea-95fe-fcd274e920ca.

69. Fiona Harvey, "Cop26: World on Track for Disastrous Heating of More than 2.4C, Says Key Report," *Guardian*, November 9, 2021, www.theguardian.com/environment/2021 /nov/09/cop26-sets-course-for-disastrous-heating-of-more-than-24c-says-key-report.

70. William Gibson and David Brin, "The Science in Science Fiction," NPR, October 22, 2018, www.npr.org/2018/10/22/1067220/the-science-in-science-fiction.

71. Benzinga, "Meet Grove, the Sustainable Product Company Richard Branson's SPAC Is Taking Public," *Markets Insider*, December 8, 2021, https://markets.businessinsider .com/news/stocks/meet-grove-the-sustainable-product-company-richard-branson-s-spac-is -taking-public-1031032978.

Chapter 1: Business's Free Lunch

1. L. Lebreton et al., "Evidence That the Great Pacific Garbage Patch Is Rapidly Accumulating Plastic," *Scientific Reports* 8, no. 1 (March 22, 2018): 4666, https://doi .org/10.1038/s41598-018-22939-w.

2. Mandy Oaklander, "Americans Eat and Inhale More Than 70,000 Plastic Particles Each Year, Study Says," *Time*, June 6, 2019, https://time.com/5601359/microplastics -in-food-air/.

3. Laura Parker, "Plastic Trash Flowing into the Seas Will Nearly Triple by 2040 Without Drastic Action," *National Geographic*, July 23, 2020, www.nationalgeographic .com/science/article/plastic-trash-in-seas-will-nearly-triple-by-2040-if-nothing-done.

4. Stefan Calimanu, "Amazon Profits Increased Nearly 200% with COVID-19," ResearchFDI, January 6, 2021, https://researchfdi.com/amazon-covid-19-pandemic-profits/.

5. "The Climate Pledge," Driving Climate Solutions, Amazon Sustainability, accessed August 25, 2022, https://sustainability.aboutamazon.com/environment/the-climate-pledge.

6. Matthew Gardner, "Amazon Avoids More Than $5 Billion in Corporate Income Taxes, Reports 6 Percent Tax Rate on $35 Billion of US Income," Institute of Taxation and Economic Policy, February 7, 2022, https://itep.org/amazon-avoids-more-than-5-billion- in-corporate-income-taxes-reports-6-percent-tax-rate-on-35-billion-of-us-income/.

7. Sarah Butler, "Amazon's Main UK Division Pays No Corporation Tax for Second Year in a Row," *Guardian*, June 1, 2023, www.theguardian.com/technology/2023/jun/01/ amazon-uk-services-main-division-pay-no-corporation-tax-for-second-year-in-row-tax -credit-government-super-deduction-scheme.

8. Michael Sainato, "'I'm Not a Robot': Amazon Workers Condemn Unsafe, Grueling Conditions at Warehouse," *Guardian*, February 5, 2020, www.theguardian.com/ technology/2020/feb/05/amazon-workers-protest-unsafe-grueling-conditions-warehouse.

9. Michael Sainato, "'They're More Concerned About Profit': Osha, DoJ Take On Amazon's Grueling Working Conditions," *Guardian*, Match 2, 2023, www.theguardian .com/technology/2023/mar/02/amazon-safety-citations-osha-department-of-justice.

10. National Council for Occupational Safety and Health, "National COSH Announces 2022 'Dirty Dozen' Unsafe Employers," news release, April 27, 2022, https:// nationalcosh.org/2022-04_Announcing_The_Dirty_Dozen.

11. Jodi Kantor, Karen Weise, and Grace Ashford, "The Amazon That Customers Don't See," *New York Times*, June 15, 2021, www.nytimes.com/interactive/2021/06/15 /us/amazon-workers.html; Richard Luscombe, "Amazon Rejects Claims It Intimidated

Alabama Workers During Union Vote," *Guardian*, April 11, 2021, www.theguardian.com/us
-news/2021/apr/11/amazon-alabama-workers-union-vote.

12. David Lumb, "Amazon Warehouse Workers Reportedly Complain of Racism
and Death Threats," *CNET*, July 28, 2022, www.cnet.com/tech/amazon-warehouse-workers
-reportedly-complain-of-racism-and-death-threats/.

13. Maria Cramer, "Investigating Amazon, the Employer," *New York Times*, July 4,
2021, www.nytimes.com/2021/07/04/insider/amazon-workers-investigation.html.

14. Grace Kay, "Amazon Tracks Warehouse Workers' Every Move Because Jeff
Bezos Thinks People Are Inherently Lazy, Report Says," *Business Insider*, June 15, 2021, www
.businessinsider.com/amazon-polices-based-jeff-bezos-belief-all-workers-are-lazy-2021-6.

15. Oxfam International, "Pandemic Profits for Companies Soar by Billions More
as Poorest Pay Price," news release, September 9, 2020, www.oxfam.org/en/press-releases
/pandemic-profits-companies-soar-billions-more-poorest-pay-price.

16. "World's Most Admired Companies," *Fortune*, accessed June 28, 2023, https://
fortune.com/ranking/worlds-most-admired-companies/.

17. David Ropeik, "Atlantic Cod and the Human 'Tragedy of the Commons,'"
WBUR, December 3, 2014, www.wbur.org/cognoscenti/2014/12/03/overfishing-georges-bank
-david-ropeik.

18. David R. Klein, "The Introduction, Increase, and Crash of Reindeer on St. Matthew Island," *Journal of Wildlife Management* (1968): 350–367; Gretchen C. Daily and Paul
R. Ehrlich, "Population, Sustainability, and Earth's Carrying Capacity," *BioScience* 42, no. 10
(1992): 761–771.

19. Earth Overshoot Day, Global Footprint Network, www.overshootday.org.

20. Peter Linebaugh, *Stop, Thief!: The Commons, Enclosures, and Resistance* (Oakland, CA: PM Press, 2014), 14.

21. Garrett Hardin, "The Tragedy of the Commons," *Science* 162, no. 3859 (1968):
1244.

22. Mariana Mazzucato, *The Value of Everything: Makers and Takers in the Global
Economy* (London: Allen Lane, 2018).

23. Raj Patel, *The Value of Nothing: How to Reshape Market Society and Redefine
Democracy* (London: Granta, 2011).

24. E. P. Thompson, *The Making of the English Working Class* (London: Penguin
Books, 2013), 95.

25. John Bellamy Foster, "The Expropriation of Nature," *Monthly Review*, March 1,
2018, https://monthlyreview.org/2018/03/01/the-expropriation-of-nature/.

26. Mazzucato, *Value of Everything*.

27. James Maitland, *An Inquiry into the Nature and Origin of Public Wealth and into
the Means and Causes of Its Increase* (Edinburgh: Archibald Constable, 1819).

28. Paul Sweezy, "Capitalism and the Environment," *Monthly Review*, October 1,
2004, https://monthlyreview.org/2004/10/01/capitalism-and-the-environment/.

29. Arthur C. Pigou, *The Economics of Welfare* (London: Macmillan, 1932).

30. "Glossary of Industrial Organization Economics and Competition Law," OECD,
accessed August 31, 2022, www.oecd.org/regreform/sectors/2376087.pdf.

31.   Adam Smith, "On Public Debts," in *An Inquiry into the Nature and Causes of the Wealth of Nations*, vol. 5, *On the Revenue of the Sovereign or Commonwealth* (New York: Random House, 1937), 3.

32.   Patel, *Value of Nothing*, 164.

33.   William P. Fifer et al., "Effects of Alcohol and Smoking During Pregnancy on Infant Autonomic Control," *Developmental Psychobiology* 51, no. 3 (April 2009): 234–242, https://doi.org/10.1002/dev.20366.

34.   Martijn van Hasselt et al., "The Relation Between Tobacco Taxes and Youth and Young Adult Smoking: What Happened Following the 2009 U.S. Federal Tax Increase on Cigarettes?," *Addictive Behaviors* 45 (June 2015): 104–109, https://doi.org/10.1016/j.addbeh.2015.01.023.

35.   Pearl Bader, David Boisclair, and Roberta Ferrence, "Effects of Tobacco Taxation and Pricing on Smoking Behavior in High Risk Populations: A Knowledge Synthesis," *International Journal of Environmental Research and Public Health* 8, no. 11 (November 2011): 4118–4139, https://doi.org/10.3390/ijerph8114118.

36.   UN, "New Study Shows Multi-Trillion Dollar Natural Capital Risk Underlining Urgency of Green Economy Transition," news release, April 15, 2013, www.unep.org/news-and-stories/press-release/new-study-shows-multi-trillion-dollar-natural-capital-risk.

37.   Patel, *Value of Nothing*, 44.

38.   Leah Garcés, *Grilled: Turning Adversaries into Allies to Change the Chicken Industry* (London: Bloomsbury Sigma, 2019).

39.   Porooshat Dadgostar, "Antimicrobial Resistance: Implications and Costs," *Infection and Drug Resistance* (2019): 3903–3910, https://doi.org/10.2147/IDR.S234610.

40.   Ian W. H. Parry, Margaret Walls, and Winston Harrington, "Automobile Externalities and Policies," *Journal of Economic Literature* 45, no. 2 (2007): 373–399, https://doi.org/10.1257/jel.45.2.373.

41.   Jarmo S. Kikstra et al., "The Social Cost of Carbon Dioxide Under Climate-Economy Feedbacks and Temperature Variability," *Environmental Research Letters* 16, no. 9 (September 2021): 094037, https://doi.org/10.1088/1748-9326/ac1d0b.

42.   "About True Price," True Price, accessed August 25, 2022, https://trueprice.org/about-us/.

43.   "Environmental Impact 'Costs' PUMA Almost 100 Million Euro," *Edie*, May 16, 2011, www.edie.net/environmental-impact-costs-puma-almost-100-million-euro/.

44.   Brad Smith, "We're Increasing Our Carbon Fee as We Double down on Sustainability," Microsoft, April 16, 2019, https://blogs.microsoft.com/on-the-issues/2019/04/15/were-increasing-our-carbon-fee-as-we-double-down-on-sustainability/.

45.   Andrew Hughes, "Carbon Pricing and Danone: This Might Just Be a Game Changer," REAL Sustainability Centre, August 18, 2020, https://realsustainability.org/carbon-pricing-and-danone-this-might-just-be-a-game-changer/.

46.   Esther Whieldon, Hana Beckwith, and So Lefebvre, "Amid Urgent Climate Warning from IPCC, Few Companies Globally Have Net-Zero Targets" S&P Global, April 26, 2023, https://www.spglobal.com/esg/insights/amid-urgent-climate-warning-from-ipcc-few-companies-globally-have-net-zero-targets.

Chapter 2: Society Pays the Bill

1.   Alfred D. Chandler Jr., *The Visible Hand* (Cambridge, MA: Harvard University Press, 1993).

2.   William G. Roy, *Socializing Capital: The Rise of the Large Industrial Corporation in America* (Princeton, NJ: Princeton University Press, 1999).

3.   Laura Sullivan, "How Big Oil Misled the Public into Believing Plastic Would Be Recycled," NPR, September 11, 2020, www.npr.org/2020/09/11/897692090/how-big-oil-misled -the-public-into-believing-plastic-would-be-recycled.

4.   Sullivan, "How Big Oil Misled the Public."

5.   William Park, "How Companies Blame You for Climate Change," BBC, May 5, 2022, www.bbc.com/future/article/20220504-why-the-wrong-people-are-blamed-for-climate-change.

6.   Chang Che, "His Recycling Symbol Is Everywhere. The E.P.A. Says It Shouldn't Be," *New York Times*, August 7, 2023, www.nytimes.com/2023/08/07/climate/chasing-arrows-recy cling-symbol-epa.html.

7.   Adrian Stacey, "Coke & Pepsi Sued Over Plastic Pollution," *Scuba Diver Mag*, March 13, 2020, www.scubadivermag.com/coke-pepsi-sued-over-plastic-pollution/.

8.   Perry Wheeler, "U.S. Companies Use Misleading 'Recyclable' Labels on Hundreds of Plastic Products," Greenpeace USA, February 18, 2020, www.greenpeace.org/usa/news /u-s-companies-use-misleading-recyclable-labels-on-hundreds-of-plastic-products/.

9.   Sullivan, "How Big Oil Misled the Public."

10.   Sharon Lerner, "Waste Only: How the Plastics Industry Is Fighting to Keep Pol-luting the World," *Intercept*, July 20, 2019, https://theintercept.com/2019/07/20/plastics -industry-plastic-recycling/; Che, "His Recycling Symbol Is Everywhere."

11.   Laura Parker, "A Whopping 91% of Plastic Isn't Recycled," *National Geographic*, December 20, 2018, www.nationalgeographic.com/science/article/plastic-produced-recycling -waste-ocean-trash-debris-environment.

12.   Karen McVeigh, "Coca-Cola, Pepsi and Nestlé Named Top Plastic Polluters for Third Year in a Row," *Guardian*, December 7, 2020, www.theguardian.com/environment /2020/dec/07/coca-cola-pepsi-and-nestle-named-top-plastic-polluters-for-third-year-in -a-row.

13.   Break Free from Plastic, *Branded: Five Years of Holding Corporate Plastic Polluters Accountable*, November 2022, https://brandaudit.breakfreefromplastic.org/wp-content /uploads/2022/11/BRANDED-brand-audit-report-2022.pdf.

14.   Break Free from Plastic, *Branded*.

15.   "The Global Commitment 2022 Progress Report," Ellen MacArthur Founda-tion, October 25, 2022, https://ellenmacarthurfoundation.org/global-commitment-2022 /overview.

16.   ExxonMobil, "Unsettled Science" (advertisement), *New York Times*, accessed Febru-ary 24, 2023, https://static01.nyt.com/images/2017/08/22/opinion/22oreskesWeb4/22oreskes Web4-superJumbo.jpg?quality=75&auto=webp.

17.   Maxine Joselow, "Exclusive: GM, Ford Knew About Climate Change 50 Years Ago," *E&E News*, October 26, 2020, www.eenews.net/articles/exclusive-gm-ford-knew-about -climate-change-50-years-ago/; Benjamin Franta, "Shell and Exxon's Secret 1980s Climate

Change Warnings," *Guardian*, September 19, 2018, www.theguardian.com/environment/climate-consensus-97-per-cent/2018/sep/19/shell-and-exxons-secret-1980s-climate-change-warnings.

18.   "Word of the Year 2022," *Merriam-Webster*, November 28, 2022, www.merriam-webster.com/words-at-play/word-of-the-year/gaslighting.

19.   Piketty, *Capital and Ideology*, 7.

20.   Chris McGreal, "How a Powerful US Lobby Group Helps Big Oil to Block Climate Action," *Guardian*, July 19, 2021, www.theguardian.com/environment/2021/jul/19/big-oil-climate-crisis-lobby-group-api.

21.   Felicity Lawrence, David Pegg, and Rob Evans, "How Vested Interests Tried to Turn the World Against Climate Science," *Guardian*, October 10, 2019, www.theguardian.com/environment/2019/oct/10/vested-interests-public-against-climate-science-fossil-fuel-lobby.

22.   Santa Barbara for Safe & Local Transport, Facebook page, accessed August 25, 2022, www.facebook.com/safetransportsb/; "Community," Safe Transport SB, accessed August 25, 2022, https://safetransportsb.com/community/.

23.   Lawrence Carter, Zach Boren, and Alexander Kaufman, "Revealed: BP and Shell Back Anti-Climate Lobby Groups Despite Pledges," *Unearthed*, September 28, 2020, https://unearthed.greenpeace.org/2020/09/28/bp-shell-climate-lobby-groups/.

24.   Graham Rapier, "Uber, Lyft, and DoorDash Have Now Spent More than $200 Million on Prop. 22—but There's Still No Guarantee It'll Pass," *Business Insider*, October 30, 2020, www.businessinsider.com/uber-doordash-lyft-prop-22-spending-200-million-close-polling-2020-10.

25.   "Deepwater Horizon—BP Gulf of Mexico Oil Spill," US Environmental Protection Agency, September 12, 2013, www.epa.gov/enforcement/deepwater-horizon-bp-gulf-mexico-oil-spill.

26.   Eric Atkins, "The Environmental Tipping Point of One-Cup Coffee Pods," *Globe and Mail*, July 5, 2015, www.theglobeandmail.com/report-on-business/the-environmental-tipping-point-of-one-cup-coffee-pods/article25308375/.

27.   Aimee Pearcy, "H&M Greenwashing Is 'Disguising the Reality' of Fast Fashion," *Big Issue*, August 5, 2021, www.bigissue.com/news/environment/hm-greenwashing-is-disguising-the-reality-of-fast-fashion/.

28.   Peter S. Goodman, "C.E.O.s Were Our Heroes, at Least According to Them," *New York Times*, January 13, 2022, www.nytimes.com/2022/01/13/business/davos-man-marc-benioff-book.html.

29.   Goodman, "C.E.O.s Were Our Heroes."

30.   Kate Yoder, "True Costs: How the Oil Industry Cast Climate Policy as an Economic Burden," *Grist*, April 7, 2022, https://grist.org/economics/climate-legislation-costs-economics-oil-industry/.

31.   Elizabeth Popp Berman, *Thinking Like an Economist: How Efficiency Replaced Equality in U.S. Public Policy* (Princeton, NJ: Princeton University Press, 2022).

32.   US Environmental Protection Agency, *Social Cost of Carbon*, December 2016, www.epa.gov/sites/default/files/2016-12/documents/social_cost_of_carbon_fact_sheet.pdf.

33.	Brad Plumer, "Trump Put a Low Cost on Carbon Emissions. Here's Why It Matters," *New York Times*, August 23, 2018, www.nytimes.com/2018/08/23/climate/social-cost -carbon.html.

34.	Benjamin Franta, "Weaponizing Economics: Big Oil, Economic Consultants, and Climate Policy Delay," *Environmental Politics* 31, no. 4 (2022): 555–575, https://doi.org/10 .1080/09644016.2021.1947636.

35.	"From Ambition to Action—the Path to Net Zero," BlackRock, accessed August 25, 2022, https://web.archive.org/web/20220831142014/www.blackrock.com/us /individual/about-us/road-to-net-zero.

36.	Sarah George, "Investors Press 1,600 'Laggard' Businesses to Report Environmental Impacts," *Edie*, May 31, 2023, www.edie.net/investors-press-1600-laggard-businesses-to -report-environmental-impacts/.

37.	"Fewer Than One in 200 Companies Have Credible Climate Plans, Says CDP," Reuters, February 8, 2023, www.reuters.com/business/sustainable-business/fewer -than-one-200-companies-have-credible-climate-plans-says-cdp-2023-02-08/.

38.	Andrew Stanley, "Energy Transitions," International Monetary Fund, December 2022, www.imf.org/en/Publications/fandd/issues/2022/12/picture-this-energy-transitions.

39.	Data source: Hannah Ritchie, Pablo Rosado, and Max Roser, "Fossil Fuels," *Our World in Data*, accessed July 18, 2023, https://ourworldindata.org/fossil-fuels.

40.	Moira Weigel, "What You Don't Know About Amazon," *New York Times*, April 21, 2022, www.nytimes.com/2022/04/21/opinion/amazon-product-liability.html.

41.	Weigel, "What You Don't Know."

42.	"Audience Ad Targeting," Meta for Business, accessed August 25, 2022, https://en -gb.facebook.com/business/ads/ad-targeting.

43.	Elizabeth Dwoskin, "Russia Is Still the Biggest Player in Disinformation, Facebook Says," *Washington Post*, May 21, 2021, www.washingtonpost.com/technology/2021/05/26 /facebook-disinformation-russia-report/.

44.	Oliver Milman, "Revealed: Quarter of All Tweets About Climate Crisis Produced by Bots," *Guardian*, February 21, 2020, www.theguardian.com/technology/2020/feb/21 /climate-tweets-twitter-bots-analysis.

45.	Aronoff, "The Right Has It In for Woke Investors."

46.	Samantha Aschieris, "ESG Is 'Terrifying,' 'Problematic' Concept in Investing. Author and Entrepreneur Vivek Ramaswamy Explains Why," *Daily Signal*, January 31, 2023, www.dailysignal.com/2023/01/31/esg-is-terrifying-problematic-concept-in-investing -author-financial-adviser-vivek-ramaswamy-explains-why/.

47.	Daniel Garrett and Ivan Ivanov, "Gas, Guns, and Governments: Financial Costs of Anti-ESG Policies" (Jacobs Levy Equity Management Center for Quantitative Financial Research paper), SSRN, May 30, 2022, https://ssrn.com/abstract=4123366.

48.	Julianne Zimmerman, "Graduating from Externalities, Ending the Grift," Reinventure Capital, February 28, 2022, https://reinventurecapital.com/graduating-from-externalities -ending-the-grift/.

49.	*Cambridge English Dictionary*, s.v., "grift (n.)," accessed June 28, 2023, https ://dictionary.cambridge.org/dictionary/english/grift.

50. Ray Anderson, "The Business Logic of Sustainability," TED, video, February 2009, www.ted.com/talks/ray_anderson_the_business_logic_of_sustainability; Gwen Kinkead and Eileen P. Gunn, "In the Future, People Like Me Will Go to Jail," *Fortune*, May 24, 1999, https://money.cnn.com/magazines/fortune/fortune_archive/1999/05/24/260285/index.htm.

51. Jane McMullen, "The Audacious PR Plot That Seeded Doubt About Climate Change," BBC, July 23, 2022, www.bbc.co.uk/news/science-environment-62225696.

51. Aaron Lammer, Max Linsky, and Evan Ratliff, "#543: Jeff Goodell," July 26, 2023, in *Longform Podcast*, 50:27, https://longform.org/posts/longform-podcast-543-jeff-goodell.

Chapter 3: Who Pays for Carbon Emissions?

1. Matt Kessler, "The Environmental Cost of Internet Porn," *Atlantic*, December 13, 2017, www.theatlantic.com/technology/archive/2017/12/the-environmental-cost-of-internet-porn/548210/.

2. Zoom, *Environmental Social Governance Report 2022*, May 2023, https://investors.zoom.us/static-files/0ddac6eb-3901-4f86-95c2-898bee9c8b95.

3. AFP, "Chill Your Netflix Habit, Climate Experts Say," France 24, October 28, 2019, www.france24.com/en/20191028-chill-your-netflix-habit-climate-experts-say.

4. Maxime Efoui-Hess, "Climate Crisis: The Unsustainable Use of Online Video" (Paris: The Shift Project, 2019), https://theshiftproject.org/wp-content/uploads/2019/07/Press-kit_Climate-crisis_The-unsustainable-use-of-online-video.pdf; Alex de Vries, "The Growing Energy Footprint of Artificial Intelligence," *Joule* 7, no. 10 (2023), https://doi.org/10.1016/j.joule.2023.09.004.

5. Sarah Griffiths, "Why Your Internet Habits Are Not as Clean as You Think," BBC, March 6, 2020, www.bbc.com/future/article/20200305-why-your-internet-habits-are-not-as-clean-as-you-think.

6. Hanna Ritchie, "Climate Change and Flying: What Share of Global CO_2 Emissions Come from Aviation?," *Our World in Data*, October 22, 2020, https://ourworldindata.org/co2-emissions-from-aviation.

7. "Cisco Annual Internet Report (2018–2023)," Cisco, last modified March 9, 2020, www.cisco.com/c/en/us/solutions/collateral/executive-perspectives/annual-internet-report/white-paper-c11-741490.html.

8. Cisco, *Global—2021 Forecast Highlights*, 2021, www.cisco.com/c/dam/m/en_us/solutions/service-provider/vni-forecast-highlights/pdf/Global_2021_Forecast_Highlights.pdf.

9. Mark Sweney, "Streaming's Dirty Secret: How Viewing Netflix Top 10 Creates Vast Quantity of CO_2," *Guardian*, October 29, 2021, www.theguardian.com/tv-and-radio/2021/oct/29/streamings-dirty-secret-how-viewing-netflix-top-10-creates-vast-quantity-of-co2.

10. Netflix, *Environmental Social Governance: 2019 Sustainability Accounting Standards Board (SASB) Report*, February 2020, https://s22.q4cdn.com/959853165/files/doc_downloads/2020/02/0220_Netflix_EnvironmentalSocialGovernanceReport_FINAL.pdf.

11. Netflix, *Environmental Social Governance Report 2021*, March 30, 2022, https://s22.q4cdn.com/959853165/files/doc_downloads/2022/03/30/2021-SASB-Report-FINAL.pdf.

12. Kelly Gilblom and Bloomberg, "Your Netflix Habit Has a Small Carbon Footprint, According to a New Study," *Fortune*, June 11, 2021, https://fortune.com/2021/06/11/netflix-streaming-small-carbon-footprint-climate-change/.

13. Sandvine, *The Global Internet Phenomena Report*, January 2023, www.sandvine.com/phenomena; Gilblom and Bloomberg, "Your Netflix Habit."

14. Sweney, "Streaming's Dirty Secret."

15. Sweney, "Streaming's Dirty Secret."

16. Agnes Walton and Kristopher Knight, "New Climate Promises, Same Old Global Warming," *New York Times*, July 12, 2022, www.nytimes.com/2022/07/12/opinion/net-zero-global-warming.html.

17. "Greenhouse Gases and Energy," National Greenhouse and Energy Reporting, Australian Government Clean Energy Regulator, April 14, 2023, www.cleanenergyregulator.gov.au/NGER/About-the-National-Greenhouse-and-Energy-Reporting-schemeGreenhouse-gases-and-energy.

18. Anne-Titia Bové and Steven Swartz, "Starting at the Source: Sustainability in Supply Chains," McKinsey, November 11, 2016, www.mckinsey.com/capabilities/sustainability/our-insights/starting-at-the-source-sustainability-in-supply-chains.

19. Sweney, "Streaming's Dirty Secret."

20. Annie Palmer, "Jeff Bezos Unveils Sweeping Plan to Tackle Climate Change," CNBC, September 19, 2019, www.cnbc.com/2019/09/19/jeff-bezos-speaks-about-amazon-sustainability-in-washington-dc.html.

21. Will Evans, "Private Report Shows How Amazon Drastically Undercounts Its Carbon Footprint," *Reveal*, February 25, 2022, https://revealnews.org/article/private-report-shows-how-amazon-drastically-undercounts-its-carbon-footprint/.

22. Gemma Bowcock, "Hollow Corporate Promises: How to Stop False Climate Claims," Carbon Market Watch, February 28, 2022, https://carbonmarketwatch.org/2022/02/28/hollow-corporate-promises-how-to-stop-false-climate-claims/.

23. Tom Greenwood, "Are We Trapped in the Jevons Paradox?," *Oxymoron* (blog), July 1, 2022, https://tomgreenwood.substack.com/p/are-we-trapped-in-the-jevons-paradox.

24. Victoria Masterson, "Degrowth—What's Behind the Economic Theory and Why Does It Matter Right Now?," World Economic Forum, June 15, 2022, www.weforum.org/agenda/2022/06/what-is-degrowth-economics-climate-change/.

25. Emma Stewart, "Our Progress on Sustainability: One Year In," Netflix, March 30, 2022, https://about.netflix.com/en/news/netflix-sustainability-progress-one-year-in.

26. Julie Creswell, "For Many Big Food Companies, Emissions Head in the Wrong Direction," *New York Times*, September 22, 2023, www.nytimes.com/2023/09/22/business/food-companies-emissions-climate-pledges.html.

27. Seventh Generation, *Driving Transformational Change: 2018 Corporate Consciousness Report*, July 2018, www.seventhgeneration.com/sites/default/files/2019-12/svgccreport2018slmreleasedollowresolution2.pdf.

28. Seventh Generation, *2020: A Year Like No Other, Seventh Generation Corporate Consciousness Update*, August 2021, www.seventhgeneration.com/sites/default/files/2021-08/svg2020-v1f-080621.pdf.

29. Rio ESG, "What Is Scope 4?," Rio, March 25, 2021, www.rio.ai/blogscope-4-emissions.

30. Akshat Rathi, Natasha White, and Demetrios Pogkas, "Junk Carbon Offsets Are What Make These Big Companies 'Carbon Neutral,'" *Bloomberg*, November 22, 2022, www.bloomberg.com/graphics/2022-carbon-offsets-renewable-energy/.

31. Rathi, White, and Pogkas, "Junk Carbon Offsets."

32. Patrick Greenfield, "Revealed: More Than 90% of Rainforest Carbon Offsets by Biggest Certifier Are Worthless, Analysis Shows," *Guardian*, January 18, 2023, www.theguardian.com/environment/2023/jan/18/revealed-forest-carbon-offsets-biggest-provider-worthless-verra-aoe.

33. Irina Ivanova, "Delta Faces Lawsuit Alleging Its 'Carbon-Neutral' Claim Is Greenwashing," CBS News, May 31, 2023, www.cbsnews.com/news/delta-lawsuit-cabon-neutral-greenwashing-carbon-offsets/.

34. Rathi, White, and Pogkas, "Junk Carbon Offsets."

35. "Permanence," Carbon Offset Guide, accessed July 27, 2023, www.offsetguide.org/high-quality-offsets/permanence/.

36. Grayson Badgley and Danny Cullenward, "California Forest Carbon Buffer Pool Update," CarbonPlan, December 1, 2022, https://carbonplan.org/blog/buffer-analysis-update.

37. Damian Carrington, "Tree Planting 'Has Mind-Blowing Potential' to Tackle Climate Crisis," *Guardian*, July 4, 2019, www.theguardian.com/environment/2019/jul/04/planting-billions-trees-best-tackle-climate-crisis-scientists-canopy-emissions; Sophie Lewis, "Planting a Trillion Trees Could Be the 'Most Effective Solution' to Climate Change, Study Says," CBS News, July 8, 2019, www.cbsnews.com/news/planting-a-trillion-trees-could-be-the-most-effective-solution-to-climate-change/.

38. US Department of Interior, "Trump Administration Furthers Commitment to One Trillion Trees Initiative," news release, October 13, 2020, www.doi.gov/pressreleases/trump-administration-furthers-commitment-one-trillion-trees-initiative.

39. UK Centre for Ecology & Hydrology, "Half of Replanted Tropical Trees Don't Survive," news release, *Science Daily*, November 14, 2022, www.sciencedaily.com/releases/2022/11/221114095347.htm.

40. Christopher Marquis, "Searching for a Solution: Ecosia Is Taking on Google and Aiding Reforestation Efforts in the Process," *Forbes*, www.forbes.com/sites/christophermarquis/2021/09/01/searching-for-a-solution-ecosia-is-taking-on-google-and-aiding-reforestation-efforts-in-the-process/.

41. "Carbon Offset Certifications," Native, accessed July 27, 2023, https://native.eco/climate-projects/certifications/.

42. Walton and Knight, "New Climate Promises."

43. BBB National Programs, "National Advertising Review Board Recommends JBS Discontinue 'Net Zero' Emissions by 2040 Claims," news release, June 20, 2023, https://bbbprograms.org/media-center/dd/narb-jbs-net-zero-emissions.

44. Alan Singer, "The List of Climate Villains Is Long—and Growing Longer," LIherald.com, November 4, 2021, www.liherald.com/stories/the-list-of-climate-villains-is-long-and-growing-longer,135965.

45. "Tree," Our Materials, Allbirds, accessed June 27, 2023, www.allbirds.co.uk/pages/our-materials-tree.

46. Maura Brannigan, "Allbirds Is Making Sustainable Shoe Soles Out of Renewable Sugarcane," *Fashionista*, August 2, 2018, https://fashionista.com/2018/08/allbirds-sweetfoam-sustainable-shoe-soles.

47. "Sugar," Our Materials, Allbirds, accessed June 27, 2023, www.allbirds.co.uk/pages/our-materials-sugar.

48. Elizabeth Segran, "Allbirds Wants to Fix Your Sole," *Fast Company*, January 8, 2018, www.fastcompany.com/90202030/allbirds-wants-to-fix-your-sole.

49. Emily Farra, "Adidas and Allbirds Are Joining Forces—and Rewriting the Rules of Competition," *British Vogue*, May 28, 2020, www.vogue.co.uk/news/article/adidas-allbirds-collaboration-sustainable-sneaker-lowest-carbon-footprint.

50. Christopher Marquis, "Making Salads Even Greener: Just Salad Is Bringing Zero-Waste Dining into the Mainstream," *Forbes*, April 6, 2021, www.forbes.com/sites/christopher marquis/2021/04/06/making-salads-even-greener-just-salad-is-bringing-zero-waste-dining-into-the-mainstream/.

51. Kate Yoder, "Why Do Oil Companies Care So Much About Your Carbon Footprint?" *Mother Jones*, August 31, 2020, www.motherjones.com/environment/2020/08/why-do-oil-companies-care-so-much-about-your-carbon-footprint/.

52. Tom Greenwood, "Whose Idea Was Carbon Footprinting?," *Oxymoron* (blog), July 22, 2022, https://tomgreenwood.substack.com/p/whose-idea-was-carbon-footprinting.

53. Simon Black, Ian Parry, and Karlygash Zhunussova, "More Countries Are Pricing Carbon, but Emissions Are Still Too Cheap," *IMF Blog*, July 21, 2022, www.imf.org/en/Blogs/Articles/2022/07/21/blog-more-countries-are-pricing-carbon-but-emissions-are-still-too-cheap.

54. Sean Bray, "Carbon Taxes in Europe," Tax Foundation, June 14, 2022, https://tax foundation.org/carbon-taxes-in-europe-2022/.

55. Jesse Klein, "3 Things Learned from Microsoft's Carbon Removal Report," *GreenBiz*, April 1, 2022, www.greenbiz.com/article/3-things-learned-microsofts-carbon-removal-report.

Chapter 4: Who Pays for Damage to the Earth?

1. Robyn O'Brien, "Robyn O'Brien | TEDxAustin 2011," YouTube video, posted by TEDx Talks, March 24, 2011, www.youtube.com/watch?v=rixyrCNVVGA.

2. "Global Greenhouse Gas Emissions Data," US Environmental Protection Agency, last modified February 15, 2023, www.epa.gov/ghgemissions/global-greenhouse-gas-emissions-data#.

3. UN Sustainable Development Goals, "UN Report: Nature's Dangerous Decline 'Unprecedented'; Species Extinction Rates 'Accelerating,'" news release, May 6, 2019, www.un.org/sustainabledevelopment/blog/2019/05/nature-decline-unprecedented-report/.

4. "Development of the Seed Patent System," Center for Food Safety, accessed June 27, 2023, www.centerforfoodsafety.org/issues/303/seeds/development-of-the-seed-patent-system.

5. S&P Global Sustainable, "How the World's Largest Companies Depend on Nature and Biodiversity," S&P Global, May 10, 2023, www.spglobal.com/esg/insights/featured/special-editorial/how-the-world-s-largest-companies-depend-on-nature-and-biodiversity.

6. Christian Bunn et al., "A Bitter Cup: Climate Change Profile of Global Production of Arabica and Robusta Coffee," *Climatic Change* 129, no. 1 (2015): 89–101, https://link.springer.com/content/pdf/10.1007/s10584-014-1306-x.pdf.

7.   "Transcript: Ezra Klein Interviews Leah Garcés," *Ezra Klein Show, New York Times,* November 29, 2022, www.nytimes.com/2022/11/29/opinion/transcript-ezra-klein-interviews -leah-garces.html.

8.   "Transcript: Ezra Klein Interviews Leah Garcés."

9.   *Animalia,* s.v. "Indian Elephant," accessed June 27, 2023, https://animalia.bio /indian-elephant.

10.   Isabelle Niang et al., "Africa," in *Climate Change 2014: Impacts, Adaptation, and Vulnerability: Part B: Regional Aspects. Contribution of Working Group II to the Fifth Assessment Report of the Intergovernmental Panel on Climate Change,* V. R. Barros et al., eds. (Cambridge: Cambridge University Press, 2014), 1206, www.ipcc.ch/site/assets/uploads /2018/02/WGIIAR5-Chap22_FINAL.pdf.

11.   "Transcript: Ezra Klein Interviews Leah Garcés."

12.   Brian Machovina, Kenneth J. Feeley, and William J. Ripple. "Biodiversity Con-servation: The Key Is Reducing Meat Consumption," *Science of the Total Environment* 536 (2015): 419–431, https://doi.org/10.1016/j.scitotenv.2015.07.022.

13.   Lisa Cox, "Beef Industry Linked to 94% of Land Clearing in Great Barrier Reef Catchments," *Guardian,* August 7, 2019, www.theguardian.com/australia-news/2019 /aug/08/beef-industry-linked-to-94-of-land-clearing-in-great-barrier-reef-catchments.

14.   Alden Wicker et al., "That Organic Cotton T-Shirt May Not Be as Organic as You Think," *New York Times,* April 12, 2022, www.nytimes.com/2022/02/13/world/asia/organic -cotton-fraud-india.html.

15.   Julius Hensel, *Bread from Stones* (Greeley, CO: AcresUSA, 1991); Regenerative Agriculture Initiative and the Carbon Underground, "What Is Regenerative Agriculture?," February 24, 2017, https://02fe55.p3cdn1.secureserver.net/wp-content/uploads/2017/02 /Regen-Ag-Definition-7.27.17-1.pdf; W. Richard Teague et al., "The Role of Ruminants in Reducing Agriculture's Carbon Footprint in North America," *Journal of Soil and Water Conservation* 71, no. 2 (2016): 156–164, https://doi.org/10.2489/jswc.71.2.156.

16.   Benedikt Bösel and Louisa B-T, "Dirt to Soil: One Family's Journey into Regenerative Agriculture," *AgFunder News,* October 15, 2018, https://agfundernews.com /dirt-to-soil-one-familys-journey-into-regenerative-agriculture.

17.   "Soil Health Nuggets," US Department of Agriculture, accessed June 27, 2023, https://indiana.clearchoicescleanwater.org/wp-content/uploads/sites/3/2020/09/Soil -Health-Nuggets_reduced.pdf.

18.   Chris Arsenault, "Only 60 Years of Farming Left if Soil Degradation Con-tinues," *Scientific American,* December 5, 2014, www.scientificamerican.com/article /only-60-years-of-farming-left-if-soil-degradation-continues/.

19.   Daphne Miller, "The Surprising Healing Qualities . . . of Dirt," *Our World* (blog), United Nations University, February 22, 2014, https://ourworld.unu.edu/en /the-surprising-healing-qualities-of-dirt.

20.   Lana Bandoim, "How President Biden's Climate Plan Will Affect Cover Crops," *Forbes,* June 18, 2021, www.forbes.com/sites/lanabandoim/2021/06/18/how -president-bidens-climate-plan-will-affect-cover-crops/.

21. Christopher Marquis, "rePlant Fuels Food System's Shift to Regenerative Agriculture with $2 Billion for Farmers to Build Soil Health," *Forbes*, www.forbes.com/sites /christophermarquis/2021/10/05/replant-fuels-food-systems-shift-to-regenerative-agri culture-with-2b-soil-fund-and-support-for-farmers/.

22. Danone North America, "Danone North America Announces Partnership with rePlant Capital," news release, *PR Newswire*, January 19, 2020, www.prnewswire .com/news-releases/danone-north-america-announces-partnership-with-replant-capital -300995276.html.

23. Christopher Marquis, "From Soap to Chocolate: Dr. Bronner's Launches into Food as Extension of Supply Chain's Positive Impact," *Forbes*, July 2, 2021, www.forbes .com/sites/christophermarquis/2021/07/02/from-soap-to--chocolate-dr-bronners-launches -into-food-as-extension-of-supply-chains-positive-impact/.

24. Tablas Creek Vineyard, "Tablas Creek Is the First Regenerative Organic Certified™ (ROC™) Winery in America," news release, August 17, 2020, https://tablascreek.com /news/2020/tablas_creek_is_the_first_regenerative_organic_certified_roc_winery_in_america.

Chapter 5: Who Pays for Cheap Goods?

1. Clarisse Magnin and Sasria Hedrich, "Refashioning Clothing's Environmental Impact," McKinsey, July 25, 2019, www.mckinsey.com/capabilities/sustainability/our -insights/sustainability-blog/refashioning-clothings-environmental-impact.

2. "Nondurable Goods: Product-Specific Data," US Environmental Protection Agency, last modified December 3, 2022, www.epa.gov/facts-and-figures-about-materials -waste-and-recycling/nondurable-goods-product-specific-data.

3. Christina Dean, "Waste—Is It 'Really' in Fashion?," Fashion Revolution, accessed June 27, 2023, www.fashionrevolution.org/waste-is-it-really-in-fashion/.

4. Rachel Monroe, "Ultra-Fast Fashion Is Eating the World," *Atlantic*, February 6, 2021, www.theatlantic.com/magazine/archive/2021/03ultra-fast-fashion-is-eating-the-world/617794/.

5. "The Environmental Impact of Fashion," ClimateSeed, October 6, 2021, https ://climateseed.com/blog/the-environmental-impact-of-fashion.

6. "Putting the Brakes on Fast Fashion," UN Environment Programme, last modified June 28, 2021, www.unep.org/news-and-stories/story/putting-brakes-fast-fashion.

7. "How Much Do Our Wardrobes Cost to the Environment?" World Bank, September 23, 2019, www.worldbank.org/en/news/feature/2019/09/23/costo-moda-medio-ambi ente; UN Climate Change, "Fashion Industry, UN Pursue Climate Action for Sustainable Development," news release, January 22, 2018, https://unfccc.int/news/fashion-industry -un-pursue-climate-action-for-sustainable-development.

8. Environmental Audit Committee, *Fixing Fashion: Clothing Consumption and Sustainability*, UK Parliament, February 19, 2019, https://publications.parliament.uk/pa/cm 201719/cmselect/cmenvaud/1952/report-summary.html.

9. Jasmin Malik Chua, "The Environment and Economy Are Paying the Price for Fast Fashion—but There's Hope," *Vox*, September 12, 2019, www.vox.com /2019/9/12/20860620/fast-fashion-zara-hm-forever-21-boohoo-environment-cost.

10. Chua, "The Environment and Economy."

11. Monroe, "Ultra-Fast Fashion."

12. Ken Miller, "Tyson, Others, Lose Oklahoma Lawsuit Over Poultry Pollution," AP, January 19, 2023, https://apnews.com/article/politics-oklahoma-state-government-illinois-tulsa-aaa56f6e60d16a9205bc3730ad1d26ed.

13. Christopher Marquis, "Sustainability with Style: Green Circle Salons Creates Community of 'Waste Warriors' Recycling," *Forbes*, January 5, 2022, www.forbes.com/sites/christophermarquis/2022/01/05/sustainability-with-style-green-circle-salons-creates-community-of-waste-warriors-recycling/.

14. Ed Boyd, "A Designer's Vision for Circularity," *Dell Blog*, Dell, December 9, 2020, www.dell.com/en-us/blog/a-designer-s-vision-for-circularity/.

15. Ken Pucker, "A Circle That Isn't Easily Squared," *Stanford Social Innovation Review* 21, no. 3 (Summer 2023): 26–39, https://doi.org/10.48558/96N0-Q813.

16. Hervé Corvellec, Alison F. Stowell, and Nils Johansson, "Critiques of the Circular Economy," *Journal of Industrial Ecology* 26, no. 2 (2022): 421–432.

17. James Kennelly, *Richard Henkel GmbH: Growing Profits, Not Sales* (Ontario, Canada: Ivey Publishing, 2022), 5, https://hbsp.harvard.edu/product/W25517-PDF-ENG?Ntt=.

18. Hartley Charlton, "iPhone 13 vs. iPhone 14 Buyer's Guide: Should You Upgrade?," *MacRumors*, April 5, 2023, www.macrumors.com/guide/iphone-13-vs-iphone-14/.

19. Apple, "Apple Expands Global Recycling Programs," news release, April 18, 2019, www.apple.com/newsroom/2019/04/apple-expands-global-recycling-programs/.

20. Fairphone, *Fairphone's Impact 2021*, July 2021, www.fairphone.com/wp-content/uploads/2022/06/Fairphone-Impact-Report-2021.pdf.

21. Guy Ryder and Houlin Zhao, "The World's e-Waste Is a Huge Problem. It's Also a Golden Opportunity," World Economic Forum, January 24, 2019, www.weforum.org/agenda/2019/01/how-a-circular-approach-can-turn-e-waste-into-a-golden-opportunity/.

22. "The Electronic Graveyard," Plastic Expert, accessed June 27, 2023, www.plasticexpert.co.uk/plastic-recycling-guiyu-graveyard/.

23. Newsfile Corp., "Back Market, the Renewed Electronics Marketplace, Raises $510 Million and Is Now Valued at $5.7 Billion," *Yahoo! Finance*, January 12, 2022, https://finance.yahoo.com/news/back-market-renewed-electronics-marketplace-172600288.html.

24. "EasyDose™ Ultra Concentrated Laundry Detergent—Free & Clear," Seventh Generation, accessed June 27, 2023, www.seventhgeneration.com/easydose-ultra-concentrated-laundry-detergent-freeclear.

25. European Commission, DG Environment, *Development of Guidance on Extended Producer Responsibility (EPR)*, 2014, www2.deloitte.com/content/dam/Deloitte/fr/Documents/sustainability-services/deloitte_sustainability-les-filieres-a-responsabilite-elargie-du-producteur-en-europe_dec-15.pdf.

26. Data source: Roland Geyer, Jenna R. Jambeck, and Kara Lavender Law, "Production, Use, and Fate of All Plastics Ever Made," *Science Advances* 3, no. 7 (2017): e1700782; Jenna R. Jambeck et al., "Plastic Waste Inputs from Land into the Ocean," *Science* 347, no. 6223 (2015): 768–771.

Chapter 6: Who Pays for Cheap Labor and Inequality?

1. Marius Wessel and P. M. Foluke Quist-Wessel, "Cocoa Production in West Africa, a Review and Analysis of Recent Developments," *NJAS: Wageningen Journal of Life Sciences* 74, no. 1 (2015): 1–7, https://doi.org/10.1016/j.njas.2015.09.001; Jeff Luckstead, Francis Tsiboe, and Lawton L. Nalley, "Estimating the Economic Incentives Necessary for Eliminating Child Labor in Ghanaian Cocoa Production," *PloS One* 14, no. 6 (2019): e0217230, https://doi.org/10.1371/journal.pone.0217230.

2. "Trafficking and Forced Labour in Global Supply Chains—The Gender Lens," Global March, accessed June 27, 2023, https://globalmarch.org/trafficking-and-forced-labour-in-global-supply-chains-the-gender-lens/.

3. Rashmila Maiti, "Fast Fashion and Its Environmental Impact," Earth.org, May 21, 2023, https://earth.org/fast-fashions-detrimental-effect-on-the-environment/.

4. James Melville, "Modern Slavery Is Never Out of Fashion: Child Labour in the Clothing Industry," *Byline Times*, July 14, 2020, https://bylinetimes.com/2020/07/14/modern-slavery-is-never-out-of-fashion-child-labour-in-the-clothing-industry/.

5. Josephine Moulds, "Child Labour in the Fashion Supply Chain," *Guardian*, accessed June 27, 2023, https://labs.theguardian.com/unicef-child-labour/.

6. Moulds, "Child Labour."

7. ILO and UNICEF, "Child Labour: Global Estimates 2020, Trends and the Road Forward," New York, 2021 (License: CC BY 4.0).

8. "Trafficking and Forced Labour in Global Supply Chains."

9. *Labour Standards in Global Supply Chains: How to Meet Them to Become More Competitive and Sustainable* (Geneva, Switzerland: International Labour Organization, 2019), www.ilo.org/wcmsp5/groups/public/---asia/---ro-bangkok/documents/instructionalmaterial/wcms_725761.pdf.

10. "The Real Impact of the Fast Fashion Industry on the World," *OurGoodBrands*, April 20, 2020, https://ourgoodbrands.com/real-impact-fast-fashion-industry-world/.

11. Alex Lintner, "How Do We Help 138 Million Adults Who Struggle Financially?," Experian, June 26, 2017, www.experian.com/blogs/news/2017/06/26/help-138-million-adults-struggle-financially/.

12. Lawrence Katz and Alan Krueger, "The Rise and Nature of Alternative Work Arrangements in the United States, 1995–2015," NBER working paper 22667 (Cambridge, MA: National Bureau of Economic Research, 2016), https://doi.org/10.3386/w22667.

13. Monica Anderson et al., "The State of Gig Work in 2021," Pew Research Center, December 8, 2021, www.pewresearch.org/internet/2021/12/08/the-state-of-gig-work-in-2021/; Emilia Istrate and Jonathan Harris, *The Future of Work* (Washington, DC: National Association of Counties, 2017), www.naco.org/sites/default/files/documents/Gig-Economy.pdf; D. B. Kelly and Mariel Loveland, "The Biggest Scandals to Ever Hit Costco," *Mashed*, July 11, 2022, www.mashed.com/143099/the-biggest-scandals-to-ever-hit-costco/.

14. Amanda Aronczyk and Ariana Tobin, "Call Center Call Out," *Planet Money*, NPR, September 29, 2020, www.npr.org/2020/09/29/918195277/call-center-call-out.

15. Ken Armstrong, Justin Elliott, and Ariana Tobin, "Meet the Customer Service Reps for Disney and Airbnb Who Have to Pay to Talk to You," ProPublica, October 2, 2020, www.propublica.org/article/meet-the-customer-service-reps-for-disney-and-airbnb-who -have-to-pay-to-talk-to-you.

16. Kris Broda, "Gig Economy—The Economic Backbone of the Future?" Brodmin, February 6, 2022, https://brodmin.com/case-studies/gig-economy-case-study/.

17. Gabriel Mac, "I Was a Warehouse Wage Slave," *Mother Jones*, March–April 2012, www.motherjones.com/politics/2012/02/mac-mcclelland-free-online-shipping-warehouses -labor/.

18. Bobby Allyn, "California Judge Orders Uber and Lyft to Consider All Drivers Employees," NPR, August 10, 2020, www.npr.org/2020/08/10/901099643/california-judge -orders-uber-and-lyft-to-consider-all-drivers-employees.

19. Andrew J. Hawkins, "Uber Argues Its Drivers Aren't Core to Its Business, Won't Reclassify Them as Employees," *Verge*, September 11, 2019, www.theverge .com/2019/9/11/20861362/uber-ab5-tony-west-drivers-core-ride-share-business-california.

20. Jason Moyer-Lee, "UK Supreme Court's Uber Decision Is a Victory for All Gig Workers," *Al Jazeera*, February 25, 2021, www.aljazeera.com/opinions/2021/2/25 /the-uk-supreme-courts-uber-decision-is-a-victory-for-all-workers.

21. Kari Paul, "Prop 22 Explained: How California Voters Could Upend the Gig Economy," *Guardian*, October 15, 2020, www.theguardian.com/us-news/2020/oct/15 /proposition-22-california-ballot-measure-explained.

22. Nicole Prchal Svajlenka, "Protecting Undocumented Workers on the Pandemic's Front Lines," Center for American Progress, December 2, 2020, www.americanprogress .org/article/protecting-undocumented-workers-pandemics-front-lines-2/.

23. James Fallows, "The Story of Ernestor," *Atlantic*, July 8, 2016, www.theatlantic .com/national/archive/2016/07/ernestor-de-la-rosa/489977/.

24. Carlos Vargas-Silva and Madeleine Sumption, "The Labour Market Effects of Immigration," Migration Observatory, March 24, 2023, https://migrationobservatory.ox.ac .uk/resources/briefings/the-labour-market-effects-of-immigration/.

25. Christopher Marquis, "Innovative Employee Practices Provide Financial Support in Good Times—and in Crisis," *Forbes*, April 16, 2020, www.forbes.com/sites /christophermarquis/2020/04/16/innovative-employee-practices-provide-financial -support-in-good-times-and-in-crisis/.

26. "Retirement in the U.S.: A History to Today," Fisher Investments, June 13, 2023, www.fisherinvestments.com/en-us/insights/business-401k/retiring-in-the-us-brief-history.

27. Liz Davidson, "The History of Retirement Benefits," Workforce.com, June 21, 2016, https://workforce.com/news/the-history-of-retirement-benefits.

28. Soo Youn, "40% of Americans Don't Have $400 in the Bank for Emergency Expenses," ABC News, May 24, 2019, https://abcnews.go.com/US/10-americans -struggle-cover-400-emergency-expense-federal/story?id=63253846.

29. Adam Tempkin and Christopher Maloney, "Expensive Loans to Desperate People Built This $90 Billion Industry," *Bloomberg*, February 14, 2019, www.bloomberg.com/news /articles/2019-02-14/expensive-loans-to-desperate-people-built-this-90-billion-industry.

30. Jessica Dickler, "With Inflation Stubbornly High, 58% of Americans Are Living Paycheck to Paycheck: CNBC Survey," CNBC, April 11, 2023, www.cnbc.com/2023 /04/11/58percent-of-americans-are-living-paycheck-to-paycheck-cnbc-survey-revealshtml#.

31. Kay, "Amazon Tracks Warehouse Workers' Every Move."

32. Harry Braverman, *Labor and Monopoly Capital: The Degradation of Work in the Twentieth Century* (New York: Monthly Review Press, 1974).

33. Li Cohen, "White House Calls Out Republicans Who Criticized Student Loan Cancellation but Had Thousands in PPP Loans Forgiven," CBS News. August 26, 2022, www.cbsnews.com/news/white-house-republican-critics-student-loan-cancellation-ppp -loan-forgiveness/.

34. Robert K. Merton, "The Matthew Effect in Science," *Science* 159, no. 3810 (January 5, 1968): 56–63, https://doi.org/10.1126/science.159.3810.56.

35. Justin Fox, "Piketty's 'Capital,' in a Lot Less than 696 Pages," *Harvard Business Review*, April 24, 2014, https://hbr.org/2014/04/pikettys-capital-in-a-lot-less-than-696 -pages.

36. Lucas Chancel et al., *World Inequality Report 2022* (Paris: World Inequality Lab, 2022), https://wir2022.wid.world.

37. Lucas Chancel, "Ten Facts About Inequality in Advanced Economies," in *Combating Inequality: Rethinking Government's Role*, eds. Olivier Blanchard and Dani Rodrik (Cambridge, MA: MIT Press, 2021), https://doi.org/10.7551/mitpress/13469.003.0003.

38. Data source: "Top 1% Personal Wealth Share in Rich Countries, 1910–2014."

39. Gabriel Zucman, "Global Wealth Inequality," *Annual Review of Economics* 11 (2019): 109–138, https://doi.org/10.1146/annurev-economics-080218-025852.

40. "Top 1% Personal Wealth Share in Rich Countries, 1910–2014," World Inequality Database, accessed July 19, 2023, https://wid.world/data/.

41. White House, "New OMB-CEA Report: Billionaires Pay an Average Federal Individual Income Tax Rate of Just 8.2%," news release, September 23, 2021, www.whitehouse .gov/omb/briefing-room/2021/09/23/new-omb-cea-report-billionaires-pay-an-average -federal-individual-income-tax-rate-of-just-8-2/.

42. "First Crisis, Then Catastrophe," Oxfam, April 12, 2022, https://oi-files-d8-prod .s3.eu-west-2.amazonaws.com/s3fs-public/2022-04/Oxfam%20briefing%20-%20First%20 Crisis%20Then%20Catastrophe_0.pdf.

43. Larry Elliott, "World's 10 Richest Men See Their Wealth Double During Covid Pandemic," *Guardian*, January 17, 2022, www.theguardian.com/business/2022/jan/17/world -10-richest-men-see-their-wealth-double-during-covid-pandemic.

44. Gelles, *Man Who Broke Capitalism*.

45. Moira Ritter, "CEOs Made 299 Times More Than Their Average Workers Last Year," CNN, July 14, 2021, https://edition.cnn.com/2021/07/14/investing/ceo-employee-pay -afl-cio-report/index.html.

46. Christopher Marquis, "Global Food Giant Adopts Stakeholder Model to Survive COVID-19 and the Long-Term," *Forbes*, June 26, 2020, www.forbes.com/sites /christophermarquis/2020/06/26/global-food-giant-adopts-stakeholder-model-to-survive -covid-19-and-the-long-term/.

47. Marquis, "Global Food Giant."

48   Nick Romeo, "How Mondragon Became the World's Largest Co-Op," *New Yorker*, August 27, 2022, www.newyorker.com/business/currency/how-mondragon-became-the-worlds-largest-co-op.

49.   Jessica Klein, "Chilean Businesses Are Committing to Lower the CEO-Worker Salary Gap as Inequality Protests Rage," *Fast Company*, November 6, 2019, www.fastcompany.com/90426096/chilean-businesses-are-committing-to-lower-the-ceo-worker-salary-gap-as-inequality-protests-rage; "¿Qué es Desafío 10X?," Desafío 10X, accessed October 2, 2023, www.desafio10x.cl.

50.   Dominic Rushe, "Biden Targets America's Wealthiest with Proposed Minimum Tax on Billionaires," *Guardian*, March 28, 2022, www.theguardian.com/us-news/2022/mar/28/biden-announces-billionaire-minimum-income-tax.

51.   Matthew Yglesias, "The Short Guide to Capital in the 21st Century," *Vox*, April 8, 2014, www.vox.com/2014/4/8/5592198/the-short-guide-to-capital-in-the-21st-century.

52.   Daniel Markovits, "Five Myths about Meritocracy," *Washington Post*, September 13, 2019, www.washingtonpost.com/outlook/five-myths/five-myths-about-meritocracy/2019/09/13/4d90d244-d4cd-11e9-9610-fb56c5522e1c_story.html.

53.   Daniel A. Gross, "How Elite US Schools Give Preference to Wealthy and White 'Legacy' Applicants," *Guardian*, January 23, 2019, www.theguardian.com/us-news/2019/jan/23/elite-schools-ivy-league-legacy-admissions-harvard-wealthier-whiter.

54.   "Low-Income Students and Elite Schools," letters to the editor by Ira Silver, Janet Belsky, and David Rubien, *New York Times*, March 22, 2013, www.nytimes.com/2013/03/23/opinion/low-income-students-and-elite-schools.html.

55.   Sean Illing, "How Elite Colleges Fail Half of the Poor Students They Admit," *Vox*, June 17, 2019, www.vox.com/policy-and-politics/2019/6/17/18647250/privileged-poor-university-admissions-anthony-abraham-jack.

56.   Michael Sandel, "Toppling the Myth of Meritocracy," *Harvard Gazette*, January 5, 2021, https://news.harvard.edu/gazette/story/2021/01/the-myth-of-meritocracy-according-to-michael-sandel/.

57.   Judy Samuelson, "Why I Don't Love the Term Stakeholder," Arthur W. Page Society, April 21, 2022, https://ma.page.org/blog/why-i-don-t-love-the-term-stakeholder.

58.   "'Complete BS': UAW President Rips Auto Company Leaders," CNN, September 19, 2023, www.cnn.com/videos/business/2023/09/15/autoworkers-strike-uaw-vpx.cnn.

59.   David Koenig, "Only 9 Percent of Americans Support Car Companies Over Striking Auto Workers, AP-NORC Polls Shows," *PBS Newshour*, October 12, 2024, www.pbs.org/newshour/nation/only-9-percent-of-americans-support-car-companies-over-striking-auto-workers-ap-norc-polls-shows.

60.   Ameilia Lucas, "Starbucks CEO Howard Schultz Says He's Not Anti-Union, but His Past Tells a Different Story," CNBC, April 9, 2022, www.cnbc.com/2022/04/09/starbucks-ceo-howard-schultz-has-history-of-opposing-unions.html; Adam Lashinsky, "Why Are Unions Such a Non-Starter in the C-Suite?," *Washington Post*, September 2, 2022, www.washingtonpost.com/opinions/2022/09/02/unions-ceos-workers-together/.

Chapter 7: Who Pays for Systemic Discrimination?

1. Marianne Bertrand and Sendhil Mullainathan, "Are Emily and Greg More Employable Than Lakisha and Jamal? A Field Experiment on Labor Market Discrimination," *American Economic Review* 94, no. 4 (2004): 991–1013, https://doi.org /10.1257/0002828042002561.

2. "Global Gender Gap Report 2020," World Economic Forum, December 16, 2019, www.weforum.org/reports/gender-gap-2020-report-100-years-pay-equality/digest/.

3. Aditya Aladangady and Akila Forde, "Wealth Inequality and the Racial Wealth Gap," *FEDS Notes* (blog), Federal Reserve, October 22, 2021, www.federalreserve.gov/econres /notes/feds-notes/wealth-inequality-and-the-racial-wealth-gap-20211022.html.

4. Emily Moss et al., "The Black-White Wealth Gap Left Black Households More Vulnerable," Brookings, December 8, 2020, www.brookings.edu/articles/the-black -white-wealth-gap-left-black-households-more-vulnerable/.

5. "What's the Gender Wealth Gap, and How Can We Close It?" *Ellevest Magazine*, March 14, 2022, www.ellevest.com/magazine/disrupt-money/closing-the-gender-wealth-gap.

6. Rashawn Ray and Alexandra Gibbons, "Why Are States Banning Critical Race Theory?" Brookings, November 21, 2021, www.brookings.edu/articles/why-are-states -banning-critical-race-theory/.

7. Pete Saunders, "Buffalo Demonstrates How Disasters Expose Cities' Racial Divides," *Washington Post*, December 31, 2022, www.washingtonpost.com/opinions/2022 /12/31/buffalo-blizzard-inequality-segregation-cities/.

8. Marianne Bertrand, Dolly Chugh, and Sendhil Mullainathan, "Implicit Discrimination," *American Economic Review* 95, no. 2 (2005): 94–98, https://doi.org/10.1257/00028 2805774670365.

9. Mario L. Small and Devah Pager, "Sociological Perspectives on Racial Discrimination," *Journal of Economic Perspectives* 34, no. 2 (2020): 49–67, https://doi.org/10.1257 /jep.34.2.49.

10. "Black and Latino Drivers File Discrimination Class Action Against Amazon," Lawyers for Civil Rights, accessed June 27, 2023, http://lawyersforcivilrights.org/our-impact/ employment/black-and-latino-drivers-file-discrimination-class-action-against-amazon/.

11. Maryam Jameel and Joe Yerardi, "Workplace Discrimination Is Illegal. But Our Data Shows It's Still a Huge Problem," *Vox*, February 28, 2019, www.vox.com/ policy-and-politics/2019/2/28/18241973/workplace-discrimination-cpi-investigation-eeoc.

12. Julia Horowitz, "JPMorgan Settles with Black Financial Advisers Who Alleged Discrimination," CNN, September 4, 2018, https://money.cnn.com/2018/09/04/news/companies /jpmorgan-settlement-race-discrimination/index.html.

13. Steven Cohen, "JPMorgan Chase Class Action Alleges Racial Discrimination," Top Class Actions, February 14, 2020, https://topclassactions.com/lawsuit-settlements/employment -labor/discrimination/jpmorgan-chase-class-action-alleges-racial-discrimination/.

14. Sonia K. Kang et al., "Whitened Résumés: Race and Self-Presentation in the Labor Market," *Administrative Science Quarterly* 61, no. 3 (2016): 469–502, https://doi.org /10.1177/0001839216639577.

15. Sandrine Devillard, Dame Vivian Hunt, and Lareina Yee, "Still Looking for Room at the Top: Ten Years of Research on Women in the Workplace," *McKinsey Quarterly*, March 8, 2018, www.mckinsey.com/featured-insights/gender-equality/still-looking -for-room-at-the-top-ten-years-of-research-on-women-in-the-workplace.

16. Anaïs Brémond, "Racism in Big Tech: Amazon Workers Speak Up," Welcome to the Jungle, July 8, 2020, www.welcometothejungle.com/en/articles/racism-big -tech-amazon-warehouse-workers-speak.

17. ACLU (@ACLU), "Cool tweet. Will you commit to stop selling face recognition surveillance technology that supercharges police abuse?," X (Twitter), May 31, 2020, https:// twitter.com/ACLU/status/1267181557195907078; ACLU (@ACLU), "Does everyone belong when you ban thousands of people from your platform because of criminal records? Will you reject the racism of a criminal legal system that disproportionately targets Black people? Supporting Black lives means changing your own policies, @airbnb," X (Twitter), June 11, 2020, https://twitter.com/ACLU/status/1271106497251065856.

18. David Gianatasio, "McDonald's Names 7 Victims of Racial Violence in Black Lives Matter Ads," *Muse by Clio*, June 4, 2020, https://musebycl.io/diversity-inclusion /mcdonalds-names-7-victims-racial-violence-black-lives-matter-ads.

19. Nicole Regalado, "McDonald's Employees Are Working Through the COVID-19 Pandemic. So Why Don't They Have Access to Paid Sick and Family Leave?," ACLU, May 1, 2021, www.aclu.org/news/racial-justice/mcdonalds-employees-are-working-through-the -covid-19-pandemic-so-why-dont-they-have-access-to-paid-sick-and-family-leave.

20. Sarah Jones, "Essential Workers Aren't Impressed by Corporate Anti-Racism," *New York*, June 13, 2020, https://nymag.com/intelligencer/2020/06/essential-workers-arent -impressed-by-corporate-anti-racism.html.

21. Frank Dobbin and Alexandra Kalev, *Getting to Diversity: What Works and What Doesn't* (Cambridge, MA: Harvard University Press, 2022).

22. "Frank Dobbin and Alexandra Kalev Explain Why Diversity Training Does Not Work," *Economist*, May 21, 2021, https://scholar.harvard.edu/files/dobbin/files/dobbin _kalev_economist_5-21-21.pdf.

23. Sundar Pichai, "Our Commitments to Racial Equity," Google, June 17, 2020, https://blog.google/inside-google/company-announcements/commitments-racial-equity/.

24. "Frank Dobbin and Alexandra Kalev Explain."

25. Christina Cheddar Berk and Jessica Golden, "Colin Kaepernick Featured in Nike's 30th Anniversary 'Just Do It' Campaign," CNBC, September 3, 2018, www.cnbc .com/2018/09/03/colin-kaepernick-featured-in-nike-just-do-it-campaign.html.

26. "About Us," As You Sow, accessed June 27, 2023, www.asyousow.org/about-us.

27. Kori Hale, "Nike Shareholders Race Towards Diversity Data," *Forbes*, September 8, 2021, www.forbes.com/sites/korihale/2021/09/08/nike-shareholders-race-towards-diversity -data/.

28. Shoshy Ciment, "Nike to Release Recruitment and Promotion Rates of Diverse Employees by 2024," *Footwear News*, July 28, 2022, https://footwearnews.com/shoes/outdoor -footwear/nike-to-release-recruitment-promotion-data-diversity-1203317814/.

29. "Open Hiring Jobs at Greyston Bakery," Greyston Bakery, accessed June 27, 2023, www.greyston.org/openhiringjobs/.

30. "Greyston Delivers $11 Million in Economic Impact to Yonkers," Business Council of Westchester, March 12, 2021, https://thebcw.org/greyston-delivers-11-million-in-economic-impact-to-yonkers/.

31. "QuickFacts: United States," US Census Bureau, accessed June 27, 2023, www.census.gov/quickfacts/fact/table/US/PST045222.

32. Cherrie Bucknor and Alan Barber, *The Price We Pay: Economic Costs of Barriers to Employment for Former Prisoners and People Convicted of Felonies* (Washington, DC: Center for Economic and Policy Research, 2016), https://cepr.net/images/stories/reports/employment-prisoners-felonies-2016-06.pdf.

33. "Open Hiring," Body Shop, accessed June 27, 2023, www.thebodyshop.com/en-gb/about-us/open-hiring/a/a00060.

34. "Frank Dobbin and Alexandra Kalev Explain."

35. "Frank Dobbin and Alexandra Kalev Explain."

36. "About Us," MaineWorks, accessed June 27, 2023, www.maineworks.us/about-us.

37. Daniel Aaronson, Daniel Hartley, and Bhashkar Mazumder, "The Effects of the 1930s HOLC 'Redlining' Maps," *American Economic Journal: Economic Policy* 13, no. 4 (2021): 355–392, https://doi.org/10.1257/pol.20190414.

38. Michele Lerner, "One Home, a Lifetime of Impact," *Washington Post*, July 23, 2020, www.washingtonpost.com/business/2020/07/23/black-homeownership-gap/.

39. David Norris and Mikyung Baek, *Full Report: H.E.A.T.* (Kansas City, KS: CHC of Wyandotte County, 2016), http://wearewyandotte.com/wp-content/uploads/2016/12/CHC_HeatReport_1130.pdf; Aaronson, Hartley, and Mazumder, "The Effects of the 1930s HOLC."

40. Richard Williams, Reynold Nesiba, and Eileen Diaz Mcconnell, "The Changing Face of Inequality in Home Mortgage Lending," *Social Problems* 52, no. 2 (2005): 181–208, https://doi.org/10.1525/sp.2005.52.2.181; Small and Pager, "Sociological Perspectives."

41. "Cities of the Future," *National Geographic*, accessed June 26, 2023, www.nationalgeographic.co.uk/cities-of-the-future.

42. Edward Goetz, "Gentrification in Black and White: The Racial Impact of Public Housing Demolition in American Cities," *Urban Studies* 48, no. 8 (2011): 1581–1604, https://pubmed.ncbi.nlm.nih.gov/21949948/.

43. Shift, *Shift 2021 Impact Report*, 2022, https://shiftworkspaces.com/wp-content/uploads/2022/03/SHIFT-Impact-Report-2021_digital.pdf.

44. "US VC Female Founders Dashboard," PitchBook, accessed June 26, 2023, https://pitchbook.com/news/articles/the-vc-female-founders-dashboard.

45. Rachel Sheppard, "Only 3% of Business Investment Goes to Women, and That's a Problem for Everyone," Crunchbase, April 8, 2020, https://about.crunchbase.com/blog/business-investment-to-women/.

46. "Diversity in U.S. Startup 2020 Edition," Sieo, accessed June 26, 2023, www.sieo.io/ratemyinvestor-report-2020.

47. Katie Abouzahr et al., "Why Women-Owned Startups Are a Better Bet," BCG, June 6, 2018, www.bcg.com/publications/2018/why-women-owned-startups-are-better-bet; Morgan Stanley, *The Growing Market Investors Are Missing: The Trillion-Dollar Case for Investing in Female and Multicultural Entrepreneurs*, 2018, www.morganstanley.com/pub/content/dam/msdotcom/mcil/growing-market-investors-are-missing.pdf.

48.   Shelley Stewart III et al., "The Economic State of Black America: What Is and What Could Be," McKinsey, June 17, 2021, www.mckinsey.com/featured-insights/diversity -and-inclusion/the-economic-state-of-black-america-what-is-and-what-could-be.

49.   DeNeen L. Brown, "40 Acres and a Mule: How the First Reparations for Slavery Were Reversed," *Washington Post*, August 15, 2021, www.washingtonpost.com/history /2021/04/15/40-acres-mule-slavery-reparations/.

50.   Soumya Karlamangla, "What to Know About California's Reparations Efforts," *New York Times*, May 9, 2023, www.nytimes.com/2023/05/09/us/california-reparations-efforts.html.

51.   Rachel Treisman, "In Likely First, Chicago Suburb of Evanston Approves Reparations for Black Residents," NPR, March 23, 2021, www.npr.org/2021/03/23/980277688 /in-likely-first-chicago-suburb-of-evanston-approves-reparations-for-black-reside.

52.   Emmanuel Felton, "Providence Offers Reparations to Address Racism. White People Can Apply," *Washington Post*, November 29, 2022, www.washingtonpost.com /nation/2022/11/29/reparations-program-providence-rhode-island/.

53.   Mary Szto, "Real Estate Agents as Agents of Social Change: Redlining, Reverse Redlining, and Greenlining," *Seattle Journal for Social Justice* 12, no. 1 (2013): 2.

54.   Hayden Coplen, "This Bike Company Launched a Black Reparations Program. Then the Lawyers Called," *Outside*, August 4, 2022, www.outsideonline.com/outdoor-gear /bikes-and-biking/rivendell-black-reparations/.

55   Logan Watts, "Rivendell Bicycle Works Offers Black Reparations Pricing (BRP)," BIKEPACKING.com, October 1, 2020, https://bikepacking.com/news/rivendell -bicycle-black-reparations-pricing/

56.   Coplen, "This Bike Company."

57.   Coplen, "This Bike Company."

Chapter 8: Governing with the Commons in Mind

1.   Marquis, "Global Food Giant Adopts Stakeholder Model."

2.   Dionysia Katelouzou and Mathias Siems, "Disappearing Paradigms in Shareholder Protection: Leximetric Evidence for 30 Countries, 1990–2013," *Journal of Corporate Law Studies* 15, no. 1 (2015): 127–160, www.tandfonline.com/doi/pdf/10.5235/14735970 .15.1.127.

3.   Shelly Williams, "Dodge v. Ford (1919) and the Doctrine of 'Shareholder Primacy,'" Move to Amend, February 9, 2021, www.movetoamend.org/dodge_v_ford_1919 _and_the_doctrine_of_shareholder_primacy.

4.   Frederick Alexander, *Benefit Corporation Law and Governance: Pursuing Profit with Purpose* (Oakland, CA: Berrett-Koehler Publishers, 2017), 27.

5.   "Q&A: How to Know Whether a Company Is Really Purposeful or Just Marketing That Way," B Lab United States & Canada, January 12, 2022, https://usca.bcorporation.ne t/zbtcz01z22/qa-how-know-whether-company-really-purposeful-or-just-marketing-way/.

6.   Robert F. Kennedy, "Day of Affirmation Address at Cape Town University," June 6, 1966 (Jameson Hall, Cape Town, South Africa), *American Rhetoric*, www.americanrhetoric .com/speeches/rfkcapetown.htm.

7. "English Information," Società Benefit, accessed October 10, 2022, www.soci etabenefit.net/english-information/.

8. Wallace Witkowski, "Lemonade Logs Best U.S. IPO Debut of 2020 with More than 140% Gain," *MarketWatch*, July 2, 2020, www.marketwatch.com/story/lemonade-logs -best-ipo-debut-of-2020-with-more-than-140-gain-2020-07-02.

9. "Access to the Public Markets Helps Us Bring Ethical Food to Tables: Vital Farms CEO on IPO Debut," *Yahoo! Finance*, July 31, 2020, https://money.yahoo.com/access-public -markets-helps-us-170436821.html.

10. Riley de León, "Coursera Closes Up 36%, Topping $5.9 Billion Market Cap in Wall Street Debut," CNBC, July 31, 2021, www.cnbc.com/2021/03/31/coursera-ipo-cour-begins -trading-on-the-nyse.html; Lauren Debter, "Allbirds Valued at Over $4 Billion After Stock Surges in IPO," *Forbes*, November 3, 2021, www.forbes.com/sites/laurendebter/2021/11/03 /allbirds-shares-soar-after-shoemaker-raises-over-300-million-in-ipo/.

11. Christopher Marquis and Laura Velez Villa, *Warby Parker: Vision of a "Good" Fashion Brand* (Cambridge, MA: Harvard Business Publishing, 2012), https://hbsp.harvard .edu/product/413051-PDF-ENG; Christopher Marquis, *Better Business: How the B Corp Movement Is Remaking Capitalism* (New Haven: Yale University Press, 2020).

12. Christopher Marquis, "Public Benefit Corporations Flourish in the Public Markets," *Forbes*, June 14, 2021, www.forbes.com/sites/christophermarquis/2021/06/14 /public-benefit-corporations-flourish-in-the-public-markets/.

13. Veeva, "Veeva Becomes First Public Company to Convert to a Public Benefit Corporation," news release, January 13, 2021, www.veeva.com/resources/veeva-becomes -first-public-company-to-convert-to-a-public-benefit-corporation/.

14. "Britain Needs Business at Its Best," Better Business Act, accessed May 23, 2023, https://betterbusinessact.org/.

15. Katie Hill and Wojciech Baginski, "One Article Could Be Struck from the EU Corporate Sustainability Directive. Actually, It's Crucial," *Euronews*, March 6, 2023, www.euronews.com/2023/03/06/one-article-could-be-struck-from-the-eu-corporate -sustainability-directive-actually-its-cr.

16. Task Force on Climate-Related Financial Disclosures, *Recommendations of the Task Force on Climate-Related Financial Disclosures*, June 2017, https://assets.bbhub.io "/company/sites/60/2021/10/FINAL-2017-TCFD-Report.pdf.

17. UK Department for Business, Energy & Industrial Strategy et al., "UK to Enshrine Mandatory Climate Disclosures for Largest Companies in Law," news release, October 29, 2021, www.gov.uk/government/news/uk-to-enshrine-mandatory-climate-disclosures -for-largest-companies-in-law; "Canada Moves Towards TCFD-Aligned Reporting," Environment Analyst, January 11, 2021, https://environment-analyst.com/global/107647 /canada-moves-towards-tcfd-aligned-reporting; Dominic Webb, "Australian Government Launches Consultation on Mandatory Climate Disclosures," *Responsible Investor*, December 12, 2022, www.responsible-investor.com/australian-government-launches-con sultation-on-mandatory-climate-disclosures/.

18. "Make Business a Force For Good," B Lab, accessed June 26, 2023, www.bcorpo ration.net/en-us.

19. Securities and Exchange Commission, The Enhancement and Standardization of Climate-Related Disclosures for Investors, March 21, 2022, www.sec.gov/rules/proposed /2022/33-11042.pdf.

20. TSC Industries v. Northway, Inc., 426 U.S. 438, 449 (1976). See Basic, Inc. v. Levinson, 485 U.S. 224 (1988). As the Supreme Court has noted, determinations of materiality require "delicate assessments of the inferences a 'reasonable shareholder' would draw from a given set of facts and the significance of those inferences to him." *TSC Industries*, 426 U.S. at 450. See also Financial Accounting Standards Board, "Chapter 3, Qualitative Characteristics of Useful Financial Information," in *Conceptual Framework for Financial Reporting*, August 2018.

21. Veronica E. Callahan et al., "Senate Banking Committee Questions Gary Gensler on His Nomination to Be Chair of the Securities and Exchange Commission," Arnold & Porter, March 4, 2021, www.arnoldporter.com/en/perspectives/advisories/2021/03/senate -banking-committee-questions-gensler.

22. Patrick Morrisey, "Comments on Proposed Rule Titled 'Enhanced Disclosures by Certain Investment Advisers and Investment Companies about Environmental, Social, and Governance Investment Practices' by the Attorneys General of the States of West Virginia, Alabama, Alaska, Arizona, Arkansas, Georgia, Idaho, Indiana, Kansas, Kentucky, Louisiana, Mississippi, Missouri, Montana, Nebraska, Oklahoma, South Carolina, Texas, Utah, Virginia, and Wyoming (SEC File No. S7-17-22)," letter to Vanessa A. Countryman, August 16, 2022, https://ago.wv.gov/Documents/2022.08.16 ESG Funds Comment.pdf.

23. David Gelles, "How Environmentally Conscious Investing Became a Target of Conservatives," *New York Times*, March 1, 2023, www.nytimes.com/2023/02/28/climate/esg -climate-backlash.html.

24. Christopher Marquis et al., *Driving Sustainability at Bloomberg L.P.* (Cambridge, MA: Harvard Business Publishing, 2010), https://hbsp.harvard.edu/product /411025-PDF-ENG.

25. Mark Purdy, *2022 ESG Survey Report*, Index Industry Association, 2022, www .indexindustry.org/wp-content/uploads/IIA-report-FINAL-7-27.pdf.

26. Connor Gibson and Frances Sawyer, *2023 Statehouse Report: Right-Wing Attacks on the Freedom to Invest Responsibly Falter in Legislatures*, Pleiades Strategy, 2023, www .pleiadesstrategy.com/state-house-report-bill-tracker-republican-anti-esg-attacks-on-freedom -to-invest-responsibly-earns-business-labor-and-environmental-opposition.

27. "Corporate Sustainability Reporting," European Commission, accessed June 26, 2023, https://finance.ec.europa.eu/capital-markets-union-and-financial-markets/company -reporting-and-auditing/company-reporting-corporate-sustainability-reporting_en.

28. Todd Wasserman, "Amazon's Biggest, Hardest-to-Solve ESG Issue May Be Its Own Workers," CNBC, August 29, 2021, www.cnbc.com/2021/08/29/amazons-biggest -hardest-to-solve-esg-issue-may-be-its-own-workers.html.

Chapter 9: Commons First Finance and Ownership

1. "Global Pension Statistics," OECD, accessed June 26, 2023, www.oecd.org/finance /private-pensions/globalpensionstatistics.htm.

2.   "Antibiotic Resistance," World Health Organization, July 31, 2020, www.who.int /news-room/fact-sheets/detail/antibiotic-resistance#:~:text=Key%20facts,animals%20is %20accelerating%20the%20process.

3.   "Antimicrobial Resistance and Its Impact on Cancer Care," Union for International Cancer Control, accessed October 2, 2023, www.uicc.org/what-we-do/areas-focus/antimicrobial -resistance-amr.

4.   Vijayalaxmi V. Mogasale et al., "A Descriptive Analysis of Antimicrobial Resistance Patterns of Who Priority Pathogens Isolated in Children from a Tertiary Care Hospital in India," *Scientific Reports* 11, no. 1 (2021): 5116, https://doi.org/10.1038/s41598 -021-84293-8; World Bank, "By 2050, Drug-Resistant Infections Could Cause Global Economic Damage On Par with 2008 Financial Crisis," news release, September 20, 2016, www .worldbank.org/en/news/press-release/2016/09/18/by-2050-drug-resistant-infections -could-cause-global-economic-damage-on-par-with-2008-financial-crisis.

5.   Mogasale et al., "A Descriptive Analysis"; World Bank, "By 2050."

6.   Shareholder Commons, "YUM! Brands, Inc.: ITEM 4*—External Public Health Cost Disclosure," Rule 14a-8 Proposal, December 3, 2020, https://theshareholdercommons .com/wp-content/uploads/2021/02/YUM-Proposal-ED-AMR.pdf.

7.   Patrick Tooher, "Britain's Biggest Asset Manager L&G Leads Shareholder Revolt at McDonald's Over 'Overuse' of Antibiotics in Mass Meat Production," MSN, May 20, 2023, www.msn.com/en-gb-money/other/britain-s-biggest-asset-manager -leading-shareholder-revolt-at-mcdonald-s-over-fast-food-giant-s-continued-overuse-of -antibiotics-in-mass-meat-production/ar-AA1bsbat.

8.   "AT&T Inc: Alignment of Stated Corporate Values with Political and Electioneering Expenditures," As You Sow, November 17, 2022, www.asyousow.org/resolutions/2022/11/17-att -alignment-of-stated-corporate-values-with-political-and-electioneering-expenditures-xh3tm.

9.   As You Sow, "AT&T Commits to Political Spending Transparency for Shareholders and Customers," news release, April 3, 2023, www.asyousow.org/press-releases/2023/4/3 /att-commits-political-spending-transparency-for-shareholders-customers.

10.   "The Cambridge Principles: System Stewardship for Universal Owners," Centre for the Study of Existential Risk, December 3, 2021, www.cser.ac.uk/news /Cambridge-principles-system-stewardship-universal-/. For more on universal ownership strategies, see Ellen Quigley, "Universal Ownership in the Anthropocene," available at SSRN 3457205 (2019).

11.   Christopher Marquis, "As You Sow Uses KPIs and Data to Help Shareholders Advocate for Long-Term Corporate Change," *Forbes*, June 7, 2022, www.forbes.com/sites /christophermarquis/2022/06/07/as-you-sow-uses-kpis-and-data-to-help-shareholders -advocate-for-long-term-corporate-change/.

12.   Marquis, "As You Sow."

13.   Andrew Ross Sorkin et al., "Reassessing the Board Fight That Was Meant to Transform Exxon," *New York Times*, May 31, 2023, www.nytimes.com/2023/05/31/business /dealbook/engine-no-1-exxon-mobil.html.

14.   Shareholder Commons, "Shareholder Lawsuit Charges Meta Platforms with Prioritizing Profits Over Shareholders," news release, *Businesswire*, October 4, 2022, www .businesswire.com/news/home/20221004005383/en/Shareholder-Lawsuit-Charges-Meta

-Platforms-with-Prioritizing-Profits-over-Shareholders; Shareholder Commons, "Meta Platforms, Inc.: ITEM 4*: Report on External Costs of Misinformation," Rule 14a-8 Proposal, November 2021, https://theshareholdercommons.com/wp-content/uploads/2021/12/2022 -FB-Proposal.pdf.

15.   Shareholder Commons, "Shareholder Lawsuit Charges Meta Platforms."

16.   Christopher Marquis, "What if a Stock Exchange Prioritized Long-Termism Instead of Short-Term Gains?," *Forbes*, March 17, 2021, www.forbes.com/sites/christopher marquis/2021/03/17/what-if-a-stock-exchange-prioritized-long-termism-instead-of -short-term-gains/; Theodore Schleifer, "America's Newest Stock Exchange Wants to Fix One of Capitalism's Fundamental Challenges," *Vox*, May 22, 2019, www.vox.com/recode /2019/5/22/18629621/long-term-stock-exchange-explainer-capitalism-quarterly-earnings.

17.   Alexander Osipovich and Dennis K. Berman, "Silicon Valley vs. Wall Street: Can the New Long-Term Stock Exchange Disrupt Capitalism?," *Wall Street Journal*, October 16, 2017, www.wsj.com/articles/silicon-valley-vs-wall-street-can-the-new-long-term-stock -exchange-disrupt-capitalism-1508151600; John Detrixhe, "Eric Ries Is on an All-or-Nothing Mission to Reform Capitalism," *Quartz*, September 9, 2020, https://qz.com/1901336/ eric-ries-long-term-stock-exchange-aims-to-reform-capitalism/.

18.   Securities and Exchange Commission, "Long-Term Stock Exchange, Inc. Notice of Filing of Application for Registration as a National Securities Exchange under Sec-tion 6 of the Securities Exchange Act of 1934," November 30, 2018, www.sec.gov/rules/ other/2018/34-84709.pdf; Heather Somerville, "U.S. Regulators Approve New Silicon Val-ley Stock Exchange," Reuters, May 10, 2019, www.reuters.com/article/us-usa-sec-silicon valley-idUSKCN1SG21K; Marquis, "What If A Stock Exchange."

19.   "Listed Companies," LTSE, accessed February 7, 2023, https://ltse.com/listings/ listings-overview.

20.   Adam Bluestein, "Silicon Valley Is Quietly Building Its Own Wall Street," *Marker* (blog), February 18, 2020, https://marker.medium.com/silicon-valley-is-quietly -building-its-own-wall-street-9c0b34f25a27.

21.   Cydney Posner, "LTSE Proposes Listing Standards to Support Long-Term Value Creation," *Cooley PubCo*, August 1, 2019, https://cooleypubco.com/2019/08/01 /ltse-proposes-listing-standards/.

22.   Bluestein, "Silicon Valley."

23.   Indiegogo, accessed October 8, 2022, www.indiegogo.com/.

24.   Alex Tabarrok, "Summers on the Wealth Tax," *Marginal Revolution*, October 21, 2019, https://marginalrevolution.com/marginalrevolution/2019/10/summers-on-the -wealth-tax.html.

25.   Douglas Kruse, "Does Employee Ownership Improve Performance?," *IZA World of Labor*, May 25, 2022, https://wol.iza.org/articles/does-employee-ownership -improve-performance/long.

26.   Romeo, "How Mondragon."

27.   Steen Thomsen and Nikolaos Kavadis, "Enterprise Foundations: Law, Taxation, Governance, and Performance," *Annals of Corporate Governance* 6, no. 4 (2022): 227–333, https://doi.org/10.1561/109.00000031.

Chapter 10: Corporate Activism for the Commons

1. David Robson, "The '3.5% Rule': How a Small Minority Can Change the World," BBC, May 14, 2019, www.bbc.com/future/article/20190513-it-only-takes-35-of-people-to -change-the-world; Erica Chenoweth, "Questions, Answers, and Some Cautionary Updates Regarding the 3.5% Rule," Carr Center discussion paper 5 (Cambridge, MA: Harvard Kennedy School, 2020).

2. "The Corporate Social Mind Research Reports," Corporate Social Mind, accessed October 2, 2023, www.thecorporatesocialmind.com/research.

3. Amanda Holpuch and Julie Creswell, "2 Executives Are on Leave After Bud Light Promotion with Transgender Influencer," New York Times, April 25, 2023, www.nytimes .com/2023/04/25/business/bud-light-dylan-mulvaney.html.

4. Alana Semuels, "Why Corporations Can No Longer Avoid Politics," Time, November 21, 2019, https://time.com/5735415/woke-culture-political-companies/.

5. Fox News, "How 'Barbie' the Movie Got the 'Bud Light Treatment,'" YouTube video, July 4, 2023, www.youtube.com/watch?v=8GA5nlnV2A; Dean Obeidallah, "Opinion: 'Barbie' Breaks Box-Office Records While Crushing Right-Wing Outrage," CNN, July 24, 2023, www.cnn.com/2023/07/23/opinions/barbie-movie-right-wing-opposition-obeidallah/ index.html.

6. "Leading Ice Cream Brands Sales U.S., 2021," Statista, accessed October 8, 2022, www.statista.com/statistics/190426/top-ice-cream-brands-in-the-united-states/.

7. "Issues We Care About," Ben & Jerry's, accessed October 8, 2022, www.benjerry .com/values/issues-we-care-about.

8. Ben & Jerry's (@benandjerrys), "(7/7) Tell Congress to pass #HR40 and start the process of healing our nation by taking action here >>> https://T.Co/SjEPkpjH9q," X (Twitter), February 17, 2021, https://twitter.com/benandjerrys/status/13620893815705 06755.

9. "Our Story," Body Shop, accessed June 26, 2023, www.thebodyshop.com/en-gb /about-us/our-story/a/a00002.

10. Katie Hope, "The Body Shop: What Went Wrong?," BBC, February 9, 2017, www .bbc.com/news/business-38905530.

11. Huw Spanner, "Body Politics: Anita Roddick," High Profiles, January 5, 1996, https://highprofiles.info/interview/anita-roddick/.

12. Krista Charles, "Food Production Emissions Make Up More Than a Third of Global Total," New Scientist, September 13, 2021, www.newscientist.com/article /2290068-food-production-emissions-make-up-more-than-a-third-of-global-total/.

13. Christopher Marquis, "Toast Ale Aims to Reduce Food Waste While Educat- ing Consumers About the Global Problem," Forbes, April 15, 2022, www.forbes.com/sites /christophermarquis/2022/04/15/toast-ale-aims-to-reduce-food-waste-while-educating -consumers-about-the-global-problem/.

14. "Companion Series," Toast Ale, October 15, 2021, www.toastale.com/blog /companion-series-cop26-beer.

15. "Race to Zero Campaign," UN Climate Change, accessed October 11, 2022, https://unfccc.int/climate-action/race-to-zero-campaign.

16. "We Mean Business Coalition Statement on the Outcomes of COP27," We Mean Business Coalition, November 20, 2022, www.wemeanbusinesscoalition.org/blog/we-mean-business-coalition-statement-on-the-outcomes-of-cop27/.

17. Christian Mumenthaler, "Global Cooperation Has Mended a Divided World Before—It Can Do It Again," World Economic Forum, January 11, 2023, www.weforum.org/agenda/2023/01/global-cooperation-fragmented-world-wef23/.

18. "The Never List™," Beautycounter, accessed October 11, 2022, www.beautycounter.com/the-never-list.

19. Beautycounter, *The Mica Toolkit*, accessed October 2, 2023, https://assets.ctfassets.net/ylsk4zpp53wa/4NaPR5v4YCAKY4ktPf9ek3/033dbd682260d4ec475ea5aea47ddadd/0125_MICA_TOOLKIT.pdf.

20. "The 1938 Food, Drug, and Cosmetic Act," FDA, January 31, 2018, www.fda.gov/about-fda/histories-product-regulation/1938-food-drug-and-cosmetic-act.

21. "About Us," Participant, accessed October 8, 2022, https://participant.com/about-us.

22. "John Lewis: Good Trouble," Participant, accessed October 8, 2022, https://participant.com/campaigns/johnlewisgoodtrouble.

23. "Slay the Dragon," Participant, accessed October 8, 2022, https://participant.com/campaigns/slaythedragon.

24. "About American Promise," American Promise, accessed October 11, 2022, https://americanpromise.net/about/.

25. Dobbs v. Jackson Women's Health Organization (2022), www.supremecourt.gov/opinions/21pdf/19-1392_6j37.pdf.

26. "The Amendments in History," ConstitutionFacts.com, accessed October 11, 2022, www.constitutionfacts.com/us-constitution-amendments/amendments-in-history/.

Chapter 11: Consumption and the Commons

1. Josie Allchin, "Case Study: Patagonia's 'Don't Buy This Jacket' Campaign," *Marketing Week*, January 23, 2013, www.marketingweek.com/case-study-patagonias-dont-buy-this-jacket-campaign/.

2. Solitaire Townsend, "Near 80% of People Would Personally Do as Much for Climate as They Have for Coronavirus," *Forbes*, June 1, 2020, www.forbes.com/sites/solitairetownsend/2020/06/01/near-80-of-people-would-personally-do-as-much-for-climate-as-they-have-for-coronavirus/.

3. "Goal 12: Ensure Sustainable Consumption and Production Patterns," UN Sustainable Development Goals, accessed October 11, 2022, www.un.org/sustainabledevelopment/sustainable-consumption-production/.

4. "Interview with Yvon Chouinard," YouTube video, posted by Lion Heart Carsten Essig, Männerseminare & Podcast, January 17, 2010, https://youtu.be/O3TwULu-Wjw.

5. Antonia Wilson, "Dutch Airline KLM Calls for People to Fly Less," *Guardian*, July 11, 2019, www.theguardian.com/travel/2019/jul/11/dutch-airline-klm-calls-for-people-to-fly-less-carbon-offsetting-scheme.

6. "Fly Responsibly," KLM, accessed October 11, 2022, https://flyresponsibly.klm.com/en.

7. "IKEA Buyback & Resell Terms and Conditions," IKEA, accessed October 11, 2022, www.ikea.com/gb/en/customer-service/terms-conditions/ikea-buy-back-terms-and-conditions-pub9e989950.

8. "Becoming Climate Positive," IKEA, accessed October 11, 2022, https://about.ikea.com/en/sustainability/becoming-climate-positive.

9. Dawn Allcot, "Ikea Will Buy Back Your Used Furniture to Save Your Wallet—and the Planet," *Yahoo! Finance*, April 1, 2022, https://finance.yahoo.com/news/ikea-buy-back-used-furniture-173534272.html.

10. Ingka Group, "World's First Second-Hand IKEA Store to Open in Sweden," news release, September 14, 2020, www.ingka.com/news/worlds-first-second-hand-ikea-store-to-open-in-sweden/.

11. Rosie Frost, "Is IKEA's New Furniture 'Buy Back' Scheme Greenwashing?," *Euronews.green*, October 19, 2020, www.euronews.com/green/2020/10/14/is-ikea-s-new-buy-back-furniture-scheme-greenwashing.

12. Cecilia Keating, "IKEA Will Buy Back Used Furniture in Stand Against 'Excessive Consumption,'" *Greenbiz*, October 15, 2020, www.greenbiz.com/article/ikea-will-buy-back-used-furniture-stand-against-excessive-consumption.

13. REI, "REI Co-Op Expands Used Gear Business with Member Gear Trade-In Program and Pilot of Standalone Used Gear Pop-up Stores," news release, October 15, 2020, www.rei.com/newsroom/article/expands-used-gear.

14. Anna Sanina, "Patagonia Calls on People to Buy Less and Resell Their Clothing on eBay," *Popsop*, October 26, 2011, https://popsop.com/patagonia-calls-on-people-to-reduce-their-clothing/.

15. Lindsay Morris, "Changing the Fabric of Our Lives," Patagonia, February 25, 2020, https://eu.patagonia.com/gb/en/stories/changing-the-fabric-of-our-lives/story79355.html.

16. Allison Engel and Margaret Engel, "Eileen Fisher Wants Those Clothes Back When You're Done," *Washington Post*, August 31, 2018, www.washingtonpost.com/business/economy/eileen-fisher-wants-those-clothes-back-when-youre-done/2018/08/31/cd873aea-ac58-11e8-b1da-ff7faa680710_story.html.

17. Maria Cristina Pavarini, "Nudie Jeans Wants to Be 'the World's Most Sustainable Denim Brand,'" *Spin Off*, May 28, 2021, www.the-spin-off.com/news/stories/The-Brands-Nudie-Jeans-wants-to-be-the-worlds-most-sustainable-denim-brand-15937.

18. Christopher Marquis, "Fors Marsh Group Takes a Data-Driven Approach to Help Build Consumer Awareness of Social Impact," *Forbes*, January 13, 2022, www.forbes.com/sites/christophermarquis/2022/01/13/fors-marsh-group-takes-a-data-driven-approach-to-help-build-consumer-awareness-of-social-impact/.

19. Brandon Stover and Cullen Schwarz, "Building the Amazon for Social Good," *Evolve Podcast*, January 4, 2021, www.evolvethe.world/episodes/cullen-schwarz.

20. Stover and Schwarz, "Building the Amazon."

21. Allyson Chiu, "Online or In-Store? A Guide to Climate-Friendly Clothes Shopping," *Washington Post*, December 13, 2022, www.washingtonpost.com/climate-solutions/2022/12/13/store-online-shop-emissions/#.

22. "We'll Be Climate Positive by 2025," Reformation, accessed September 2, 2022, www.thereformation.com/sustainability/climate-positive.html.

23. "Carbon Is Canceled," Reformation, accessed September 2, 2022, www.thereformation.com/sustainability/carbon-is-canceled.html.

24. Jon Henley, "Many Europeans Want Climate Action—but Less So If It Changes Their Lifestyle, Shows Poll," *Guardian*, May 2, 2023, www.theguardian.com/environment/2023/may/02/many-europeans-want-climate-action-but-less-so-if-it-changes-their-lifestyle-shows-poll.

25. Marquis, "Fors Marsh Group."

26. Christopher Marquis, "Risk-Averse Real Estate Investing Is Turning to Sustainability for Strong, Long-Term Financial Returns," *Forbes*, January 5, 2021, www.forbes.com/sites/christophermarquis/2021/01/05/risk-averse-real-estate-investing-is-turning-to-sustainability-for-strong-long-term-financial-returns/.

27. "The 17 Goals," Sustainable Development, UN Department of Economic and Social Affairs, accessed October 11, 2022, https://sdgs.un.org/goals.

28. Cyril Ip, "China Consumption: How Important Is It to the World's No 2 Economy?," *South China Morning Post*, October 30, 2021, www.scmp.com/economy/china-economy/article/3154119/china-consumption-how-important-it-worlds-no-2-economy.

29. Umair Irfan, "Consumers, Not Corporations, Saved the Power Grid. What Else Can We Do?," *Vox*, October 31, 2022, www.vox.com/science-and-health/23340991/power-demand-response-blackout-consumer-climate-change-california-texas-cop27.

30. Li Cohen, "Companies Say They're Going Green. Here's How to Tell If They Measure Up," CBS News, April 22, 2022, www.cbsnews.com/news/companies-say-theyre-going-green-sustainability-marketing-earth-day/.

31. "Responsible Consumption and the Benefits of Local Consumption," Sustainability for All, accessed October 12, 2022, www.activesustainability.com/sustainable-life/responsible-consumption-benefits-local-consumption/.

32. David J. Hardisty, Katherine White, and Rishad Habib, "5 Ways to Shift Consumers Towards Sustainable Behaviour," *Conversation*, August 11, 2019, http://theconversation.com/5-ways-to-shift-consumers-towards-sustainable-behaviour-120883.

Conclusion

1. Zimmerman, "Graduating from Externalities."

2. Eric Cline, *1177 B.C.: The Year Civilization Collapsed* (Princeton, NJ: Princeton University Press, 2014).

3. Quoted in Marjorie Kelly, *Wealth Supremacy: How the Extractive Economy and the Biased Rules of Capitalism Drive Today's Crises* (Oakland, CA: Berrett-Koehler Publishers, 2023).

4. Doug McAdam, John D. McCarthy, and Mayer N. Zald, eds., "Introduction: Opportunities, Mobilizing Structures, and Framing Processes—Toward a Synthetic, Comparative Perspective on Social Movements," in *Comparative Perspectives on Social Movements: Political Opportunities, Mobilizing Structures, and Cultural Framings* (Cambridge: Cambridge University Press, 1996), 1–20.

INDEX

Christopher Marquis is the Sinyi Professor of Chinese Management at the University of Cambridge Judge Business School and the author of the award-winning books *Better Business: How the B Corp Movement Is Remaking Capitalism* and *Mao and Markets: The Communist Roots of Chinese Enterprise.*

Chris is passionate about how academic research can help people around the world address our most significant challenges. He examines how some of the biggest crises of our day—including climate change, inequality, and racism—are intimately connected to how our current form of capitalism has prioritized accumulating and concentrating wealth for the few over the concerns and needs of everyone and everything else. His research and writing focus on the need to rebalance the interactions between corporations, governments, and civil society to deliver socially and environmentally beneficial outcomes to all.

A second set of his research examines entrepreneurship and market development in China, and how China has developed an economic system that is profoundly different from the West.

Prior to joining Cambridge, Chris was the Samuel C. Johnson Professor in Sustainable Global Enterprise at Cornell University.

Before that, he spent ten years as a professor at Harvard Business School and also worked for eighteen months at Harvard Kennedy School as a professor of social innovation and public policy. Chris received a PhD in sociology and business administration from the University of Michigan, and since then has authored more than twenty peer-reviewed academic articles and more than fifty Harvard business cases on topics related to social innovation, sustainable business, and doing business in China. Before his academic career, he was a vice president and technology manager at JPMorgan Chase.

PublicAffairs is a publishing house founded in 1997. It is a tribute to the standards, values, and flair of three persons who have served as mentors to countless reporters, writers, editors, and book people of all kinds, including me.

I. F. STONE, proprietor of *I. F. Stone's Weekly*, combined a commitment to the First Amendment with entrepreneurial zeal and reporting skill and became one of the great independent journalists in American history. At the age of eighty, Izzy published *The Trial of Socrates*, which was a national bestseller. He wrote the book after he taught himself ancient Greek.

BENJAMIN C. BRADLEE was for nearly thirty years the charismatic editorial leader of *The Washington Post*. It was Ben who gave the *Post* the range and courage to pursue such historic issues as Watergate. He supported his reporters with a tenacity that made them fearless and it is no accident that so many became authors of influential, best-selling books.

ROBERT L. BERNSTEIN, the chief executive of Random House for more than a quarter century, guided one of the nation's premier publishing houses. Bob was personally responsible for many books of political dissent and argument that challenged tyranny around the globe. He is also the founder and longtime chair of Human Rights Watch, one of the most respected human rights organizations in the world.

·   ·   ·

For fifty years, the banner of Public Affairs Press was carried by its owner Morris B. Schnapper, who published Gandhi, Nasser, Toynbee, Truman, and about 1,500 other authors. In 1983, Schnapper was described by *The Washington Post* as "a redoubtable gadfly." His legacy will endure in the books to come.

Peter Osnos, *Founder*